D1535875

C# Programmer's Handbook

GREGORY S. MACBETH

Apress™

C# Programmer's Handbook
Copyright ©2004 by Gregory S. MacBeth

ISBN (pbk): 1-59059-270-0

Printed and bound in the United States of America 10987654321

Trademarked names may appear in this book. Rather than use a trademark symbol with every occurrence of a trademarked name, we use the names only in an editorial fashion and to the benefit of the trademark owner, with no intention of infringement of the trademark.

Editorial Board: Dan Appleman, Craig Berry, Gary Cornell, Tony Davis, Steven Rycroft, Julian Skinner, Martin Streicher, Jim Sumser, Karen Watterson, Gavin Wray, John Zukowski

Assistant Publisher: Grace Wong

Copy Editor: Marilyn Smith

Production Manager: Kari Brooks

Proofreader: Lori Bring

Compositor: Susan Glinert Stevens

Indexer: Michael Brinkman

Cover Designer: Kurt Krames

Manufacturing Manager: Tom Debolski

Distributed to the book trade in the United States by Springer-Verlag New York, Inc., 175 Fifth Avenue, New York, NY 10010 and outside the United States by Springer-Verlag GmbH & Co. KG, Tiergartenstr. 17, 69112 Heidelberg, Germany.

In the United States: phone 1-800-SPRINGER, email orders@springer-ny.com, or visit http://www.springer-ny.com. Outside the United States: fax +49 6221 345229, email orders@springer.de, or visit http://www.springer.de.

For information on translations, please contact Apress directly at 2560 Ninth Street, Suite 219, Berkeley, CA 94710. Phone 510-549-5930, fax 510-549-5939, email info@apress.com, or visit http://www.apress.com.

The information in this book is distributed on an "as is" basis, without warranty. Although every precaution has been taken in the preparation of this work, neither the author(s) nor Apress shall have any liability to any person or entity with respect to any loss or damage caused or alleged to be caused directly or indirectly by the information contained in this work.

The source code for this book is available to readers at http://www.apress.com in the Downloads section. You will need to answer questions pertaining to this book in order to successfully download the code.

To Paige, Welby, and Sumner,
who I love more than they will ever know.

Contents at a Glance

Contents

About the Author

Gregory S. MacBeth is currently employed by Microsoft as a Solution Integration Engineer in Charlotte, North Carolina, where he helps customers realize the potential of Microsoft products. He specifically aids customers in resolving complex problems where multiple products are involved. In addition, he often assists customers in developing first-class software using C# and .NET. He holds MCAD, MCSD (.NET and VS 6), MCSE, MCDBA, MCT, N+, and A+ certifications.

Acknowledgments

TO MY WIFE PAIGE and my sons Welby and Sumner, thanks for your patience and love, and the sacrifices that you made during the time it took me to complete this work.

To my father Mac, Major Allen D. Broussard, Captain Kenneth Poteet, and the United States Marine Corps for making me the man I am today.

To Ken Burns, my former manager at Microsoft, thanks for being understanding, supportive, and helping me to develop my career. But most of all, thanks for being a friend!

Thanks to the staff members at Apress for all their help.

Preface

I WAS INSPIRED to write this book because when I needed to transition from C++ to C#, I found few books that helped. All I really wanted was a book that defined the language and showed me simple examples of how to use the .NET Framework. I hope that you will find this book helpful and useful in learning C#.

As you read this book, please keep in mind that my goal was to provide you with simple samples showing you how to use this language to do common tasks. I stripped out all but the essential code. Specifically, I removed safeguards such as exception handling that would normally be present in all good code. I advise you strongly to use exception handling in your own code.

I have also included in this book material that will be in the next major release of C#, such as generics, anonymous methods, iterators, and more.

I wish you the best of luck in your coding.

Part One

C# Language Basics

Common Type System

- Identifiers and Naming Conventions

- Variables

- Value Types

- Reference Type Variables

- Constant and Static Values

- Scopes

- Casting and Class Conversion

Identifiers and Naming Conventions

Identifiers are used to describe allocated memory types such as integer, longs, classes, and other types defined by C# or by you, as the developer. The rules for identifiers are simple:

- Identifiers can start with any Unicode letter or an underscore.

- Identifiers are case-sensitive.

- Identifiers must be unique within a particular scope: namespace, class, method, or code block.

Typically, identifiers should be descriptive and use whole words without abbreviations. Your identifiers, whether they are for types or methods, should describe the intent that you have in mind when you develop the type or method. The focus should be on the readability of the code.

CAUTION Make sure that you do not create methods, fields, or properties that have the same identifiers that differ only in case. If you do this, languages that are not case-sensitive, such as Visual Basic, will have difficulties in using your code.

Your identifiers become the symbolic name that identifies the memory location of the given type when a declaration is made. If an identifier is used in the namespace/global part of the code, you cannot use it again throughout any scope within that namespace, including child parts.

In addition to identifier names, there is also the issue of naming conventions for identifiers. In C#, there is a defined set of naming conventions and recommendations. C++ programmers are familiar with Hungarian notation, which required that identifiers be prefixed with their type. Ironically, Hungarian notation is no longer a recommended naming convention. The following are the two recommended naming conventions for C#:

- **Pascal casing:** This convention capitalizes the first character of each word, as in int `MyInt`. Pascal casing is the default convention for all names with the exception of protected instance fields and parameters.

- **Camel casing:** This convention capitalizes the first character of each word except the first word, as in int `myInt`. This convention is used only for protected instance fields and parameters.

The following example shows the use of identifiers in C#.

Code Example: Identifiers and Naming Conventions

```
//Adds System namespace
using System;
//Defines a new namespace
namespace Client.Chapter_1___Common_Type_System
{
    //Defines a new class
    class MyMainClass
    {
        //Defines a static method that serves as an entry point
        //for the application
        static void Main(string[] args)
        {
            //Declares an instance of variables
            int MyInt = 12345;
            long MyLong = MyInt;
            short MyShort = (short)MyInt;
            My2ndFunction(MyInt);
        }
        //Defines a public static method
        public static int My2ndFunction(int myInt)
        {
            return myInt;
        }
    }
}
```

Variables

When a variable is declared in a statement, the compiler is told to reserve that type's amount of memory. The declaration statement does not place any value in that memory other than inheriting the value on the stack that currently occupies that memory. This is why C# requires that you initialize all variables prior to using them. After you have declared a variable type, you must initialize that variable with a value. If you do use a local variable without initializing that value, the compiler will let you know about it!

There are many ways to assign a value to a variable, including the following:

- One approach is to use an *expression*. An expression combines operators to define a computation that results in a value.

- Another route is to use assignment. An assignment statement requires three parts: the variable name, an equal (=) operator, and the data to be placed into the memory location of the variable.

- Finally, a variable can be assigned by receiving a value from a returning method using the `return` keyword.

 CAUTION If you do try to use a local variable without initializing that value, you will get an error at compile time. For example, if you use `c:\class\Test\SimpleTester.cs`, the message will be, "An object reference is required for the nonstatic field, method, or property 'Test.SimpleTester.Test(int)'."

The following is an example of using variables.

Code Example: Using Variables

```
using System;

namespace Client.Chapter_1___Common_Type_System
{
    class UsingVariables
    {
        static void Main(string[] args)
          {
                //Assignment
            int MyInt = 12345;
            //Using an expression
            int MyInt2 = MyInt + 1;
            int MyInt3;
            //Initializing through a return value from a method
              MyInt3 = My2ndFunction(MyInt2);
          }
          static public int My2ndFunction(int myInt2)
          {
            myInt2 = myInt2 * 2;
            //The value of myInt2 will be assigned to MyInt3 above
              return myInt2;
          }
    }
  }
```

Value Types

Value types are the built-in types provided by C# that you can use to store simple values and combine to build your own types called classes. Table 1-1 describes some of the common types you will encounter in C#, as well as their memory allocation requirements. You will find all of these simple value types on the stack when they are used by themselves, without being in a class. It is important to realize that all the types listed in Table 1-1 are aliases; for example, System.int32 is the real name for int.

Table 1-1. Common Value Types

Symbolic Name	Description
sbyte	8-bit signed integer
short	16-bit signed integer
int	32-bit signed integer
long	64-bit signed integer
byte	8-bit unsigned integer
ushort	16-bit unsigned integer
uint	32-bit unsigned integer
ulong	64-bit unsigned integer
float	Single-precision floating point
double	Double-precision floating point
bool	True or false
char	Unicode character, 16 bytes
decimal	Precise decimal with 28 digits

NOTE   Since all value types inherit from System.Object, you will always see the GetHashCode, ToString, CompareTo, Equals, GetType, and GetTypeCode methods available to value types. Their exact functionality will be described in later chapters.

The following example shows common value types.

Code Example: Value Types

```csharp
using System;
namespace Client.Chapter_1___Common_Type_System
{
    class ValueType
    {
        static void Main(string[] args)
        {
            //Declares an instance of a value type. These objects will be
            //placed on the stack. All value types inherit from
            //System.ValueType, which in turn inherits from
            //System.Object. Common value types include all basic types
            //such as int, long, struct, and enum.

            int MyInt = 12345;
            long MyLong = MyInt;
            short MyShort = (short)MyInt;
        }
    }
}
```

Using Bool

A bool is a variable that holds one of two values, true or false, and consumes 1 byte. In C#, a bool is a true type, not just an integer that stores a zero for false and a nonzero value for true. Therefore, a bool cannot be converted to a numeric type. The following shows an example of using a bool type.

Code Example: Using Bool

```
using System;

namespace Client.Chapter_1___Common_Type_System
{
    class UsingBool
    {
        static void Main(string[] args)
        {
            bool MyBool = false;
            //Use bool in if statement
            if (MyBool)
            {
                //Writes true to console
                Console.WriteLine(MyBool);
            }
            else
            {
                //Writes false to console
                Console.WriteLine(MyBool);
            }
        }
    }
}
```

Using Integers

The int keyword is used to store integer values or whole numbers. When an integer is defined, the compiler will reserve enough memory to hold an integer in C#, which is 4 bytes. One byte is large enough to hold 8 bits (or 8 ones or zeros).

In C#, the valid ranges of value for an int are –2,147,483,648 to +2,147,483,648. In addition to the int type, there are several other types of varying size that can be used to store whole numbers. Table 1-2 shows these types, the smallest and largest values each can hold, and the memory they require.

Table 1-2. Types That Store Whole Numbers

Type	Smallest Value	Largest Value	Memory
short	–32,768	32,768	2 bytes – 16 bits
ushort	0	65,536	2 bytes – 16 bits
int	–2,147,483,648	2,147,483,648	4 bytes – 32 bits
uint	0	4,294,967,296	4 bytes – 32 bits
long	–9,223,372,036,854,775,808	9,223,372,036,854,775,808	8 bytes – 64 bits
ulong	0	18,446,744,073,709,551,616	8 bytes – 64 bits

A feature of C# is that it protects against placing a value in a type that is beyond the range that it can hold. This is done by using the keyword checked, which will cause an OverflowException to occur at runtime if a type is assigned a value beyond its limits.

checked (*expression*) or (*statement block*)

The unchecked statement disables this functionality, but it is rarely useful unless you want to force an assignment of data that is beyond a type's accepted range.

unchecked (*expression*) or (*statement block*)

The following shows an example of using integers.

Code Example: Using Integers

```
using System;
namespace Client.Chapter_1___Common_Type_System
{
    class UsingIntegers
    {
        static void Main(string[] args)
        {
            int MyInt = 12345;
            long MyLong = MyInt;


        }

        public long My2ndFunction(long myLong)
        {
            //Creates a try block
            try
            {
                //If the value calculated for MyLong exceeds the maximum
                //value for a long, you will get an OverflowException
                long c = checked(myLong * 500);
            }
            catch (OverflowException e)
            {
                Console.WriteLine(e);
            }
            return 0;
        }
    }
}
```

Using Char

C# provides support for Unicode char types. A char is an integer value that is an interpretation of an integer type that has a defined value based on the Unicode standard. You may use char types to store a single character or in an array to store an entire string. However, the easiest way to store a string is to use the built-in string class for nonmutable strings, or maybe a StringBuilder class if the string needs to be mutable.

In C#, char types reserve 2 bytes of memory and expect a Unicode string as opposed to an ASCII (American Standard Code Information Interchange) string, which C++ expects in a char type. C# char types are similar to C++'s wchar_t types.

If you need to do manipulations from Unicode strings to ASCII, you may wish to examine the System.Runtime.InteropServices.Marshal class. For example, you can take a managed string and move it to an array of ASCII char types by doing the following:

```
sbyte* pServer = (sbyte*)Marshal.StringToCoTaskMemAnsi("My Managed String");
```

The following example shows how to use char types.

Code Example: Using Char

```
using System;

namespace Client.Chapter_1___Common_Type_System
{
    class UsingChar
    {
        static void Main(string[] args)
        {
            //Declares and initializes a char to the value of A
            char MyChar = 'A';
            //Here the Unicode value of 65 is cast to a char, which is A
            MyChar = (char)65;
            char[] MyChar2 = { 'H', 'e', 'l', 'l', 'o', '\0' };
            char[] MyChar3 = new char[5];
            //Fills a char array
            MyChar3[0] = 'H';
            MyChar3[1] = 'e';
            MyChar3[2] = 'l';
            MyChar3[3] = 'l';
            MyChar3[4] = 'o';
            MyChar3[5] = '\0';
        }
    }
}
```

Using Strings

In C++, Microsoft provided a string class in the Microsoft Foundation Classes (MFC), and the Standard Template Library (STL) provided one as well. It was so helpful to developers that a string class was built into C# to let programmers avoid the common use of string pointers and char arrays, as well as needing to depend on an extension. C#'s explicit type called string can be used to store an entire string. It is important to realize that this type is an alias for System.String.

 CAUTION Keep in mind that the string type is only used for nonmutable strings. If you plan to use a string and make a lot of changes to it, you will want to examine the System.Text.StringBuilder class. This will save your application many performance woes. For more information, see the Microsoft Knowledge Base article, "PRB: High CPU Utilization in Web Service or Web Form" (http://support.microsoft.com/default.aspx?scid=kb;en-us;307340).

The great thing about having a string type is the built-in methods supported by this type. These methods, listed in Table 1-3, allow you to manipulate the string.

Table 1-3. Built-in Methods That Support Strings

Method Name	Description
CompareTo	Compares the current instance with a specified object
CopyTo	Copies a specific number of characters to a specific position in a Unicode array
EndsWith	Determines if the end of this string matches a given string
Remove	Deletes characters from this string, given a specific index to start
Replace	Replaces all characters that match a specified string
Split	Identifies substrings within a string

Table 1-3. Built-in Methods That Support Strings (Continued)

Method Name	Description
StartsWith	Determines if a given string matches the beginning of the current string
Substring	Returns a substring from the given string
ToCharArray	Returns a Unicode char array
ToLower	Returns an all lowercase string
ToUpper	Returns an all uppercase string
Trim	Removes all instances of a specified string from the beginning or end of the current string
TrimEnd	Removes characters from the end of the current string
TrimStart	Removes characters from the beginning of the current string

The following example shows the use of string values.

Code Example: Using Strings

```
using System;
namespace Client.Chapter_1___Common_Type_System
{
    class UsingStrings
    {
        static void Main(string[] args)
        {
            string MyString = "Hello World";
            string Path = @"c:\Program Files";
            string Path2 = "c:\\Program Files";
            string Name = "Joe";
        }
    }
}
```

Using Escape Characters

Escape characters are used in char and string types to tell the compiler to ignore the normal meaning of the next character and to recognize some special functionality or special meaning. The escape character in C# is the backslash (\). This escape character is used in conjunction with the characters listed in Table 1-4.

Table 1-4. Escape Characters

Escape Character	Meaning	Hex Value
\'	Single quote	0x0027
\"	Double quotes	0x0022
\\	Backslash	0x005C
\0	Null termination	0x0000
\a	Alert	0x0007
\b	Backspace	0x0008
\f	Form feed	0x000C
\n	New line	0x000A
\r	Carriage return	0x000D
\t	Horizontal tab	0x0009
\v	Vertical tab	0x000B

A feature of C# that allows you to avoid using escape characters in some cases is the @ symbol syntax. A string object could use the following syntax to assign the exact string, without using the \\ escape character.

```
string MyString = @"c:\Program Files\My Program\strings.exe";
```

 CAUTION You must still use the escape sequence for double quotation marks! For example, use string MyString = " \"To Be or Not To Be, That Is The Question\" ";.

The following example shows the use of escape characters.

Code Example: Escape Characters

```
using System;
namespace Client.Chapter_1___Common_Type_System
{
    class EscapeCharacters
    {
        static void Main(string[] args)
        {
            char MyChar='\0';
            //The @ symbol tells C# to take the string literally
            string MyString=@"C:\MyFiles";
            string MYString2="c:\\Program Files";
            //Even with the @ symbol, you must still escape quotation marks
            string MyString3=" \"To Be or Not To Be, That Is The Question\" ";
        }
    }
}
```

Using Floats, Doubles, and Decimals

Since integer data types can store only whole numbers, there must be a way to store very large fractional numbers. C# provides the float, double, and decimal types to handle large fractional numbers. A float is 4 bytes, and a double uses 8 bytes. The decimal type is a new feature to C#. It is used for calculations in which rounding errors caused by floating points are unacceptable. The decimal type holds 28 digits and the position of the decimal point. Table 1-5 shows the lowest and highest values for these types.

Table 1-5. Float, Double, and Decimal Type Values

Type	Lowest	Highest
float	+/−1.5 × 10^-45	+/−3.4 × 10^38
double	+/−5.0 × 10^-324	+/−1.7 × 10^308
decimal	+/−1.0 × 10^-28	−7.9 × 10^28

The following example shows the use of float, double, and decimal types.

Code Example: Using Floats, Doubles, and Decimals

```
using System;
namespace Client.Chapter_1___Common_Type_System
{
     class UsingFloats
     {
          static void Main(string[] args)
          {
               float MyFloat = 3.281f;
               double MyDouble = 5E-02;
          }
     }
}

using System;
namespace Client.Chapter_1___Common_Type_System
{
     class UsingDecimals
     {
          static void Main(string[] args)
          {
               decimal MyDecimal = 3.50m;
          }
     }
}
```

Reference Types

Reference types are instances of classes in C#. These are found on the managed heap. To create a new instance of a class reference type, use the new keyword.

 NOTE   One of the great things about C# is that you no longer need to take care of cleanup for the object by using delete. The garbage collector does this for you automatically when the object is no longer reachable. The garbage collector is discussed in later chapters.

Inheriting from System.Object

All reference types inherit from System.Object. If you were to dump the MethodTable (discussed in Chapter 16), you would see an object is made up of the following:

```
0:000> !dumpmt -MD 00932140
EEClass : 06be6a90
Module : 0015ba48
Name: System.Object
mdToken: 02000002  (c:\windows\microsoft.net\framework\v1.1.4322\mscorlib.dll)
MethodTable Flags : 2080000
Number of IFaces in IFaceMap : 0
Interface Map : 009321a4
Slots in VTable : 14
---------------------------------------
MethodDesc Table
  Entry  MethodDesc   JIT
      Name
0093203b 00932040    None
[DEFAULT] [hasThis] String System.Object.ToString()
     009320fb 00932100    None
[DEFAULT] [hasThis] Boolean System.Object.Equals(Object)
     791f4a07 791f4a0c    None
[DEFAULT] [hasThis] Boolean System.Object.Equals(Object)
     0093207b 00932080    None
[DEFAULT] [hasThis] Void System.Object.Finalize()
     0093202b 00932030    None
[DEFAULT] [hasThis] Void System.Object..ctor()
     009320cb 009320d0    None
```

```
[DEFAULT] [hasThis] Class System.Type System.Object.InternalGetType()
        009320e3 009320e8    None
[DEFAULT] [hasThis] Class System.Type System.Object.FastGetExistingType()
        0093204b 00932050    None
[DEFAULT] Boolean System.Object.Equals(Object,Object)
        0093205b 00932060    None
[DEFAULT] Boolean System.Object.ReferenceEquals(Object,Object)
        0093206b 00932070    None
[DEFAULT] [hasThis] Class System.Type System.Object.GetType()
        0093212b 00932130    None
[DEFAULT] [hasThis] Object System.Object.MemberwiseClone()
        0093208b 00932090    None
[DEFAULT] [hasThis] Void System.Object.FieldSetter(String,String,Object)
        0093209b 009320a0    None
[DEFAULT] [hasThis] Void System.Object.FieldGetter(String,String,ByRef Object)
        009320ab 009320b0    None
[DEFAULT] [hasThis] Class System.Reflection.FieldInfo
System.Object.GetFieldInfo(String,String)
```

The following example shows the use of reference types.

Code Example: Reference Type

```
using System;
namespace MyNamespace
{
      class MyMainClass
      {
            static void Main(string[] args)
            {
                  My2ndMainClass My2ndClass = new My2ndMainClass();
            }
      }
      class My2ndMainClass
      {
            public void MyFunction()
            {
                  int MyInt = 0;
            }
      }
}
```

Converting Reference Types: Boxing and Unboxing

Boxing describes a situation where a value type needs to be converted to a reference type. When this is done, an object is created to hold the value and the value is copied into the object.

Unboxing is the reverse of boxing. In this situation, the object created when the value type was boxed is copied back into a value type.

 CAUTION   Be very careful when you box and unbox, because these actions can cause the managed heap to be thrashed. Every time you box an object, you force the object to be copied to the heap. When you unbox it, the object is moved back to the stack. You will most often see this when you call methods that accept an Object as the type and you are passing a value type. If you try to unbox an underlying value type, and the type you are unboxing to is not compatible with the type you boxed, you will get InvalidCastException.

The following shows an example of boxing and unboxing.

Code Example: Boxing and Unboxing

```
using System;
namespace Client.Chapter_1___Common_Type_System
{
    class BoxandUnbox
    {
        static void Main(string[] args)
        {
            long MyLong = 1005;
            //Boxes
            object MyObject = MyLong;
            //Unboxes
            long MyLong2 = (long)MyObject;
        }
    }
}
```

Constant and Static Values

A *constant* is a value that cannot be modified after it is assigned. Constants can be divided into two broad categories:

- *Literal constants* are numbers (integers and floats), single characters, or character strings.

- *Named constants* are created using the const qualifier and must be initialized at the time of declaration.

These variables are typically given identifiers that are in all uppercase letters to help signify that they are read-only. You should use the const statement in cases where you would use the #define statement in C++.

The static keyword tells the compiler that the value of the variable will never be destroyed and a single instance is always stored. These variables are initialized to zero by default.

The following examples demonstrate using constant and static values.

Code Example: Constants

```
using System;

namespace MyNamespace
{
        class MyMainClass
        {
                static void Main(string[] args)
                {
                        //const tells the compiler that the value can't be modified
                        //after it is assigned
                        const int MyInt = 0;
                        //This is invalid and would be caught by the compiler
                        MyInt = 5;
                }
        }
}
```

Code Example: Static

```
using System;
namespace MyNamespace
{
        class MyMainClass
        {
                //There will always be one value for this member variable
                public static int MyClassInt;
                static void Main(string[] args)
                {
                }

                MyMainClass()
                {
                        MyClassInt++;
                }
        }
}
```

Scopes

In C#, the life or accessibility of an object or type is determined by its *scope*. C# has the following scopes:

- Namespace

- Class

- Method

- Curly braces ({}) inside a method

We will discuss scope and accessibility in Chapter 5, which covers classes and methods. But to give you an idea of how scopes work, the following shows examples of namespace, class, and method-level scopes.

Code Example: Scopes

```
using System;

//Defines namespace scope
namespace MyNamespace
{
      //Defines class scope
      class MyMainClass
      {
          public int MyClassInt;
          public long MyClassLong;
          static void Main(string[] args)
          {
                //Defines method-level scope
                int MyInt = 5;
          }
      }
}
```

Casting and Class Conversion

Casting is used to convert a particular object type to another type. There are two dominant casting types: implicit/upcast and explicit/downcast.

The *implicit/upcast* type of cast is used to convert a smaller type into a larger type. This is done automatically for you in C#, and there is no need to explicitly cast, except to better describe your intentions, which is a good idea. Here is an example:

```
int X = 123456;
long Y = X;
```

The *explicit/downcast* type of cast is used to convert a larger type into a smaller type. You must do this to get the conversion to work. With this type of casting, you are converting from a more specific type to a less specific type, and you will lose some of the exactness of the object. Here is an example:

```
int X = 12345;
short Y = (short) X;
```

In addition, C# also provides two special operators to help with casting:

- The as operator allows a downcast that will result in null, rather than an exception, if the casting fails.

- The is operator tests if an object is or derives from a specific class or implements a specific interface.

The following example demonstrates casting.

Code Example: Casting

```
using System;

namespace Client.Chapter_1___Common_Type_System
{
    class Casting
    {
        static void Main(string[] args)
        {
            int MyInt = 12345;
            //Implicit cast
            long MyLong = MyInt;
            //Explicit cast
            short MyShort = (short)MyInt;
        }
    }
}
```

Expressions and Operators

- Expressions

- Arithmetic Operators

- Relational Operators

- Logical Operators

- Bitwise Operators

- Shift Operators

- Precedence Table

Expressions

Chapter 1 demonstrated how to use statements to get the computer to do something. The statements were made up of keywords and symbols that end with a semicolon. The next step is to examine *expressions*.

An expression uses *operators* and *operands* to instruct the compiler to perform a computation. Operators act on operands. Operators come in three flavors:

- **Unary:** A unary operator has one operand.

- **Binary:** A binary operator has two operands.

- **Ternary:** A ternary operator has three operands.

The operands consist of variables, constants, and method calls. The following shows examples of expressions.

Code Example: Expressions

```
using System;

namespace Client.Chapter_2___Expressions_and_Operators
{
    class Expressions
    {
        static void Main(string[] args)
        {
            int MyInt = 12345;
            int MyInt2 = 10000;
            int Sum = 0;
            long MyLong = MyInt;
            short MyShort = (short)MyInt;
            //Bool expression
            if (MyInt == MyInt2)
            {
                //Simple calculation
                Sum = MyInt + MyInt2;
            }
            else
            {
                Sum = MyInt - MyInt2;
            }
        }
    }
}
```

Arithmetic Operators

C#, like any other business language, offers a broad range of mathematical operators. Table 2-1 lists the C# arithmetic operators.

Table 2-1. C# Arithmetic Operators

Operator	Description
-	Subtraction or unary minus
+	Addition or unary plus
*	Multiplication
/	Division
%	Modulus division (remainder)
-=	Subtraction assignment
+=	Addition assignment
*=	Multiplication assignment
/=	Division assignment
%=	Modulus division assignment
--	Decrement
++	Increment

The following example shows the use of arithmetic operators in C#.

Code Example: Arithmetic Operators

```
using System;

namespace Client.Chapter_2___ Expressions_and_Operators
{
    class MyMainClass
    {
        static void Main(string[] args)
        {
            int a,b,c,d,e,f;

            a = 1;
            //Addition
            b = a + 6;
            //Subtraction
            c = b - 3;
            //Multiplication
            d = c * 2;
            //Division
            e = d / 2;
            //Modulus
            f = e % 2;
        }
    }
}
```

Multiple-Function Operators (+=, -=, *=, /=, and %=)

In addition to the normal arithmetic operators, C# provides several multiple-function operators. These operators include the following:

- Addition assignment (+=)

- Subtraction assignment (-=)

- Multiplication assignment (*=)

- Division assignment (/=)

- Modulus assignment (%=)

These multiple-function assignment operators instruct the compiler to add the value of the variable on the left side of the operator to the value of the expression to the right, and then assign the results of the computation to the variable on the left.

Unary Operators (++ and --)

The increment (++) and decrement (--) operators are unary operators that act on a single operand. If the ++ or -- operator is placed before the operand, the value of the operand will be incremented or decremented before the rest of the expression is evaluated. If this operator is placed after the operand, the value of the operand is assigned first, and then incremented or decremented after the assignment.

 CAUTION Be careful where you place a unary arithmetic operator. The position of the ++ or -- operator can affect the results of the operation.

The following is an example of using the multiple-function and unary operators.

Code Example: Multiple-Function and Unary Operators

```
using System;

namespace Client.Chapter_2___ Expressions_and_Operators
{
    class NumericOperators1
    {
        static void Main(string[] args)
        {
            int a, b, c, d, e;

            a = 1;
            //a = a + 1
            a += 1;
            b = a;
            //b = b - 2
            b -= 2;
            c = b;
            //c = c * 3
            c *= 3;
            d = 4;
            //d = d / 2
            d /= 2;
            e = 23;
            //e = e % 3
            e %= 3;
        }
    }
}
```

```
using System;

namespace Client.Chapter_2___Operators_and_Expressions
{
    class NumericOperators2
    {
        static void Main(string[] args)
        {
            int a,b,c,d,e,f;

            a = 1;
            b = a + 1;          //b = 2
            b = b - 1;          //b = 1
            c = 1; d = 2;
            ++c;                //c = 2
            --d;                //d = 1
            e = --c;            //e = 1 c =1
            f = c--;            //f = 1 c= 0
        }
    }
}
```

Relational Operators

Relational operators include the following:

- Comparison operators (<, <=, >, and >=) are used to compare two expressions or two values. This comparison results in either a true or false result.

- An equivalence operator (==) can be used to evaluate if two values are the same.

- The not equal (!=) operator can be used to determine if a value is not equal to another value.

The following is an example of using relational operators.

Code Example: Relational Operators

```
using System;

namespace Client.Chapter_2___ Expressions_and_ Operators
{
    class RelationalOperators
    {
        static void Main(string[] args)
        {
            int a, b;
            a = 1;
            b = 2;
            if (a > b)
               b = 10;
            if (b < a)
                    a = 10;
            if (a >= b)
                    b = 20;
            if (b <= a)
                    a = 20;
            if (a == b)
                    b = 5;
            if (b != a)
                    b = a;
        }
    }
}
```

Logical Operators

Logical operators are used to combine two expressions into logical expressions. There are three logical operators:

- The AND operator (&&) operator results in true if both expressions are true; it results in false if either one is false.

- The OR operator (||) results in true if either of the expressions are true; it results in false only if both expressions are false.

- The NOT operator (!) results in true only if the expression itself evaluates to false; it results in false only if the expression evaluates to true.

The following is an example of using logical operators.

Code Example: Logical Operators

```
using System;

namespace Client.Chapter_2___ Expressions_and_Operators
{
    class RelationalOperators2
    {
        static void Main(string[] args)
        {
            int a = 10, b = 20, c = 30;
            if (a < 15 && b < 20)
                c = 10;
            if (a < 15 || b < 20)
                c = 15;
            if (!(a == 15))
                c = 25;
        }
    }
}
```

Bitwise Operators

Bitwise operators allow you to evaluate the bits of a value directly. There are six operators that you can use to work with bits: AND, OR, XOR, NOT, shift left, and shift right. This section describes the AND, OR, XOR, and NOT operators. The shift operators are described in the next section. Only the NOT operator is unary, the other bitwise operators are binary.

AND (&)

The bitwise AND (&) compares every bit of each operand. If the bit in the same position of each operand is one, the resulting bit is one. However, if either bit in the same position is zero, the resulting bit is set to zero.

OR (|)

The bitwise OR (|) is also referred to as the inclusive OR operator. The bitwise OR operator works similarly to the AND operator in that it evaluates the bit in the same position. The difference is that if either bit is set to one, the result is a one; otherwise, it results in the bit being set to zero.

XOR (^)

The second type of the OR operator is the exclusive OR (^), which is also referred to as the XOR operator. This operator compares each bit and creates a resulting bit. If it is in the same position, the bit is set to 0, and the other operand bit is set to 1, the result is that the bit is set to 1; otherwise, it is set to zero.

NOT (!)

The bitwise NOT (!) is also called the complement operator. This operator is used to reverse the bit setting of the operand. So, if a bit is set to one, the bit is set to zero and vice versa.

The following is an example of using bitwise operators.

Code Example: Bitwise Operators

```csharp
using System;

namespace Client.Chapter_2___ Expressions_and_Operators
{
    class BitwiseOperators
    {
        static void Main(string[] args)
        {
            long MyBit = 0x1;
            long MyBitResult = 0;
            MyBitResult = MyBit & 0x1;
            MyBitResult = MyBit | 0x2;
            MyBitResult = MyBit ^ 0x4;
        }
    }
}
```

Shift Operators

The shift operators are used to shift bits either left or right, essentially performing a multiplication or division operation.

Shift Left

The shift left operator (`<<`) shifts bits to the left. The bits of the left operand are the integral number of positions specified to the right operand. As bits are shifted left, the low-order bits are brought to zero. Bits shifted beyond the high-order bits are lost. This basically means that you *multiply* the value by a power of 2. For example, `a = 8 << 3` really means 8×2^3.

Shift Right

The shift right operator (`>>`) performs the same operation as the shift left operator, but the bits are shifted right. If the value being shifted is unsigned, the value of the leftmost bit is set to zero; otherwise, it is set as the sign bit. This means you *divide* the number by a power of 2. For example, `a = 32 >> 4` really means $32/2^4$.

The following is an example of using the shift operators.

Code Example: Shift Operators

```
using System;

namespace Client.Chapter_2___ Expressions_and_Operators

{
    class ShiftOperators
    {
        static void Main(string[] args)
        {
            uint a = 0;
            uint b = 0;

            //a = 64
            a = 8 << 3;
            //b = 2
            b = 32 >> 4;
        }
    }
}
```

Precedence Table

In C#, operators are acted on based on the order of precedence of the language. As a developer, you should use parentheses to specifically set the order of precedence, as well as to make your code easier to read (see the "Logical Operators" section earlier in this chapter for examples of using parentheses).

When the compiler encounters an expression with multiple operators, the precedence table is used to evaluate the order of operations. If an operand is between two operators that have the same precedence, the associativity of the operators is used to determine the order of operations. Except for the assignment operator, all binary operators are left associative. The assignment operator (=) and the ternary operator (?:) are right associative. For example, the following:

```
a = b = c;
```

is equal to

```
a = (b = c);
```

Table 2-2 shows the precedence table for C# operators.

Table 2-2. C# Precedence Order

Category	Operator	Description
Primary	(x)	Grouping
	x.y	Member access
	->	Struct pointer member access
	f(x)	Method call
	a[x]	Indexing
	x++	Postincrement
	x--	Postdecrement
	new	Constructor
	stackalloc	Array stack allocation
	typeof	Type retrieval
	sizeof	Struct size retrieval
	checked	Arithmetic check on
	unchecked	Arithmetic check off
Unary	+	Positive value
	-	Negative value
	!	Not
	~	Bitwise complement
	++x	Preincrement
	--x	Predecrement
	(T)x	Type casting
Value at address—dereference		
	&	Address of value

Table 2-2. *C# Precedence Order (Continued)*

Category	Operator	Description
MultiplicativeMultiply		
	/	Division
	%	Division remainder
Additive	+	Add
	-	Subtract
Shift	<<	Shift left
	>>	Shift right
Relational	<	Less than
	>	Greater than
	<=	Less than or equal
	>=	Greater than or equal
	is	Type equality
Equality	==	Equal
	!=	Not equal
Logical Bitwise	&	AND
	^	XOR
	|	OR
Logical Boolean	&&	And
	||	Or
	?:	Returns one of two values depending on the value of a Boolean expression
Assignment	= *= /=	Assign/modify
	+= -= <<=	
	>>= &= ^=	
	|=	

Structs, Enums, Arrays, and Collections

- Structs

- Enums

- Arrays

- System.Collections: ArrayList, Hashtable, Queue, and Stack

- Iterators (new to 2.0)

Structs

A struct is a way to organize a group of unlike variable types under a single name. Structs are a carryover from C++. Although they are not as valuable as they once were, they still provide some usefulness in creating user-defined types (UDTs).

Structs are most useful in situations where you want the information to be stored on the stack or you do not want to incur the overhead of a class (calling an allocator and calling the constructor for the class).

Structs can be nested inside a class or a namespace. The following example includes the struct in the namespace so it will be available to all classes in the namespace. Notice how MyStruct is now a type, and an instance can be declared in the class. To access members of the class, you use the dot operator (.). The syntax is instance_name.member_ name.

NOTE   It is very important to know that there are no unions in C#. This means that if you want to simulate a union in C#, you must use some built-in attributes. A sample of doing this is in Chapter 10.

Code Example: Struct

```
using System;

namespace Client.Chapter_3___Structs__Enums__Arrays_and_Collections
{
    //Declares a struct
    public struct MyStruct
    {
        public int MyInt;
        public long MyLong;
        public string MyString;
    }
    class Structs
    {
        static void Main(string[] args)
        {
            //Defines an instance of a struct
            MyStruct TheStruct;
            TheStruct.MyInt = 0;
            TheStruct.MyLong = 0;
            TheStruct.MyString = "Hello World";
        }
    }
}
```

Enums

C# offers another way to group data: an *enumeration*. This allows the developer to establish a set of values for an instance of the group. Any single instance of an enumeration can have only a value that is defined within the group.

The compiler automatically assigns each member of the enumeration an integer value. The first member is always assigned a zero, followed by a one. However, you can start the sequence with any integer value you choose by explicitly setting the value of the member.

The names used for enumerations must be distinct from those of other identifiers. After you have defined an enumeration, the name of the enumeration is used to declare an instance of the enumeration. In the following example, MyWeek is an instance of the enum DaysOfWeek. This example also shows how to make an enum start with a value other than zero by assigning values to each member.

```
public enum Months
{
    January = 1,
    February = 2,
    March = 3
}
```

You can also use an enum to define bit flags by using the [Flags] attribute, as in this example:

```
[Flags] enum MyBits
{
    On = 1,
    Off = 2,
    Broken = 4
}
```

The following example demonstrates the use of enum.

Code Example: Enums

```
using System;

namespace Client.Chapter_3___Structs__Enums__Arrays_and_Collections
{
    //Defines an enum
    enum DaysOfWeek
    {
        Monday,
        Tuesday,
        Wednesday,
        Thursday,
        Friday,
        Saturday,
        Sunday
    }
    class Enums
    {
        static void Main(string[] args)
        {
            //Declares an instance of the enum
            DaysOfWeek Today = DaysOfWeek.Monday;
            //Prints Monday
            Console.WriteLine(Today);
        }
    }
}
```

Arrays

An *array* is a collection of like data types that can be referenced by a single name. Each member of the collection is called an *element* or a *member* of the array. Elements of an array are identified by the name of the array, followed by a unique index number contained in square brackets.

Arrays are of a specific fixed size, which is determined at the time the array is declared. All arrays start with an index number of zero. The actual amount of memory that an array takes up is the number of elements times the number of bytes that the type requires. Furthermore, all arrays are stored on the heap in C# and thus are reference types. This provides a great advantage because it removes the most common cause of stack corruption by forcing arrays to be on the heap. Finally, arrays are initialized automatically to zero for all members.

The following is an example of declaring and instantiating an instance of a single-dimension array:

```
int[] numbers = {1,2,3,4,5};
```

NOTE   C# arrays provide a means to prevent you from writing beyond the end of the array. When this occurs, you will throw an exception of IndexOutOfRangeException.

Jagged Arrays

Some arrays contain an array of other arrays. These are called *jagged arrays*. Here is an example of declaring and instantiating an instance of a jagged array:

```
int[][] numbers = new int[5];
for(int x = 0; x < numbers.Length; x++)
{
        numbers[x] = new int[4];
}
```

Multidimensional Arrays

C# also allows for *multidimensional arrays*. These are declared in the same way as single-dimension arrays, except that you specify the number of columns and number of rows in square brackets. For example, [2,3] declares an array that has two columns, each with three rows. Here is an example of declaring and instantiating an instance of a multidimensional array:

```
int[,] numbers = new int[5,4]
```

NOTE All arrays and most collections implement the IEnumerable interface, which allows for the simple use of the foreach loop. This interface contains the MoveNext, Reset, and Current methods.

The following example demonstrates the use of arrays.

Code Example: Arrays

```
using System;

namespace Client.Chapter_3___Structs__Enums__Arrays_and_Collections
{
    class Arrays1
    {
        static void Main(string[] args)
        {
            //Note the location of the brackets indicating this is an
            //array
            string[] MyStaticArray = { "Hello", "World" };
            //Creates an array with 5 members
            int[] MyIntArray = new int[5];
              int i, z;
              for (int x = 0; x < 5; x++)
              {
                  MyIntArray[x] = 0;
              }
```

```
                    //An array of arrays, or jagged array
                    int[][][] MyIntArray2 = new int[3][][];
                    for (i = 0; i < 5; i++)
                        MyIntArray2[i] = new int[4][];
                    for (z = 0; z < 10; z++)
                        MyIntArray2[i][z] = new int[5];
                }
            }
        }
        using System;

        namespace Client.Chapter_3___Structs__Enums__Arrays_and_Classes
        {
            class Arrays2
            {
                static void Main(string[] args)
                {
                    //Multidimensional array
                    int[,] MyIntArray = new int[5, 5];
                    for (int x = 0, y = 0; x < 5; x++, y++)
                    {
                        MyIntArray[x, y] = 0;
                    }
                }
            }
        }
```

System.Collections

The System.Collections namespace contains interfaces and classes that define various collections of objects, such as lists, queues, arrays, hash tables, and dictionaries. Table 3-1 describes the nonstrong-typed collection classes.

Table 3-1. Nonstrong-Typed Collections

Class	Description
ArrayList	A dynamically sized array that can contain any sort of object.
BitArray	A compact array of bit values whose value can be either true or false.
Hashtable	A hash table that maps given keys to values allowing for buckets of segmented data. A hash table maintains a sorted list of key/value pairs that can be accessed by a key value.
Queue	Represents a first-in, first-out collection of objects.
Stack	Represents a last-in, first-out collection of type Object.

 CAUTION Each of these nonstrong-typed collection classes stores its contents as objects, which forces the contents to be boxed and placed on the heap. This could cause performance problems in your applications. Therefore, it is recommended that you use strong-typed collections or build your own collection with generics (see Chapter 5 for information about generics).

The strong-typed collection classes are described in Table 3-2.

Table 3-2. Strong-Typed Collections

Class	Description
CollectionBase	Provides an abstract base class, allowing you to derive your own strong-typed collection.
DictionaryBase	Provides an abstract base class, allowing you to create a derived class that stores a specific type. This type uses the associated key/value pairs.
ReadOnlyCollectionBase	Another abstract class. This type allows for read-only access.

We will discuss each major collection type in detail over the next few pages.

ArrayLists

An ArrayList is an array that has a dynamic size, so it can grow as necessary. ArrayLists can be used to store any type, including built-in types and custom types defined as classes.

A useful feature of an ArrayList is that it can be expanded on demand, if necessary. C# does this by creating a new instance of an ArrayList for the new size and copying the current members of the smaller ArrayList to the new ArrayList.

 CAUTION Expanding an ArrayList on demand comes at a price. An ArrayList is a reference type, and when it is expanded by creating a new ArrayList, you must not count on the reference always being at the same address.

You can add members of an ArrayList using two methods: Add and Insert. You can remove members from an ArrayList by using the Remove, RemoveAt, or Clear method. These and other useful methods provided by an ArrayList are described in Table 3-3.

Table 3-3. Useful ArrayList Methods

Method	Description
Add	Adds a new member to the end of the array
Insert	Allows you to place the new member in the ArrayList at whatever location you choose
Remove	Removes the first occurrence of the parameter that you pass
RemoveAt	Removes a specific member at a specific location in the ArrayList
Clear	Removes all members of the ArrayList
Clone	Creates a shallow copy of the list
Equals	Determines if two objects are equal
Reverse	Reverses the order of the array
ToArray	Copies the members to a new array
ToString	Returns a string that represents the current object

The ArrayList also provides a field called count, which will tell you how many members are in the ArrayList at a given time.

To iterate through an ArrayList, you can use any of the iterator statements defined in Chapter 4. The foreach or for statements are recommended, because they will define your intent more clearly than the other iterator statements.

The following example demonstrates declaring an instance of an ArrayList that will contain an initial ten members. This example uses a foreach loop. Notice the first operand of the foreach loop is of the type placed in the ArrayList, and the second operand is the name given to the instance of the ArrayList.

Code Example: ArrayList

```
using System;
using System.Collections;

namespace Client.Chapter_3___Structs__Enums__Arrays_and_Collections
{
    class MyArrayList
    {
        static void Main(string[] args)
        {
            //Creates an array with 10 members
            ArrayList a = new ArrayList(10);
            int x = 0;
            //Adds a member to the end of the array
            a.Add(x);
            //Adds the value of 1 to position 2
            a.Insert(1, ++x);
            foreach (int y in a)
            {
                Console.WriteLine(y);
            }

            //Removes the last member of the array
            a.Remove(x);
            //Removes the member at position 0
            a.RemoveAt(0);
            //Removes all members of the array
            a.Clear();
        }
    }
}
```

Hashtables

Hashtables are a collection of associated keys and values that are organized based on the hash code of the key.

When an entry is added to the Hashtable, the entry is placed into a bucket based on the hash code of the key. Subsequent lookups of the key use the hash code of the key to search in only one particular bucket, thus substantially reducing the number of key comparisons required to find an entry.

The load factor of a Hashtable determines the maximum ratio of entries to buckets. Smaller load factors cause faster average lookup times, at the cost of increased memory consumption. The default load factor of 1.0 generally provides the best balance between speed and size. You can specify a different load factor when the Hashtable is instantiated.

As entries are added to a Hashtable, the actual load factor of the Hashtable increases. When the actual load factor reaches the default or specified load factor, the number of buckets in the Hashtable is automatically increased to the smallest prime number that is larger than twice the current number of Hashtable buckets.

To declare an a new Hashtable, you must call new with the number of entries that you expect, like this:

```
Hashtable a = new Hashtable(10);
```

You can add entries to a Hashtable by calling the Add method and supplying the key as the first parameter, followed by the value in the second, as in these examples:

```
a.Add(100, "Arrays");
a.Add(200, "Classes");
```

There are three types of exceptions that can be thrown when adding a new key to the Hashtable:

- If you pass a null key, you will throw an exception of ArgumentNullException.

- If you try to add an entry that already exists, an ArgumentException will be thrown.

- If the Hashtable is read-only or of fixed length, a NotSupportedException will be thrown.

NOTE IDictionary is the underlying interface used to create Hashtables, DictionaryBase, and SortedList collections. This interface provides support for associated key/value pairs. It also allows for enumeration but does not imply a sorted collection. Some common methods supported by this interface are Add, Clear, Contains, GetEnumerator, and Remove.

Since each element of the Hashtable is a key/value pair, the element type is not the type of the key or the type of the value. Therefore, you must use a DictionaryEntry object as the type to iterate through the collection, as in this example:

```
foreach(DictionaryEntry d in a)
{
        Console.WriteLine(d.Value);
}
```

Finally, you can call the Remove and Clear methods to remove entries.

```
a.Remove(100);
a.Clear();
```

NOTE The Hashtable is the only built-in collection that has some thread safety. Specifically, it supports multiple readers and a single writer.

The following example demonstrates the use of Hashtables.

Code Example: Hashtables

```
using System;
using System.Collections;

namespace Client.Chapter_3___Structs__Enums__Arrays_and_Collections
{
    class HashTables
    {
        static void Main(string[] args)
        {
            Hashtable a = new Hashtable(10);
            //Marks the Hashtable as thread-safe
            Hashtable.Synchronized(a);

            //Adds a member to the table
            a.Add(100, "Arrays");
            a.Add(200, "Classes");

            foreach(DictionaryEntry d in a)
            {
                Console.WriteLine(d.Value);
            }
            //Removes all members with the key of 100
            a.Remove(100);
            a.Remove(200);
            //Removes all members
            a.Clear();
        }
    }
}
```

Queues

A Queue represents a first-in, first-out (FIFO) collection of objects. Queues should be used when the sequence of objects with regard to their order of entry is important to maintain. Queue entries are entered in one end of the collection and removed from the other end.

 CAUTION Note that Queues are not thread-safe by default. Therefore, you must use the Synchronize method or lock keyword to ensure two threads do not access the same Queue simultaneously.

To create a new Queue, you must declare a new instance with the number of entries as the first parameter, like this:

```
Queue a = new Queue(10);
   int x = 0;
```

You add entries to a Queue by using the Enqueue method and passing the item to be queued as the first parameter, as in this example:

```
a.Enqueue(x);
x++;
a.Enqueue(x);
```

To iterate through a Queue, you can use a foreach statement. The first operand of the foreach loop is of the same type that was inserted into the queue with the Enqueue method. The second operand is the name of the Queue collection that was declared. Here is an example of using foreach to iterate through a Queue:

```
foreach(int y in a)
{
    Console.WriteLine(y);
}
```

To remove items from the Queue, call the Dequeue method. The oldest items are always removed from the Queue first.

```
a.Dequeue();
```

If you want to clear the whole Queue at once, you can use the Clear method.

```
a.Clear();
```

The following example demonstrates how to use Queues.

Code Example: Queue

```csharp
using System;
using System.Collections;

namespace Client.Chapter_3___Structs__Enums__Arrays_and_Collections
{
    class Queues
    {
        static void Main(string[] args)
        {
            //Creates a queue with 10 members
            Queue a = new Queue(10);
            int x = 0;
            //Adds members to the queue
            a.Enqueue(x);
            x++;
            a.Enqueue(x);
            foreach (int y in a)
            {
                Console.WriteLine(y);
            }
            //Removes members from the queue
            a.Dequeue();
            //Removes all members from the queue
            a.Clear();
        }
    }
}
```

Stacks

A Stack represents a simple last-in, first-out (LIFO) collection of type. A Stack is implemented as a circular buffer, where the last item in is always the first item out.

 CAUTION   Like a Queue, a Stack is not thread-safe, and it requires the Synchronize method to prevent simultaneous access.

To create a new Stack, you must declare and pass it the number of items that you expect to add to the Stack, like this:

```
Stack a = new Stack(10);
int x = 0;
```

To add items, call the Push method, passing it the item to be added to the Stack as the first parameter. You can add items, as long as the property count does not exceed the maximum size of the Stack when it was declared. Here is an example of adding items to the Stack:

```
a.Push(x);
x++;
a.Push(x);
```

To iterate through a Stack, you can use a foreach loop. The first operand is the same type that you are pushing onto the Stack, and the second operand is the Stack object itself, as shown in this example:

```
foreach(int y in a)
{
        Console.WriteLine(y);
}
```

To remove items from the top of the Stack, call the Pop method.

```
a.Pop();
```

You can also call the Clear method to remove all items from the Stack.

```
a.Clear();
```

The following example demonstrates using Stacks.

Code Example: Stacks

```
using System;
using System.Collections;

namespace Client.Chapter_3___Structs__Enums__Arrays_and_Collections
{
      class Stacks
      {
            static void Main(string[] args)
            {
                  //Creates a stack with 10 members
                  Stack a = new Stack(10);
                  int x = 0;
                  //Adds members to the stack
                  a.Push(x);
                  x++;
                  a.Push(x);
                  foreach (int y in a)
                  {
                        Console.WriteLine(y);
                  }
                  //Removes members from a stack
                  a.Pop();
                  //Removes all members of the stack
                  a.Clear();
            }
      }
}
```

Choosing the Right Collection

Do you need temporary storage?

- If yes, use a Queue or Stack.

- If no, consider another collection.

Do you need to access elements of the collection in a specific order, LIFO or FIFO?

- A Queue provides an FIFO order.

- A Stack provides an LIFO order.

The other collections provide random access.

Do you need to access elements by an index?

- ArrayList and StringCollection provide zero-based index access.

- Hashtable, SortedList, ListDictionary, and StringDictionary provide access via keys.

- NamedObjectCollectionBase and NameValueCollectionBase provide access by both zero-based index and by key/value pairs.

Will elements store a single value or a key/value pair?

- For one value, use any collection based on IList.

- For a key/single-value pair, use any IDictionary-derived class.

- For a key/multivalued pair, use or derive from NameValueCollection or a class in Collections.Specialized.

Do you need to sort elements differently from how they were entered into the array?

- Hashtable sorts by the hash code of the key.

- SortedList sorts by the value of key.

- ArrayList provides a Sort method that takes an IComparer-derived class.

Do you need fast searches?

- ListDictionary is best for small collections of ten or fewer items.

- Use a Hashtable.

Do you need a collection that accepts only strings?

- Use StringCollection, StringDictionary, or Collections.Specialized.

Iterators

In the past, to enumerate through an object that held a collection, your objects needed to inherit and implement IEnumerable. In addition, they needed to support an internal means of storing the state of the object being enumerated. This approach works in versions 1.0 and 1.1 of C#, but new functionality has been added to greatly simplify this process. Today, we have the foreach statement. You no longer need to do all the work to get your objects to enumerate with the foreach-style iterators.

Iterators handle the messy chore of implementing the enumerator pattern on your behalf. Rather than needing to create the classes and build the state machine, the C# compiler will place the code you have written in your iterators into the appropriate classes. The following example illustrates how iterators work.

Code Example: Iterators

```
using System;
using System.Collections;

namespace Client.Chapter_3___Structs__Enums__Arrays_and_Collections
{
    public class List
    {
        internal object[] elements;
        internal int count;
        public IEnumerable Elements()
        {
            foreach (object o in elements)
            {
                yield o;
            }
        }
    }
    public class ListUser
    {
        static void Main(string[] args)
        {
            List list = new List();
            foreach (object obj in list.Elements())
            {
                //Do something with obj
            }
        }
    }
}
```

CHAPTER 4
Program Control

- Selection Statements: if … else and switch … case

- Iterator Statements: for, foreach, while, and do … while

- Jump Statements: continue, break, and goto

Selection Statements

You can use the if statement or the if … else combination to select code to be executed. However, there is a practical limit to the number of selection-based if statements that you can combine. In these cases, if for no other reason than code readability, you should use a switch … case statement instead of multiple if statements.

if and if … else

By itself, the if statement means that if an expression to be evaluated is true, then execute this/these statements. The if statement evaluates an expression contained within the parentheses.

```
if(expression)
{
      Statement
      Statement
}
```

The parentheses help the compiler to identify the expression to be evaluated. If the expression evaluates to true, then the statements in the code block of the if statement are executed. If the expression evaluates to false, then the statements in the code block of the if statement are not executed.

If the if statement is followed by a single statement, the braces after the if statement are optional.

```
if(expression)
      Statement
```

An if statement can be used in conjunction with an else statement. This allows the first block to be executed for a true result of the if expression and the second set of statements following the else block to be executed for a false result.

```
if(expression)
      Statement - Expression evaluates to true
else
      Statement - Expression evaluates to false
```

You can nest if statements within if statements to produce a series of selection statements.

```
if(expression)
{
        if(expression)
        {
        }
}
```

You can also use logical operators (&& and ||) to combine multiple expression statements.

```
if(expression && expression)
```

The following example demonstrates the use of if … else selection statements.

Code Example: if … else

```
using System;

namespace Client.Chapter_4___Program_Control
{
     class ifelse
     {
          static void Main(string[] args)
          {
               int a = 5, b = 5, c = 10;
              //Compares a to b. If they are equal, then the expression
              //is true and WriteLine is called.
               if (a == b)
                      Console.WriteLine(a);
               else
                      Console.WriteLine(b);
              //Compares a > c and if a equal to b
               if ((a > c) || (a == b))
                      Console.WriteLine(b);
              //If a is greater than or equal to c and
              //b is less than or equal to c
               if ((a >= c) && (b <= c))
                      Console.WriteLine(c);
          }
     }
}
```

switch ... case

The switch ... case statement accepts a single integral value in the switch statement, and then compares that value with other values that are defined in the case statement.

```
switch(value)
{
    case value:
        break;
    default:
        break;
}
```

 NOTE   Unlike the C++ implementation of switch ... case statements, in C#, there is no fall-through between case statements. You must provide a break.

In the following example, a switch statement is declared where the value examined is the variable a. The execution will then flow through the case statements until it gets to the case statement that matches the value inside the switch statement.

Code Example: switch ... case

```
using System;
namespace Client.Chapter_4___Program_Control
{
    class MyMainClass
    {
        static void Main(string[] args)
        {
            int a = 0;
            Console.ReadLine();

            //Evaluates the value of a and compares to the value of the case
            //statements below
            switch (a)
            {
                case 1:
                    Console.WriteLine("One");
                    break;
                case 2:
                    Console.WriteLine("Two");
                    break;
                //Default is called when no match is made
                default:
                    Console.WriteLine("?");
                    break;
            }
        }
    }
}
```

Iterator Statements

As mentioned in Chapter 3, the foreach statement can be used to iterate through collections or arrays of objects. Other iterator statements include for, while, and do … while.

for

The simplest loop or iterator statement is the for statement.

```
for(value; condition expression; incrementor/decrementor)
{
        Statements
}
```

The for loop has three parts:

- A value, which assigns the starting count for the loop

- Followed by a conditional expression, which determines the end count for the loop

- And finally, an incrementor/decrementor, which increments or decrements the count of the first value

You may also nest for loops if you desire.

foreach

A new addition to C# is the foreach statement, which is another type of iterator.

```
foreach(type Identifier in collection/array)
{
        Statements
}
```

In a foreach statement, the first operand is always the type that is being added to the collection or array defined in the second operand.

The following example demonstrates the use of for and foreach loops. (Also see Chapter 4 for more examples of using foreach with arrays and collections.)

Code Example: for and foreach

```csharp
using System;

namespace Client.Chapter_4___Program_Control
{
    class Fors
    {
        static void Main(string[] args)
        {
            //a is set to zero and incremented with each iteration until
            //a is less than 10
            for (int a = 0; a < 10; a++)
            {
                Console.WriteLine(a);
            }
        }
    }
}
using System;
using System.Collections;
namespace Client.Chapter_4___Program_Control
{
    class ForEaches
    {
        static void Main(string[] args)
        {
            ArrayList a = new ArrayList(10);
            //Each member of the ArrayList will be iterated
            foreach (int x in a)
            {
                Console.WriteLine(x);
            }
        }
    }
}
```

while

The while loop executes statements within the code block of the while loop only if the expression within the parentheses evaluates to true. If the statement within the code block evaluates to false, then the block of while code is ignored, and control passes to the first statement following the while block.

 CAUTION   When using a while loop, make sure that the condition of the while loop is such that it will eventually be false and exit, or else you will have a spinning thread and your application will become unresponsive. You should also make sure that you increment or decrement the iterator if you are using one inside the loop.

---

do … while

Another version of the while loop is the do … while loop. The big difference between the while loop and the do … while loop is that the do … while loop code block is guaranteed to execute at least once.

In the following example, the while loop will print 1 through 10 using Console.WriteLine.

Code Example: while and do … while

```
using System;

namespace Client.Chapter_4___Program_Control
{
    class Whiles
    {
        static void Main(string[] args)
        {
            int a = 0;
            //While the value of a is greater than 10,
            //the inner code will be executed
            while(a > 10)
            {
                a++;
                Console.WriteLine(a);
            }
        }
    }
}
using System;

namespace Client.Chapter_4___Program_Control
{
    class DoWhile
    {
        static void Main(string[] args)
        {
            int a = 0;
            //The do loop is a normal while loop with one exception:
            //the code in the block is guaranteed to be executed
            //at least once
            do
            {
                a++;
                Console.WriteLine(a);
            } while (a < 10);
        }
    }
}
```

Jump Statements

The jump statements allow you control program flow by specifying which code blocks should be executed at a certain point in the code. These statements include continue, break, and goto.

continue

There are situations when the execution of code inside a code block should return to the evaluation expression. In C#, this behavior is controlled by the use of the continue statement. When the continue statement is encountered, the conditional expression in the while loop or other flow-control code is evaluated again, and the rest of the code block is skipped.

break

A break statement causes the execution of the code to exit the code block. This statement is usually used in conjunction with a selection statement (if or switch), and it is occasionally used with an iterator statement.

goto

There are two parts to using a goto statement:

- The first part is a goto command followed by a label.

- The second part is a label in the method, followed by a semicolon.

 CAUTION   Be very careful in using the goto statement, because it makes the code much less readable and more difficult to understand.

Upon execution of the goto command, the flow of execution will skip to the first statement following the label.

The following example demonstrates the use of the continue, break, and goto statements.

Code Example: continue, break, and goto

```
using System;

namespace Client.Chapter_4___Program_Control
{
    class MyMainClass
    {
        static void Main(string[] args)
        {
            WhileContinue();
            WhileBreak();
            WhileGoto();
        }
        static void WhileContinue()
        {
            int a = 0;
            while(a < 10)
            {
                a++;
                if (a == 5)
                {
                    //Force the execution back to the iterator
                    a++; continue;
                }
            }
        }
        static void WhileBreak()
        {
            int a = 0;
            while (a < 10)
            {
                a++;
                if (a == 5)
                    //Force the code to leave the iterator
                    break;
            }
            a++;
        }
        static void WhileGoto()
        {
            int a = 0;
            while (a < 10)
            {
```

```
            if (a == 5)
                //Force the code to the code label
                    goto cleanup;
        }
        cleanup :
            Console.WriteLine(a);
    }
  }
}
```

CHAPTER 5
Building Your Own Classes

- Object Methods

- Class Declaration and Definitions

- Constructors and Initialization

- Destroying Objects

- Passing by Value and by Reference

- Class Instances

- Overloading

- Core OOP Concepts

- Virtual Methods

- Overriding

- Interfaces

- Generics (new to 1.2)

- Partial Types (new to 1.2)

Object Methods

All nonvalue type objects inherit from the Object class, which provides four basic functions. Therefore, all objects have the following four methods: GetHashCode, ReferenceEquals, Equals (==), and ToString.

GetHashCode

The GetHashCode method returns a number that will always correspond to the value of an object. This hash code can then be used in collections to drastically reduce the overall number of objects searched for, because you can always look for this number. The collection classes do this by gathering all objects with the same hash code, and then eliminating the rest from the search.

NOTE   When you call the GetHashCode method on two objects that are equal in value, you should always get the same response.

It is very common for this class to be overridden, like this:

```
public override int GetHashCode()
```

ReferenceEquals

Given two references, ReferenceEquals can tell you if you are working on the same object. This functionality is a lot like comparing the controlling IUnknown in COM. Under the hood, this method just looks at the pointers being used to access the object and compares them. If the objects are the same object, this method returns true; otherwise, it returns false.

Equals

The Equals method is used to tell if two objects are the same in value. You will most certainly wish to override this method, because the default functionality is to call ReferenceEquals. This means that, by default, it will compare the objects, not the values of the objects.

```
public override bool Equals(Object obj)
```

If you override this method, you will also want to override GetHashCode.

When doing this kind of work, it is common to override the == and != operators as well. In fact, it is recommended that if you override these operators, you also override the Equals method.

```
public static bool operator == (Object A, Object B)
public static bool operator != (Object A, Object B)
```

ToString

All objects support a ToString method, which, by default, returns type information, rather than the value of the object. In most cases, you will wish to override this method as well, so that it returns data rather than type information.

Class Declaration and Definition

C# is a language designed to interpret "real-life" objects into syntax the computer can understand. Real-life objects are made up of data and functionality. Since C# is designed to be a true object-oriented language, all code is based on the *class*. The class is the name of the type that you use to define the relationship between data and functions or methods. The class declaration in C# also includes the class definition, so it is the one-stop place where everything about the class is defined.

 NOTE The declaration of a class does not result in memory being reserved. Memory will not be allocated until an instance of the class is created. Each instance of a class contains unique memory locations for data members of the instance.

Another key feature of classes in C# is the idea of *encapsulation*. Encapsulation is the process of controlling what is publicly available to clients that instantiate the class. (See the "Core OOP Concepts" section later in this chapter for more information about encapsulation.)

If you were to examine a class, you would find that it has six main parts, as shown in Table 5-1.

Table 5-1. The Main Components of a Class

Component	Description
Fields	Used to store variables in a class
Properties	Used to expose fields to client code
Methods	Provide actions for the class by manipulating fields and properties
Constructors	Initialize fields to values preferred for a class
Destructors	Called by garbage collectors
Dispose methods	Called by clients to clean up objects on their time schedule

When you are declaring a new class, you should set the accessibility of its members by using the access specifiers listed in Table 5-2.

Table 5-2. Access Specifiers for Classes

Access Specifier	Description
public	No access limitation
protected	Access limited to containing classes or derived classes
internal	Access limited to this program
protected internal	Access limited to this program or derived classes
private	Access limited to containing types

The following example demonstrates declaring and defining a class.

Code Example: Declaring and Defining a Class

```
using System;

namespace Client.Chapter_5___Building_Your_Own_Classes
{
    //Class definition
    public class DeclaringandDefiningClasses
    {
        //Fields
        static private int MyInt = 5;
        //Access Specifiers
        static public int MyInt2 = 10;
        static public int[] MyIntArray;
        static private int ObjectCount = 0;
        //Methods
        static void Main(string[] args)
        {
            MyIntArray = new int[10];
            ObjectCount++;
        }
        public static int MyMethod(int myInt)
        {
            MyInt = MyInt + myInt;
            return MyInt;
        }
        private static long MyLongMethod(ref int myInt)
        {
            return myInt;
        }
    }
}
```

Constructors and Initialization

Whenever an instance of a class is allocated, the compiler automatically executes a special method called a *constructor*. The purpose of the constructor is to initialize the fields within a class. It is common to use a constructor to initialize new reference types, as well as to pass existing objects to be acted on by the class.

Defining a constructor is optional but typically recommended. Also, you may overload the constructor with as many methods as needed, as long as the method signature is unique. If you do create your own constructor, make sure that you also create a default constructor that takes no parameters.

A constructor signature requires that the name of the constructor be the same as the name of the class and that the method contains no return value. The variable part is the number and order of the parameters. This is where you have the power to overload the constructor.

NOTE   If you choose to write your own constructor, you must provide at least a minimum method definition for the constructor, if you wish to use a simulated default constructor.

The following example demonstrates a constructor and initialization.

Code Example: Constructors and Initialization

```
using System;

namespace Client.Chapter_5___Building_Your_Own_Classes
{
    class CTOR
    {
        public int[] MyIntArray;
        public int Y;
        //Initialization can take place here
        private int ObjectCount = 0;
        static void Main(string[] args)
        {
            CTOR X = new CTOR();
            X.ObjectCount++;
            CTOR YY = new CTOR(10);
        }

        //Default CTOR
        CTOR()
        {
            MyIntArray = new int[10];
            //Do work necessary during object creation
        }

        //Overloads the CTOR allowing you to initialize Y
        CTOR(int myY)
        {
            Y = myY;
        }

    }
}
```

Destroying Objects

Objects are freed automatically by the garbage collector (GC). However, you can control some of this behavior by using `Dispose` or a finalizer.

Dispose

If you want to explicitly release resources such as file handles, mutexes, and so on, you can provide a public function called `Dispose` or `Close`, which will do this on demand. If you do write this function, you should call `SuppressFinalize` if you have a finalizer method, so the GC does not try to free the resources twice. To use this method, you must inherit from `IDisposable`.

NOTE   If you have derived the class, make sure to call the base class `Dispose` method.

Finalizer

The finalizer (*~classname*) method is called by the GC asynchronously when the object is being destroyed. It allows you to customize the destruction of the object when called by the GC. It is extremely important to remember that when you use this method, your object will always survive the first garbage collection and will not be freed until the next garbage collection cycle.

CAUTION   Use the finalizer *only* to release unmanaged resources, and avoid doing this if you can. The order in which objects that have a finalizer are freed by the GC is not defined. This makes freeing managed resources in the finalizer dangerous. You can use Performance Monitor counters to determine the effect of using finalizers in your code. Use FinalizationSurvivors to determine the unmanaged resources that are consuming memory. Use Promoted Finalization-Memory from Gen X to determine the number of bytes that were promoted to this generation (note that this specific counter is not cumulative; it's reset with each sample).

The following example demonstrates destroying objects.

Code Example: Destroying Objects

```csharp
using System;

namespace Client.Chapter_5___Building_Your_Own_Classes
{
    class DTOR: IDisposable
    {
        public static int[] MyIntArray;
        private static int ObjectCount = 0;
        private bool Disposed = false;
        static void Main(string[] args)
        {
            MyIntArray = new int[10];
            ObjectCount++;
        }
        //Used to clean up and free unmanaged resources.

        //Never mark this class as virtual, because you do not want
        // derived classes to be able to override it.
        public void Dispose()
        {
            //If this class is derived, call the base
            //class Dispose.
            base.Dispose();
            //Call the overloaded version of Dispose
            Dispose(true);
            //Tell the CLR not to run the finalizer this way.
            //You do not free unmanaged resources twice.
            GC.SuppressFinalize(this);
        }
        //If the user calls Dispose, both managed and unmanaged
        // resources are freed.
        //If the finalizer is called, only unmanaged resources are freed.
        private void Dispose(bool disposing)
        {
            if(!this.Disposed)
            {
                if(disposing)
                {
                    //Free any managed resources.
                }
```

```
                    //Free unmanaged resources.
            }

        Disposed = true;
    }
    //This finalizer method is called by the GC,
    //not the user. The net result of having this is that
    //the object will always survive the first GC cycle and
    //will be collected the next time GC1 is collected.
    ~DTOR()
    {
        Dispose(false);
    }
    }
}
```

Passing by Value and by Reference

Arguments can be passed in two fashions: by value or reference. If you pass an argument by value, you are essentially creating a copy of the existing variable to the method being called.

 CAUTION It is extremely important to know that any changes made to the variable will not be returned to the calling function when you pass a variable by value!

Arguments can also be passed by reference. This requires a couple of steps:

- The variable passed must be passed by reference by using the ref keyword when you call the method.

- The prototype of the method being called must expect a reference type and have the ref keyword in the method prototype.

By passing arguments by reference, you are allowing the called function to make modifications to the object being passed, and those modifications will be present when the called function returns.

Table 5-3 describes the keywords used for passing arguments.

Table 5-3. Keywords for Passing Arguments

Keyword	Description
in	Passes a parameter by value to the called method. Modifications made to the object inside the called method will not be reflected after returning.
out	Used to specify that the called method will create the object being returned.
ref	Passes a reference of an object that can be modified to the called method.
params	Allows you to pass an unknown number of parameters of a single type. This can be used by only one parameter in a method. You can pass a single argument of a type, an array, or a variable number of arguments.

NOTE   Methods in C# have the ability to receive a value back for error checking or modification if you desire. It is important to note that conducting error checking with return values is not the preferred method in C#. It is recommended to throw exceptions instead. We will look at exceptions in a Chapter 8.

The following example demonstrates passing arguments by value and by reference.

Code Example: Passing by Value and by Reference

```csharp
using System;

namespace Client.Chapter_5___Building_Your_Own_Classes
{
    class PassingParametersByValueandByRef
    {
        static private int MyInt = 5;
        static public int MyInt2 = 10;
        static public int[] MyIntArray;
        private static int ObjectCount = 0;
        static void Main(string[] args)
        {
            int MyInt = 5;
            MyIntArray = new int[10];
            ObjectCount++;
            Method2();
            Method2(1, 2);
            MyMethodRef(ref MyInt);
            Method2(new int[] { 1, 2, 3, 4 });
        }
        //Pass by reference
        static public int MyMethodRef(ref int myInt)
        {
            MyInt = MyInt + myInt;
            return MyInt;
        }
        //Pass by value
        static public int MyMethod(int myInt)
        {
            MyInt = MyInt + myInt;
            return MyInt;
        }
        static private long MyLongMethod(ref int myInt)
        {
            return myInt;
        }
        static public void Method2(params int[] args)
        {
            for (int I = 0; I < args.Length; I++)
                Console.WriteLine(args[I]);
        }
    }
}
```

Class Instances

To declare a class instance, include the class name, followed by an identifier of the particular instance of the class. In addition, you must use the new keyword, followed by calling a constructor for the object.

When a class is instantiated, memory is reserved for those objects members on the managed heap.

The following is an example of declaring class instances.

Code Example: Declaring Class Instances

```
using System;

namespace Client.Chapter_5___Building_Your_Own_Classes
{
    class DeclaringClassInstances
    {
        static void Main(string[] args)
        {
            //Creates an instance of a class
            ClassInstantiated MyClass = new ClassInstantiated();
        }
    }
    public class ClassInstantiated
    {
        public void Display()
        {
            Console.WriteLine("Hello World");
        }
    }
}
```

Overloading

Overloading allows you to have a class that has multiple methods with the same name, but with a different number and order of arguments that accomplish a similar task. You should use overloading sparingly and only when doing so makes it easier for other developers to better understand your intentions. Furthermore, your overloaded method's behavior should be consistent across all methods that you are overloading.

The following example demonstrates overloading.

Code Example: Overloading

```
using System;

namespace Client.Chapter_5___Building_Your_Own_Classes
{
    class OverloadingClasses
    {
        static void Main(string[] args)
        {
            A MyA = new A();
            MyA.Display();
            MyA.Display(10);
        }
    }
    public class A
    {
        //Overloaded method calls
        public void Display()
        {
            Console.WriteLine("No Params Display Method");
        }
        public void Display(int A)
        {
            Console.WriteLine("Overloaded Display {0}", A);
        }
    }
}
```

Core OOP Concepts

At the very heart and soul of object-oriented programming (OOP) are five concepts: abstraction, encapsulation, inheritance, polymorphism, and containership.

Abstraction

The idea of *abstraction* is to reduce an object to its core essence so that only the most essential elements are represented. An example of this would be a simple phone number (803)222-5555. This number is made up of three parts: the area code, the prefix, and the number. It is much easier to deal with one object as the phone number, while knowing that it is actually made up of these three parts.

Encapsulation

The term *encapsulation* is used to describe the process of controlling the contents of an object directly, as well as making the implementation of an object unknown to its consumer. Let's say that we create a class called `PhoneNumber`. The idea of encapsulation allows us to not really care about what the three parts of a phone number are, or for that matter, how they are generated. The consumer just wants to be able to create an instance of our class and get a valid number in return. We control access to our objects by using the access modifiers: `public`, `protected`, `internal`, and `private`.

Inheritance

Inheritance allows for the reuse of a class. The traditional example is that of creating a simple base class of type `Animal`. This class contains the basic functionality that is consistent across all animals, such as breathing, eating, mating, and so forth. We can then generate new objects by deriving a new class from our existing class `Animal`, without needing to provide the basic functionality of an `Animal`. This allows us to focus on the `Dog` class that we are trying to create. But this doesn't mean that we do not have the option of overriding the behavior that we inherit from `Animal`, because we can use polymorphism, as described in the next section.

C# allows for only single inheritance of classes and multiple inheritance of interfaces. It also provides a means to prevent inheritance by using the `sealed` keyword.

Polymorphism

Polymorphism allows for you to define base classes that include common functionality via methods on groups of related objects, without regard to the type of the particular object. To implement this functionality, use the `virtual` keyword in the base class, which allows you to call the correct method on the basis of object type, rather than the reference type. For example, suppose that we create an instance of a `Dog` class that inherits from an `Animal` base class. The `Animal` base class provides for basic functionality such as eating. If we wish to ensure that the `Dogs.Eat` method is always called, regardless of the type that holds a reference to the `Dog` object, we will need to mark the `Animals::Eat` method as virtual and the `Dog:Eat` methods as `override`.

Containership

You may extend a class by using the concept of *containership* in addition to inheritance. The idea is that, instead of deriving a new class from an existing base class, you just include the class as a member of the new class.

The following example demonstrates OOP concepts.

Code Example: Inheritance

```csharp
using System;

namespace Client.Chapter_5___Building_Your_Own_Classes
{
    class Inheritance
    {
        static void Main(string[] args)
        {
            //Creates an instance of D objects
            B MyB = new D();
            D MyD = new D();
            //Both result in D's instance of Display being called
            MyB.Display();
            MyD.Display();
        }
    }
    public class B
    {
        public virtual void Display()
        {
            Console.WriteLine("Class B's Display Method");
        }
    }
    public class C: B
    {
        public override void Display()
        {
            Console.WriteLine("Class C's Display Method");
        }
    }
    public class ContainedClass
    {
        int MyInt = 0;
    }
    public class D: C
    {
        public ContainedClass MyClass = new ContainedClass();
        public override void Display()
        {
            Console.WriteLine("Class D's Display Method");
        }
    }
}
```

Virtual Methods

Polymorphism is the idea that you can call a particular method based on the class that was used to create the instance of the object. In C#, you must use the override and virtual keywords explicitly to gain this functionality.

A *virtual method* is a method in a base class that can be ignored in favor of a derived class's version of the same method.

 CAUTION   It is quite easy to confuse the concept of *overriding* with that of *overloading*. The big difference between these two concepts is the basis of polymorphism. A virtual method can be overridden by a method of a derived class that has the exact same prototype or method signature. Overloading a method is when the method has the same name but not the same arguments in the same order.

Pure virtual methods are used in abstract classes, and they do not have a method definition. They exist solely as a placeholder for a derived class to implement that inherits from the abstract class.

The following example demonstrates the use of virtual methods.

Code Example: Virtual Methods

```csharp
using System;

namespace Client.Chapter_5___Building_Your_Own_Classes
{
    class MyMainClass
    {
        static void Main(string[] args)
        {
         //The function called is based on the type called by new.
          //The variable MyB is actually a C object, and when you call a method
         //marked as override, it calls that object's method rather than the
            //method inherited.
             B MyB = new C();

            MyB.Display();          //Calls C's Display
        }
    }
```

```
//Marks a class as abstract or a method as abstract, which means a class instance
//cannot be made. In this instance, virtual is implied.
abstract class A
{
    public abstract void Display();
}
class B : A
{
    //Marks a method as overriding a method that was inherited.
    public override void Display()
    {
        Console.WriteLine("Class B's Display Method");
    }
}
class C : B
{
    public override void Display()
    {
        Console.WriteLine("Class C's Display Method");
    }
}
class D : C
{
    public override void Display()
    {
        Console.WriteLine("Class D's Display Method");
    }
}
}
```

Overriding

Three keywords are related to overriding methods: override, base, and new. These allow you to use polymorphism, access an overridden method, and indicate a method override.

override

The override keyword is used to invoke polymorphism. It allows a derived class to provide a method with the same name and parameters. The derived class may enhance or modify a method that is inherited through a base class.

base

The base keyword is used to access the base method that has been overridden. Remember that C# supports only single inheritance. If you have class C derived from class B, which is derived from class A, and each class has a virtual or overridable version of the same method, you can call only the method that is in the base class, not in the base class of the base class.

new

The new keyword, in addition to being used to allocate memory, can also be used to hide data members, methods, and type members of a base class. The new keyword is implied and is used to signal that a method has been replaced in the derived class. This keyword is not required, but it is recommended for code readability. Any derived class that implements a method with the same signature will be treated as if it had been marked as new.

The following example demonstrates overriding.

Code Example: Overriding

```
using System;

namespace Client.Chapter_5___Building_Your_Own_Classes
{
    class MyMainClass
    {
        static void Main(string[] args)
        {
```

```
                //The function called is based
                //on the type called by new
                 A MyA = new D();
                 B MyB = new C();

                MyA.Display();          //Calls D Display
                MyB.Display();          //Calls C Display
                //Followed by B's Display via the base keyword
        }
}
class A
{
        public virtual void Display()
        {
                Console.WriteLine("Class A's Display Method");
        }
}
class B : A
{
        public override void Display()
        {
                Console.WriteLine("Class B's Display Method");
        }
}
class C : B
{
        public override void Display()
        {
                Console.WriteLine("Class C's Display Method");
                base.Display();
        }
}
class D : C
{
        public override void Display()
        {
                Console.WriteLine("Class D's Display Method");
        }
}
}
```

Interfaces

Interfaces are used to describe a common set of methods. An interface in or of itself cannot be instantiated, but it can be used as a base class. In fact, only interfaces can be used in multiple inheritance of a derived class.

 CAUTION Be very careful when you derive a new class from two interfaces that contain the same method signatures. Under these circumstances, you must use explicit interface implementation, as well as make sure you call the method using a reference type of that interface.

If you derive a new class from interfaces with the same method signatures, you must use explicit interface implementation, and then call the method using a reference type of that interface. For example, suppose you derived a class like this:

```
interface IFoo
{
        void DoSomething()
}
interface IFoo2
{
        void DoSomething()
}
public class MyFoo : IFoo, IFoo2
{
        void IFoo.DoSomething()
        {
                //Do work
        }
        void IFoo2.DoSomething()
        {
                //Do work
        }
}
```

To use this class, you must use the interface to access the object.

```
public static void Main()
{
        MyFoo F = new MyFoo();
        IFoo F1 = (IFoo)F;
        IFoo2 F2 = (IFoo2)F;
        F1.DoSomething();
        F2.DoSomething();
}
```

The following example demonstrates using interfaces.

Code Example: Interfaces

```
using System;

namespace Client.Chapter_5___Building_Your_Own_Classes
{
    class MyMainClass
    {
        static void Main(string[] args)
        {
            //The function called is based
            //on the type called by new
             B MyB = new C();
             D MyD = new D();

            MyB.Display();          //Calls C Display
            MyD.Display();          //Calls D Display
        }
    }
    //Creates a public interface that classes may inherit
    public interface A
    {
        void Display();
    }
    class B : A
    {
        public virtual void Display()
        {
            Console.WriteLine("Class B's Display Method");
        }
    }
    class C : B
    {
        public override void Display()
        {
            Console.WriteLine("Class C's Display Method");
        }
    }
    class D : C
    {
        public override void Display()
        {
            Console.WriteLine("Class D's Display Method");
        }
    }
}
```

Generics

C++ templates have come to C#! The 1.2 version of the framework and the product currently known as Whidbey (Visual Studio 8) have a new feature that lets you build classes that can accept and work with any type of data.

The idea is simple: Take a class such as a simple `Queue` object and be able to use strong-typed objects in the class. That sounds easy enough, but to do this using the 1.0 or 1.1 versions of the framework, you would need to write a new `Queue` object for each type or do casting to object types and back to your type. You would need to rely on `Hashtables`, `Stacks`, `Queues`, and so forth always returning the base type object of `Object`. With *generics,* this is no longer necessary. You write one class that takes a parameterized value, and that type will be used throughout the class.

Generics increase the usability of your code greatly and add the coolest feature to the language. The 1.2 version of C# will have new generic versions of the common collection classes, such as `Hashtable`, `Queue`, and so on.

Generics support one or multiple parameters of types. This means that you can do something like the following:

```
public class MyDictionary<KeyType, ValType>
```

Generics also support the idea of constraints. These constraints are implemented using the `where` keyword after defining the types in `<>`. You can declare one or multiple constraints per parameter. The basic idea is that you can specify which types you will to allow to be passed to the parameters. Here is an example of using constraints:

```
public class MyDictionary<KeyType, ValType> where
KeyType : IComparable,
KeyType : IEnumerable,
ValType : MyProduct
```

With generics, value type and reference type parameters are handled as follows:

- For each type passed as parameter that is a value type, the runtime will generate a specific instance of that class, with the specific type being substituted for the parameter that was passed.

- When you pass a reference type, the runtime will produce one instance of the class and use that instance for every instance of the generic class created.

The following example demonstrates the use of generics.

Code Example: Generics

```
using System;

namespace Client.Chapter_5___Building_Your_Own_Classes
{
    public class MyQueue<ItemType>
    {
        private ItemType[] items;
        //Adds an item to the queue
        public void Enqueue(ItemType data)
        {
            //Do stuff
        }
        //Removes an item from the queue
        public ItemType Dequeue()
        {
            return items[0];
        }
    }
    class MyServer
{
        [MTAThread]
        static void Main(string[] args)
        {
            MyQueue<MyProduct> queue = new MyQueue<MyProduct>();
            queue.Enqueue(new MyProduct());
            MyProduct c = queue.Dequeue();
        }
    }
    public class MyProduct
    {
    }
}
```

Partial Types

Partial types allow you to break up types consisting of a large amount of source code into several different source files for easier development and maintenance. The partial keyword allows you to define a C# class in multiple files, similar to the way C++ did. It's about time!

The following examples demonstrate the use of partial types.

Code Example: Partial Types, Test1.cs

```
public partial class Test
{
        public void MyFirstMethod()
        {
                //Do stuff
        }
}
```

Code Example: Partial Types, Test2.cs

```
public partial class Test
{
        public void MySecondMethod()
        {
                //Do stuff
        }
}
```

CHAPTER 6
Strings

- String Creation

- String Concatenation

- Substrings: Finding and Extracting

- Character Manipulation: Changing Case, Replacing, and Removing

- Joining and Splitting Strings

- Trimming and Padding Strings

- String Formatting

String Creation

Strings are a way to combine a group of characters for presentation to the user. In C#, we have the benefit of a built-in string class in .NET, but we can also use traditional C-style strings in arrays. The big advantage of using the .NET string is that it has built-in support for common methods that you may wish to use on a string, such as copy, concatenate, and so forth.

Another advantage of the .NET string class is that it produces nonmutable strings. This prevents a string from being overwritten because a pointer was being used to access the string, as sometimes occurred with C++ strings. If you truly desire to have a mutable string, you should use the StringBuilder class from the System.Text namespace, as demonstrated in several examples in this chapter.

C-style strings are nothing more than an array of chars that is null-terminated. Remember that an array is a block of contiguous memory of the same type and is a reference variable. To declare and define a C-style string, create a char array, as in this example:

```
char[] MyString = new char[6] {'H', 'e', 'l', 'l', 'o', '\0'};
```

This creates a string that looks very similar to the following in memory:

0	1	2	3	4	5
H	e	l	l	o	\0

Another and more preferred way to handle strings is to use the built-in string class, which provides a variety of methods that perform common tasks. To define and declare a new string class, use the string keyword, as in the following example:

```
string MyString = new string("Hello");
```

This creates a new string that is initialized with the word "Hello" that is automatically null-terminated (\0).

 NOTE   By default, strings are Unicode in C#. It is also important to remember that the C# string keyword is an alias for System.String.

The following example demonstrates creating strings.

Code Example: Creating Strings

```csharp
using System;

namespace Client.Chapter_6___Strings
{
    class CreatingStrings
    {
        static void Main(string[] args)
        {
            char MyChar = 'A';

            MyChar = (char)65;
            //Creates a Unicode array
            char[] MyChar2 = {'H','e','l','l','o','\0'};

            char[] MyChar3 = new char[5];
            MyChar3[0] = 'H';
            MyChar3[1] = 'e';
            MyChar3[2] = 'l';
            MyChar3[3] = 'l';
            MyChar3[4] = 'o';
            MyChar3[5] = '\0';
        }
    }
}

using System;

namespace MyNamespace
{
    class MyMainClass
    {
        static void Main(string[] args)
        {
            //Creates a string
            string MyString = "hello";
        }
    }
}
```

String Concatenation

String concatenation is used to add characters to the end of a string. The `string` class provides two methods for adding characters to a string:

- The `Insert` method allows you to specify where to place the new characters in the string. It has two parameters: the location where you would like to add to the string, followed by the string to be added to the existing string.

- The `Append` method allows you to add a string to the end of an existing string. The only parameter you pass to this method is the string to be added.

The `StringBuilder` class is convenient for string concatenation, as well as other types of string modifications, such as removing, replacing, or inserting characters. Unlike the `string` class, which creates an entire new object for each change to the string, with the `StringBuilder` class, you can avoid creating a new string subsequent to each modification. The methods contained within this class do not return a new `StringBuilder` object, unless you specify otherwise. This makes the `StringBuilder` class a much better solution for operating on strings.

The following examples demonstrate string concatenation with mutable and nonmutable strings, as well as comparing strings.

Code Example: String Concatenation

```
using System;
using System.Text;

namespace Client.Chapter_6___Strings
{
    class StringConcatenation
    {
        static void Main(string[] args)
        {
            //Creates a mutable string
            StringBuilder MyString = new
            StringBuilder("Hello");

            MyString.Insert(0, "My");
            MyString.Append("World");

            Console.WriteLine(MyString);

        }
    }
}
```

Code Example: Nonmutable String

```
using System;

namespace Client.Chapter_6___Strings
{
    class StringConcatenation2
    {
        static void Main(string[] args)
        {
            Console.WriteLine("Enter Your Password?");
            string UserPassword = Console.ReadLine();
            //Creates a nonmutable string
            string Password = "Victory";
            //Compares the value of the string
            if(Password.CompareTo(UserPassword) == 0)
            {
                    Console.WriteLine("Bad Password");
             }

            Console.WriteLine("Good Password!");
        }
    }
}
```

Substrings

You can work with strings within strings, or *substrings*, in several ways. These include searching for substrings and extracting substrings.

Searching for Substrings

There are many ways to find a string within a string. The string class provides two methods that will determine if a string contains a particular substring:

- The StartsWith method returns true if the string passed as the first parameter is contained at the beginning of the string being searched.

- The EndsWith method returns true if the string passed as the first parameter is found at the end of an existing string.

The following example demonstrates searching for substrings.

Code Example: Searching for Substrings

```
using System;

namespace Client.Chapter_6___Strings
{
    class Substrings
    {
        static void Main(string[] args)
        {
            //Creates an array of strings
            string[] FootballTeams = new string[3] {
                "Miami, Dolphins", "Oakland, Raiders", "Seattle, Seahawks"
            };
            //Iterates through each string in the array
            foreach (string s in FootballTeams)
            {
                //Returns Awesome if the string starts with Miami
                if (s.StartsWith("Miami"))
                    Console.WriteLine("Awesome!");
                else
                    Console.WriteLine("Bummer Dude!");
            }
        }
    }
}
```

Extracting Substrings

The substring method of the string class allows you to provide a parameter that will retrieve the specified number of characters from the beginning of an existing string. There are many overloaded forms of this method that provide even more functionality.

The following example demonstrates extracting substrings.

Code Example: Extracting Substrings

```
using System;

namespace Client.Chapter_6___Strings
{
    class ExtractingSubstrings
    {
        static void Main(string[] args)
        {
            string MyClasses = "Math 101 - Algebra";
            //Creates a string that is made up of the first six chars of
            //MyClasses
            string MySubstring = MyClasses.Substring(6);

            Console.WriteLine(MySubstring);
        }
    }
}
```

Character Manipulation

Along with working with substrings, you can also manipulate characters within the string. You can easily convert the case of characters, replace characters, and remove characters.

Changing Character Case

The string class provides two methods that allow you to change an existing string into all uppercase or all lowercase characters:

- The ToUpper method changes an existing string to all uppercase characters.

- The ToLower method changes a string to all lowercase characters.

The following example demonstrates using these methods to change character case.

Code Example: Changing Character Case

```
using System;

namespace Client.Chapter_6___Strings
{
    class ChangingCharacters
    {
        static void Main(string[] args)
        {
            string MyString = "Miami, Dolphins";

            Console.WriteLine(MyString);
            //Converts all characters to uppercase
            MyString.ToUpper();
            Console.WriteLine(MyString);
            //Converts all characters to lowercase
            MyString.ToLower();
            Console.WriteLine(MyString);
        }
    }
}
```

Replacing Characters

You easily replace characters in a StringBuilder class by using the Replace method. The first parameter is the character you would like to replace, and the second parameter is the replacement character. The string will then be searched for all instances of that character, and that character will be replaced with the one you specified.

The following example demonstrates how to replace characters in a string.

Code Example: Replacing Characters

```
using System;
using System.Text;

namespace Client.Chapter_6___Strings
{
    class ReplacingCharacters
    {
        static void Main(string[] args)
        {
            StringBuilder MyString = new StringBuilder("AAAAABBB");

            Console.WriteLine(MyString);
            //Replaces all the As with Fs
            MyString.Replace("A", "F");
            Console.WriteLine(MyString);
        }
    }
}
```

Removing Characters

The Remove method of the string class allows you to remove characters from a string. It takes two parameters. The first parameter is the zero-based index into the string, specifying where you wish to start. The second parameter is the count of the number of characters you would like to remove.

The following example removes characters from an existing string, printing a string that says "Hello World."

Code Example: Removing Characters

```
Using System;

namespace Client.Chapter_6___Strings
{
    class RemovingCharacters
    {
        static void Main(string[] args)
        {
            string MyString = "Hello UnderWorld";

            Console.WriteLine(MyString.Remove(7, 5));
        }
    }
}
```

Joining and Splitting Strings

The easiest way to join two strings together is to use the overloaded + operator to form a new string. Another approach is to use the Join method of the string class, which combines two strings with a separator that you define.

The Split method of the string class allows you to break an existing string into an array of strings by searching for a particular character, such as a space.

The following examples demonstrate how to join and split strings. In the first example, the two strings are joined together by using the + operator to form a new string, which is passed to WriteLine.

Code Example: Joining Strings

```
Using System;

namespace Client.Chapter_6___Strings
{
    class JoiningStrings
    {
        static void Main(string[] args)
        {
            string MyString = "Hello";
            string MyString2 = "World";
            string JoinedString = MyString + MyString2;

            Console.WriteLine(JoinedString);

            string[] A = new string[2] {
                "Hello", "World"
            };
            //Combines all the strings in the string array with a space
            //in between each string
            string Joined = string.Join(" ", A);

            Console.WriteLine(Joined);
        }
    }
}
```

Code Example: Splitting Strings

```
using System;

namespace Client.Chapter_6___Strings
{
    class SplittingStrings
    {
        static void Main(string[] args)
        {
            string MyString = "The quick brown fox ran around!";
            string[] MyStringSplit = new string[6];

            MyStringSplit = MyString.Split(new char[] { ' ' }, 6);
            Console.WriteLine(MyStringSplit[1] + MyStringSplit[3]);
        }
    }
}
```

Trimming and Padding Strings

The `string` method provides three methods that allow you to trim spaces or characters from a string:

- The `TrimStart` method allows you to trim the leading empty or space characters from a string.

- The `TrimEnd` method removes trailing spaces from the end of a string.

- The `Trim` method allows you to remove specific characters from a string.

If you want to add spaces or a specific character to the beginning or end of a string, you can use the `PadLeft` or `PadRight` method. The only parameter that these methods take is the number of characters with which to pad the existing string. This is the simplest way to pad a string. An overloaded version of the method allows you to add a parameter that defines the padding character.

The following examples demonstrate trimming spaces from a string and adding spaces to the beginning of a string.

Code Example: Trimming Spaces

```
using System;

namespace Client.Chapter_6___Strings
{
    class TrimmingSpaces
    {
        static void Main(string[] args)
        {
            string MyString = "   Hello, World !   ";

            //Removes whitespace from the front of the string
            MyString.TrimStart();
            Console.WriteLine(MyString);
            //Removes whitespace from the end of the string
            MyString.TrimEnd();
            Console.WriteLine(MyString);
            //Removes the "!" character
            MyString.Trim(char.Parse("!"));
            Console.WriteLine(MyString);
        }
    }
}
```

Code Example: Padding Strings

```csharp
using System;

namespace Client.Chapter_6___Strings
{
    class PaddingStrings
    {
        static void Main(string[] args)
        {
            string MyString = "Hello World";

            Console.WriteLine(MyString.PadLeft(5));
        }
    }
}
```

String Formatting

The Parse method allows numeric types to be converted from string types. Here is an example:

```
string X = "12345";
int Y = int.Parse(X);
```

Parse also has the ability to work with some formatting of strings, such as the following:

```
string X = "23,456";
int Y = Int.Parse(X, System.Globalization.NumberStyles.AllowThousands);
```

This example converts the string 23,456 to an int of 23456.

C# provides several built-in ways to format a string. For example, let's say we have an int with a value of 100 and we wish to present this value to the user as currency. We could accomplish this by doing one of the following:

```
int X = 100;
string Y = int.ToString("C");
```

or

```
int X = 100;
Console.WriteLine("{0:C}", X);
```

Both examples would print $100.00

The following are some of the common formatters:

- Address

- Currency

- Date

- Numerals

- Phone numbers

- Time

- Units of measure

All of this formatting is built on the globalization settings. You can learn more about string formatting through the following MSDN library articles:

- The article about functions for localizing Web forms: `http://` `msdn.microsoft.com/library/en-us/vbcon/html/` `vbconculture-specificfunctionsforlocalizingwindowsformswebforms.asp`, or if you have installed the MSDN DVD, using the URL `ms-help://` `MS.VSCC.2003/MS.MSDNQTR.2003FEB.1033/vbcon/html/` `vbconCulture-SpecificFunctionsForLocalizingWindowsFormsWebForms.htm`.

- The article about formatting issues: `http://msdn.microsoft.com/library/` `default.asp?url=/library/en-us/vsent7/html/vxconFormattingIssues.asp`, or if you have installed the MSDN DVD, using the URL `ms-help://MS.VSCC.2003/MS.MSDNQTR.2003FEB.1033/vsent7/html/` `vxconFormattingIssues.htm`.

Memory Management

- Virtual Memory and Address Space

- Heap and Stack Memory

- References and Pointers

- The Garbage Collector (GC)

Virtual Memory and Address Space

In Intel-compliant systems running Windows NT, Windows 2000, or Windows XP, programmers use *virtual memory* to access physical memory. In these systems, each process is given 4GB of virtual memory that maps to either the physical memory or the paging file. This virtual memory is split into two parts: *user mode*, which is the low 2GB (0x00000000 to 0x7fffffff) of memory, and *kernel mode*, which is the high 2GB (0x80000000 to 0xffffffff) of memory. For the most part, applications are written to operate in user mode, and drivers are written to operate in kernel mode. We will focus on user mode memory, since this is where most C# endeavors will operate.

In user mode address space (0x00000000 to 0x7fffffff), the memory of most applications is split into several parts:

- There is process information block, which contains data about the process.

- There are one or more thread environment blocks, which contain data that describes a thread.

- There is at least one block of memory that is used as the default heap.

- Finally, there is memory set aside to load assemblies such as executables (EXEs) or dynamic link libraries (DLLs).

Under the hood, the use of virtual memory allows for items like assemblies to be loaded into physical memory once, and then each process will map its virtual memory to the same physical memory. This greatly reduces the amount of memory used, since the DLL or EXE is loaded into physical memory only once.

Virtual memory comes in one of three flavors:

Free memory: Memory that has not been requested for use in the virtual memory of the application. You may not use or access free memory.

Reserved memory: Memory that has been set aside for an application but has not been committed, and thus there is no backing to the memory in pagefile.sys.

Committed memory: Memory that has been reserved and does have space allocated in the pagefile.sys. You may not use reserved memory until it is committed. Fortunately, the operating system does this process for you, unless you want to get down and dirty with API calls to methods such as VirtualAlloc.

Heap and Stack Memory

Within virtual memory, there are two very important areas of memory:

Stack memory: This memory is used to store a variety of items, including local variables, return addresses, and base pointers in nonoptimized code. When it is created, each thread reserves 1MB of memory and commits 4KB of it for active use. As the thread is used, memory is committed in 4KB increments on an as-needed basis. Interestingly enough, with stack memory, the address space used goes down from a large address to a small address.

Heap memory: This is another allocation of memory that can be use by reference-based variables, such as classes and arrays. Typically, a heap is used when the size of the allocation would be too large to place on the stack or the duration in use of the object may extend beyond the current local scope of the function. The really nice feature of C# is that the garbage collector (GC) does all the work of freeing used objects automatically that have a reference count of zero. This allows the developer to make allocations and to not need to worry about freeing the memory, as was required in C++.

The following example shows the use of heap and stack memory.

Code Example: Heap and Stack Memory

```csharp
using System;

namespace Client.Chapter_7___Memory_Management
{
    class HeapandStackMemory
    {
        static void Main(string[] args)
        {
            //Creates a reference type
            MyClass ThisClass = new MyClass();
        }
    }
    public class MyClass
    {
        public int MyInt;
        private long MyLong;
        public void DoSomething()
        {
            Console.WriteLine(MyInt);
            Console.WriteLine(MyLong);
        }
    }
}
```

References and Pointers

Reference variables are the user-defined classes and arrays you have created. References are the default description of what was a pointer in C or C++, and for that matter, is the same as a reference was in C++: a const pointer to memory. One big difference, however, is that, unless you use the fixed keyword, it is possible for the value of a reference to be changed by the GC as it optimizes the use of memory and moves allocations around.

Because a C# reference location might change, you cannot do pointer arithmetic on a reference. To use pointers, you must mark the code as unsafe. Then you declare a pointer type using the following syntax:

```
MyClass* pMyClass = new MyClass();
```

This will return a pointer to an instance of MyClass. With this pointer, you can do all the tricks that you could do with C pointers.

Although you can use C-style pointers, it is highly recommended that you use references in lieu of pointers, because they are inherently much safer. For instance, you can use the ++ and -- operators to walk through a pointer to an array. Each time you encounter the ++ or -- operator, you will increment the pointer by the size of the type associated with the pointer. So, if you were using a char*, you would increment the pointer by 2 bytes each time you ran the statement with ++.

The following example demonstrates the use of references and pointers.

Code Example: References and Pointers

```csharp
using System;
using System.Runtime.InteropServices;

namespace Client.Chapter_7___Memory_Management
{
    class ReferencesandPointers
    {
        static void Main(string[] args)
        {
            UsePointers();
        }
        //Creates an unsafe block, which allows for the use of C-style pointers
        static unsafe public void UsePointers()
        {
            char * pMyArray = (char*)Marshal.AllocCoTaskMem(6);

            while (*pMyArray != '\0')
            {
                Console.WriteLine(*pMyArray);
                pMyArray++;
            }

            Marshal.FreeCoTaskMem((IntPtr)pMyArray);
        }
    }
}
```

The Garbage Collector (GC)

In the .NET world, the GC is the component that manages memory. Every time you use the new keyword to allocate a new object, it is the GC that allocates memory from the managed heap. The GC also is responsible for efficiently freeing memory from the managed heap. This action is based on allocation needs and which objects are ready for removal from the managed heap.

The function of the GC frees the developer from needing to manage memory, which is great. However, when you use unmanaged components—such as a file, window, network, and synchronization objects—you must provide a means for the GC to clean up these items. This process is done by writing a finalizer method (~ClassName), which cleans up the objects for you by releasing or closing them. By default, this method does nothing and is automatically generated for you, similar to how a default destructor is handled in C++. If you do need to write your own finalizer method, you must override the existing one and write code that cleans up your unmanaged resources. The GC will then call this method when it becomes time to release the object or remove it from the heap.

The .NET runtime does provide a class that will allow you to manage the GC directly, but it is *highly recommended* that you avoid this if possible. The GC class provides this functionality for you. In the GC class, you can call the Collect method to force the GC to clean up immediately and call objects' finalizer methods.

 CAUTION It is recommended to call the GC Collect method only when there is a significant amount of memory that has recently been freed and needs to be restored immediately to active use for new allocations. It is very important that you use the Collect method sparingly, because overuse of the method could cause significant performance problems.

By default, the GC is run on specific generations of the managed heap at specific thresholds, as follows:

Objects move through generations from generation 0 to generation 2 by surviving a garbage collection cycle, meaning that they remain in use and strongly rooted through a garbage collection cycle. The idea is that objects that remain in use the longest will end up in generation 2, where the garbage collection process runs the least.

Objects that exceed 85KB are placed in the large object heap. Memory in this heap is never freed. You can reuse this memory after freeing up previous objects, but it will always be present in the process. The only way to free this memory in version 1.0 of C# is to stop the process.

NOTE The behavior of the large object heap never being compacted was changed in version 1.1 of the framework.

You can easily determine if your memory leaks in managed or unmanaged code by using Performance Monitor. If you see Memory:Private Bytes grow and .NET Memeory:.NET # of Bytes in all Heaps remain flat, you are dealing with an unmanaged leak; otherwise, you are seeing a managed leak. You can easily use windbg with Son Of Strike (SOS) or AllocationProfiler to determine the leak.

How does the GC know when an object is ready for garbage collection? Take a look at the following code snippet:

```
static void Main(string[] args)
{
    IClassA A;
    IClassB B;
    IClassC C;
    IClassB XXX;

    Console.WriteLine("Waiting to Debug....");
    Console.ReadLine();

    A = New ComObjectsLib.ClassA();
    B = A.CreateB();
    C = B.CreateC(); //At this point, A is considered as not being
        //referenced in code again and is eligible for cleanup?
        //.NET is smart enough to know the object is not used again in
        //the method, and thus we really don't base lifetime on
        //scope, but rather its use in a method or lack thereof.

    GC.Collect();
    XXX = C.DoBug();

    Console.ReadLine();
}
```

This example illustrates when objects are available for cleanup. The problem is simple. In this code snippet, if object C had a reference to object B, and a method of object C called a method in object B, you would have an access violation (AV), because object A and B would be freed. (This same problem occurs with the WindowsIdentity class.) You can prevent this behavior by using GC.KeepAlive(object) at the end of the method.

NOTE   The example shown here is documented in the following C# specifications: http://msdn.microsoft.com/library/default.asp?url=/library/en-us/csspec/html/vclrfCSharpSpec_3_9.asp.

The important point to remember here is that an object's lifetime is based on usage, not scope.

Delegates, Events, and Namespaces

- Delegates

- Events

- Anonymous Methods (new to 2.0)

- Namespaces and the using Keyword

Delegates

A *delegate* is a type that defines a function signature, so that an instance of a delegate can call methods that match it. In C++ terms, a delegate is a fancy way to describe a function pointer.

Declaring a Delegate

A delegate declaration consists of four parts:

- The keyword `delegate`

- Followed by the return type of the function to be called

- Followed by a name that will be generic to the function to be called

- Followed by a parameter list

In the following example, the delegate called `MyDelegate` can call any function that returns an `int` and is passed a single string:

```
delegate int MyDelegate(string s);
```

You can use delegates to fire a single method, or you may multicast methods. You may initialize a new delegate using static or instance methods, using the following syntax:

```
MyDelegate Del1 = new MyDelegate(DoSomething);
```

You can also initialize a delegate using this syntax for multicasting:

```
MyDelegate Multicast = null;
m += new MyDelegate(DoSomething);
m += new MyDelegate(DoSomething2);
```

After you have initialized your delegate with values, you use it by calling the delegate, as follows:

```
del1(MyString);
```

In the multicast case, you call the delegate as follows:

```
m(MyString);
```

This will result in the DoSomething method being called, followed by the DoSomething2 method.

To remove a method from the delegate list, use this syntax:

```
m -= new MyDelegate(DoSomething2);
```

This will remove DoSomething2 from the delegate known as m.

NOTE All delegates support asynchronous and synchronous calls of their invocation list via the methods BeginInvoke, EndInvoke, and Invoke.

You can also iterate through a list of all the delegates via the following code:

```
foreach(Delegate D in MyInstanceDelegate(GetInvocationList())
{
        (cast)D(params);
}
```

It is also important to realize that every time you declare a delegate, a new class is generated. This class does the work for you under the hood.

When to Use a Delegate

You should consider using a delegate in the following situations:

- You want to use a C-style function pointer.

- You desire a single callback invocation.

- You want the callback function registered at construction time rather than via a method call.

You should use an *interface* if the callback function involves complex behavior or when using Remoting.

The following example demonstrates using delegates.

Code Example: Delegates

```
using System;

namespace Client.Chapter_8___Delegates_Events_and_Namespaces
{
    class Delegates
    {
        //Creates a method pointer
        delegate int MyDelegate(string s);
        static void Main(string[] args)
        {
            MyDelegate Del1 = new MyDelegate(DoSomething);
            MyDelegate Del2 = new MyDelegate(DoSomething2);
            string MyString = "Hello World";

            Del1(MyString);
            Del2(MyString);

            //Or you can multicast delegates by doing this
            MyDelegate Multicast = null;

            Multicast += new MyDelegate(DoSomething);
            Multicast += new MyDelegate(DoSomething2);

            //Both DoSomething & DoSomething2 will be fired
            //in the order they are added to the delegate
            Multicast(MyString);
            Multicast -= new MyDelegate(DoSomething2);
        }
        static int DoSomething(string s)
        {
            return 0;
        }
        static int DoSomething2(string s)
        {
            return 0;
        }
    }
}
```

Events

Events allow one object to notify another object that something has occurred. You can implement events using the following steps:

1. Define a delegate in the namespace scope.

```
delegate int MyDelegateEventHandler(MyEventArgs e);
```

2. Define a class to hold arguments that need to be passed in the event.

```
public MyEventArgs :EventArgs
    {
            public int MyInt;
            public long MyLong;
            public string MyString;
    }
```

3. Define a class that will publish events.

```
public class MyEventPublisher
{
        public event MyDelegateEventHandler MyEvent;
        public int DoSomething(MyEventArgs e)
        {
            //Fire events to subscribers
              MyEvent(MyString);
        }
}
```

4. Define a class that will subscribe and handle the events.

```
class MyEventSubscriber
{
    static void Main(string[] args)
    {
        MyEventPublisher EventPublisher =
          new MyEventPublisher();
        MyEventArgs MyArgs = new MyEventArgs();
        MyArgs.Mystring = new string("Hello World");
        EventPublisher.MyEvent +=
          new MyDelegateEventHandler (MyHandler);
        EventPublisher.DoSomething(MyArgs);
    }
    static int MyHandler(object myObject, MyEventArgs e)
    {
        Console.WriteLine(e.MyString);
    }
}
```

Events Best Practices

The following are some guidelines for using events:

- Name your events using a verb and use Pascal casing.

- Use the term *raised,* rather than *fire,* to describe your events.

- For an events declaration of a delegate, always return void and pass two parameters: an object called sender, followed by an EventArgs called e. This will help to maintain the strategy of all the built-in events.

- Create an invoking method to raise events.

- Remember that an event can be raised only from within the class that declared it. This affects base classes as well. The suggested strategy for doing this is to declare a protected virtual method that raises the event.

- Name the method that fires the event OnEventName.

When to Use an Event

You should consider using events in the following cases:

- Client code registers for an event prior to the event being fired.

- You want to notify more than one client.

- You want end users to easily add listeners.

The following example demonstrates implementing events.

Code Example: Events

```
using System;

namespace Client.Chapter_8___Delegates_Events_and_Namespaces
{
    //Creates a method pointer
    public delegate int MyDelegateEventHandler(MyEventArgs e);
    class MyEventSubscriber
    {
        static void Main(string[] args)
        {
            MyEventPublisher EventPublisher = new MyEventPublisher();
            MyEventArgs MyArgs = new MyEventArgs();

            MyArgs.MyString = "Hello World";
            //Subscribes to an event
            EventPublisher.MyEvent += new MyDelegateEventHandler(MyHandler);
            EventPublisher.DoSomething(MyArgs);
        }
        static int MyHandler(MyEventArgs e)
        {
            Console.WriteLine(e.MyString);
            return 0;
        }
    }
    public class MyEventArgs: EventArgs
    {
        public int MyInt;
        public long MyLong;
        public string MyString;
    }
    public class MyEventPublisher
    {
        public event MyDelegateEventHandler MyEvent;
        public int DoSomething(MyEventArgs e)
        {
            //Raises an event
            MyEvent(e);
            return 0;
        }
    }
}
```

Anonymous Methods

Anonymous methods, new to version 2.0 of the framework, act a lot like C++ macros in that they allow you to create delegated methods that are inline when you add a new delegate to an event. One big difference is that you have type safety when you use anonymous methods.

In the following example, you can see that the anonymous delegate is automatically added to the event, without the need for a new method, as was used in the example in the previous section.

Code Example: Anonymous Methods

```
using System;

namespace Client.Chapter_8___Delegates_Events_and_Namespaces
{
    //Creates a method pointer
    public delegate void MyDelegateEventHandler(int i);
    class MyEventSubscriber
    {
        static void Main(string[] args)
        {
            MyEventPublisher EventPublisher = new MyEventPublisher();


            MyDelegateEventHandler MyAnonymousDelegate = delegate(int x)
            {
                Console.WriteLine("Anonymous Event FIRED!");
            };

            EventPublisher.MyEvent += MyAnonymousDelegate;

            EventPublisher.DoSomething();
        }
    }
    public class MyEventPublisher
    {
        public event MyDelegateEventHandler MyEvent;
        public int DoSomething()
        {
            MyEvent(5);
            return 0;
        }
    }
}
```

Namespaces and the using Keyword

A *namespace* is used to collect a hierarchy of objects into a single name. Namespaces may span .cs files, but not assemblies. The main purpose of a namespace is to collect and build an object hierarchy that is easy to use and navigate.

The `using` keyword allows you to use class objects that are deeply nested in namespaces, without needing to use their fully qualified names. For example, suppose that we wanted to access the `RemotingConfiguration` class. We could do this:

```
System.Runtime.Remoting.RemotingConfiguration...
```

Or we could do this:

```
using System.Runtime.Remoting;
RemotingConfiguration...
```

The `using` keyword can also be used to control ambiguity. Let's say that we have two assemblies: `MyAssembly` and `YourAssembly`. Both assemblies possess a class called `Dog`. Suppose we do the following:

```
using MyAssembly;
using YourAssembly;
```

Now if we tried to use the `Dog` class, we would get compiler errors. This is because the compiler would not know which class to use, `MyAssembly.Dog` or `YourAssembly.Dog`. There are a couple of solutions to this type of problem. The first would be to use fully qualified names: `MyAssembly.Dog` and `YourAssembly.Dog`. A quicker route would be to use an alias. C# supports this by using the following syntax:

```
using MyDog = MyAssembly.Dog;
using YourDog = YourAssembly.Dog;
```

Exception Handling and Application Domains

- Exception Handling: try/catch, finally, and throw

- The .NET Exception Class

- Application Domains

- Fusion Basics

Exception Handling

Exception handling allows you to handle an event in a manner that does something about the exception or shuts down an application gracefully.

Using try/catch

To use exception handling, you must place the code that you want to guard against an exception in a try block:

```
try
{
    //Code to be guarded
}
```

After you have the code to be guarded identified, you need to write a block of code that will handle the exception:

```
catch(exception type)
{
    //Handle the event

}
```

You can also use what is called a default exception handler, catch(…), to catch all exceptions, but this is not advisable. You should have some idea of the type of exceptions that could occur in your code. In most cases, catching all exceptions is not best practice, because it allows you to not be concerned with the exact exceptions being thrown. You should always try to catch the most specific exceptions that you can.

Using finally

Another approach to ensure that code will be executed prior to shutting down the application is to use the finally keyword. The finally keyword will be executed immediately after the catch block is executed. If a catch block is not present, the finally keyword will execute after the try block completes or an exception is thrown in the try block.

```
finally
{
    //Code that is guaranteed to run regardless of the exception being thrown

}
```

Using throw

The throw statement is used to force an exception of a specified type.

```
throw new MyException("My Exception has been thrown!");
```

The following example demonstrates exception handling with try/catch, finally, and throw.

Code Example: Try/Catch/Finally

```
using System;
using System.IO;

namespace Client.Chapter_9___Exception Handling_and_Application Domains
{
    class MyMainClass
    {
        delegate int MyDelegate(string s);
        static void Main(string[] args)
        {
            StreamWriter MyStream = null;
            string MyString = "Hello World";
            //Creates a guarded code block
            try
            {
                MyStream = File.CreateText("MyFile.txt");
                MyStream.Write(MyString);
            }
            //Catches IOException
            catch (IOException e)
            {
                Console.WriteLine(e);
            }
```

```
                //Catches generic exceptions
                catch (Exception e)
                {
                        Console.WriteLine(e);
                }
                //Guarded code block that is guaranteed to be executed
                finally
                {
                        if (MyStream != null)
                                MyStream.Close();
                }
        }
    }
    public class MyFile
    {
        public StreamWriter WriteText(string s)
        {
            if (!Valid(s))
                //Throws an exception
                throw new IOException("Can't Write String");
            else
                return new StreamWriter("c:\\test.txt");
        }
        public bool Valid(string s)
        {
            return false;
        }
    }
```

The .NET Exception Class

The .NET Framework provides a built in Exception class that you can use to catch almost all exceptions. You can also use this built-in class to derive new exception classes that have built-in support for a variety of fields. The Exception class provides the fields listed in Table 9-1 for you to use in your own exceptions.

Table 9-1. .NET Exception Class Fields

Field	Description
StackTrace	String that stores the current stack
Message	This property should be set with a descriptive error message
HelpLink	Contains a link to a help file
HResult	Gets or sets an error code
Source	Contains the name of the application or object that caused the error
TargetSite	Gets the method that throws the exception

Application Domains

Application domains (AppDomains) allow you to have one Win32 process that can be divided into separate areas of execution that are protected from each other. Suppose that you have a task that needs to be done, but you want to make sure that if that task fails and throws an unhandled exception, the entire process does not shut down. This is exactly what application domains do for you. They allow you to create separate execution contexts inside the same Win32 process.

The downside to using application domains is that you must use Remoting to communicate among the domains. The fact that you are using Remoting isn't bad; it's the cost of marshaling data and traversing the domains via the CrossAppDomainSink that impacts performance. You could make the performance even worse if you were to use full-blown Remoting and the TCP or HTTP channels.

An interesting fact about application domains is how threads are used. A single thread does not belong to a single application domain. Instead, threads can cross to and from application domains on demand. So, if you were to debug the following example, you would see the call to the remoted object occur on the same thread that handles that call. Another interesting fact is that the only way you can unload an assembly in a .NET project is to use application domains.

There are numerous overloads that allow you to provide evidence and setup information for the domain as well. The evidence sets the security policy for the domain. The setup information allows you to configure the configuration file information and the application base path.

The following example demonstrates how to create an AppDomain.

Code Example: How to Create an AppDomain

```csharp
using System;
using System.Runtime.Remoting;

namespace Client.Chapter_9___Exception Handling_and_Application Domains
{
    class MyServer
    {
        [MTAThread]
        static void Main(string[] args)
        {
        //Creates AppDomain
        AppDomain Domain2 = AppDomain.CreateDomain("AppDomainB");
            RemoteObj MyRemoteObj =
                (RemoteObj)Domain2.CreateInstanceAndUnwrap
                        ("Server", "Server.RemoteObj");

            MyRemoteObj.Test();
            Console.WriteLine("Finshed");
        }
    }
    public class RemoteObj: MarshalByRefObject
    {
        public RemoteObj()
        {
            Console.WriteLine("CTOR Called");
        }
        public void Test()
        {
            Console.WriteLine("RemObj Test Method Called");
        }
    }
}
```

Fusion Basics

Fusion is the name of the technology that we use to load assemblies into a process or an application domain. The basic procedure used to find assemblies is the following:

- Determine the version number of the requested assembly.

- Check to see if we have loaded that assembly already.

- Check the Global Assembly Cache (GAC).

- Search for the assembly.

In the search for the assembly, if there are no configuration or publisher policies in effect, and the bind request was generated using `Assembly.LoadFrom`, we use the path given to the `LoadFrom` method. If a codebase attribute is found in the configuration file, we check its path. If we do not find the assembly, we need to probe for the assembly. We check the application base—the location where the executable (EXE) was loaded from, using the culture and name of the assembly. We search the `privatePath` followed by the `AppendPrivatePath` values.

It is important to remember that we check the GAC only for assemblies that are strong-named. The GAC is used to store assemblies that are used by more than one application. *Strong-named assemblies* are those that have been signed using the sn.exe tool. If your assemblies are not strong-named, you have the luxury of not needing to worry about this; just make sure that you place your assemblies in the same directory as the EXE.

As you probably have guessed, the most common error in loading assemblies is the dreaded `FileNotFoundException`. To troubleshoot this, you should use the fusion logs, which you can view in Visual Studio or by using fuslogvw.exe. If you use fuslogvw.exe, select its Settings option and enable Log Bind Failures to Disk. Then run the process and get the error. Finally, select the Refresh option in fuslogvw.exe, and you should be able to see the appropriate log. Fuslogvw.exe modifies the Registry path `HKLM\Software\Microsoft\Fusion`.

There are several methods that are provided to enhance the loading of managed assemblies, such as the following:

- The `Assembly.LoadFrom` method allows you to load an assembly given a filename and path.

- The `Assembly.Load` method loads an assembly and searches the GAC, application base, and private bin paths.

Part Two

Common Tasks

COM and .NET Interoperability

- COM Interop Reference: Type Conversion, Variants for .NET Types, COM Attributes, and Marshal Class Methods

- COM Interop Rules and Facts

- Consuming COM Objects from .NET Clients—Early Binding

- Consuming COM Objects from .NET Clients—Late Binding

- `QueryInterface` and Casting

- Consuming .NET Objects from COM Clients

- Subscribing and Publishing to Events

- Using Platform Invoke to Call Native DLL Functions

- Creating .NET COM+ Objects

- Using Role-Based Security in Managed COM+ Applications

- Advanced Customizing of Structures: Simulating Unions in .NET and Passing an Array of Interface Pointers

- Using Arrays in COM Interop

COM Interop Reference

For easy COM interoperability (COM interop) reference, the following sections present tables of .NET type conversions, variants for .NET types, COM attributes, and Marshal class methods.

Type Conversion

Table 10-1 shows .NET type conversions for Interface Definition Language (IDL) types and Visual Basic 6 (VB6) types.

Table 10-1. .NET Type Conversions

.NET Type	IDL Type	VB6 Type
System.SByte	char	N/A
System.Int16	short	Integer
System.Int32	long	Long
with UnmanagedType.Error	HRESULT	Long
System.Int64	int64	N/A
System.IntPtr	long	Long
System.Char		
default parameters	unsigned short	N/A
default for struct fields (ANSI)	unsigned char	Byte
default for struct fields (Unicode)	unsigned short	N/A
with UnmanagedType.U1	unsigned char	Byte
with UnmanagedType.U2	unsigned.short	N/A
System.UInt16	unsigned short	N/A
System.UInt32	unsigned long	N/A
with UnmanagedType.Error	HRESULT	Long
System.UInt64	uint64	N/A
System.UIntPtr	unsigned long	N/A
System.Single	single	Single
System.Double	double	Double

Table 10-1. .NET Type Conversions (Continued)

.NET Type	IDL Type	VB6 Type
System.Boolean		
default for parameters	VARIANT_BOOL	Boolean
default for struct fields	long	Long
with UnmanagedType.Bool	long	Long
with UnmanagedType.I1	unsigned char	Byte
with UnmanagedType.U1	unsigned char	Byte
with UnmanagedType.VariantBool	VARIANT_BOOL	Boolean
System.DateTime	DATE	Date
System.Guid	GUID	N/A
System.Decimal		
default	DECIMAL	N/A
with UnmanagedType.Currency	CURRENCY	Currency
System.String		
default for parameters	BSTR	String
default for struct fields	LPSTR	String
with UnmanagedType.LPStr	LPSTR	String
with UnmanagedType.LPWStr	LPWSTR	String
with UnmanagedType.CustomMarshaler	long	Long
System.Text.StringBuilder	LPSTR	String
with UnmanagedType.LPStr	LPSTR	String
with UnmanagedType.LPWStr	LPWSTR	String
with UnmanagedType.CustomerMarshaler	IUnknown*	Unknown
System.Object	VARIANT	Variant
default parameters	IUnknown*	Unknown
default for struct fields	IUnknown*	Unknown
with UnmanagedType.IUnknown	IUnknown*	Unknown
with UnmanagedType.IDispatch	IDispatch*	Object

Table 10-1. .NET Type Conversions (Continued)

.NET Type	IDL Type	VB6 Type
with `UnmanagedType.Struct`	`VARIANT`	Variant
with `UnmanagedType.CustomerMarshaler`	`IUnknown*`	Unknown
with `UnmanagedType.Interface`	`IUnknown*`	Unknown
AnInterface	`AnInterface*`	SomeClass or Interface
with `UnmanagedType.CustomMarshaler`	`IUnknown*`	Unknown
SomeClass	`DefaultInterface*`	SomeClass
with `UnmanagedType.CustomerMarshaler`	`IUnknown*`	Unknown
SomeFormattedClass	`SomeStruct*`	ByRef SomeUDT
with `UnmanagedType.CustomMarshaler`	`IUnknown*`	Unknown
SomeDelegatedClass		
default parameters	`DefaultInterface*`	SomeDelegatedClass
default for `struct` fields	`int`	Long
with `UnmanagedType.FunctionPtr`	`int`	Long
with `UnmanagedType.CustomMarshaler`	`IUnknown*`	Unknown
SomeValueType	`SomeStruct`	SomeUDT
SomeEnum		
with 32-bit underlying type	`SomeEnum`	SomeEnum
with any other underlying type	underlying type	underlying type
array of some type		
default parameters	`SAFEARRAY(Type)`	*SomeType*()
with `UnmanagedType.ByValArray`	*SomeType*[*size*]	*SomeType*(0 to -1)
with `UnmanagedType.LPArray`	(parameters only)	*SomeType**
SomeType		
with `UnmanagedType.SafeArray`	`SAFEARRAY(Type)`	*SomeType*()
with `UnmanagedType.CustomMarshaler`	`long`	Long

Variants for .NET Types

Table 10-2 lists the .NET types and their corresponding variant types. When calling methods that have optional variant types, you must use `Type.Missing`, because C# does not support optional/default parameters.

Table 10-2. .NET to Variant Types

.NET Type	Variant Type
null	VT_EMPTY
System.DBNull	VT_NULL
System.Runtime.InteropServices.CurrencyWrapper	VT_CY
System.Runtime.InteropServices.UnknownWrapper	VT_UNKNOWN
System.Runtime.InteropServices.DispatchWrapper	VT_DISPATCH
System.Runtime.InteropServices.ErrorWrapper	VT_ERROR
System.Reflection.Missing	VT_ERROR
System.String	VT_BSTR
System.Decimal	VT_DECIMAL
System.Boolean	VT_BOOL
System.Char	VT_U2
System.Byte	VT_U1
System.SByte	VT_I1
System.Int16	VT_I2
System.Int32	VT_I4
System.Int64	VT_I8
System.IntPtr	VT_INT

Table 10-2. .NET to Variant Types (Continued)

.NET Type	Variant Type
System.UInt16	VT_U2
System.UInt32	VT_U4
System.UInt64	VT_U8
System.UIntPtr	VT_UINT
System.Single	VT_R4
System.Double	VT_R8
System.DateTime	VT_DATE
Array	VT_ARRAY
System.Object or other .NET class	VT_DISPATCH

COM Attributes

Table 10-3 lists COM attributes with their descriptions.

Table 10-3. COM Attributes

Attribute	Description
AutomationProxy	Sets if an object should be custom marshaled or marshaled using the automation marshaler
ClassInterface	Sets the type of interface generated for a class
CoClass	Identifies the original CLSID for an object
ComImport	Indicates that a class or interface was imported to managed code
ComRegisterFunction	Sets a method to be called when an assembly is registered for use with COM
ComSourceInterfaces	Identifies the source interface for events
ComUnregisterFunction	Sets a method to be called when an assembly is unregistered for COM
ComVisible	Sets or determines if an object is visible to COM
DispId	Sets the dispatch ID for a method or property
FieldOffset	Sets the physical position of a field within a class or struct
Guid	Sets a GUID on a class or an interface
IDispatchImp	Sets which IDispatch implementation is used by managed code when exposing dual interfaces or dispinterfaces
LCIDConversion	Sets an unmanaged method signature LCID parameter
MarshalAs	Sets how data is marshaled to COM
Optional	Sets a parameter to be optional
Out	Sets a parameter as optional
PreserveSig	Suppresses HRESULT or retval signature when making COM calls
ProgId	Sets the program ID of a class
StructLayout	Sets or controls the physical layout of structs

Marshal Class Methods

The Marshal class is used to interact with unmanaged code. Table 10-4 lists the Marshal class methods.

Table 10-4. Marshal Class Methods

Method	Description
AddRef	Adds a reference to an interface
AllocCoTaskMem	Allocates an unmanaged memory chunk
BindToMoniker	Get an interface moniker from a specified moniker
CreateWrapperOfType	Wraps a COM type with a designated type
Destroy Structure	Frees substructures of an unmanaged clock
FreeCoTaskMem	Frees an unmanaged memory chunk
GetActiveObject	Obtains an instance from the running object table (ROT)
GetComInterfaceForObject	Returns an IUnknown pointer for an object
GetFunctionPointerForDelegate	Used to pass a function pointer for a managed object to unmanaged code
IsComObject	Determines if an object is a native COM object
OffsetOf	Returns the field offset of an unmanaged object
PtrToStringXXXX(Ansi, Bstr, or Uni)	Given a pointer to an unmanaged string, returns a string object
PtrToStructure	Given a pointer to an unmanaged struct, returns a managed struct
QueryInterface	Returns a COM interface
Release	Releases a reference to an interface
StructureToPtr	Given a managed struct, returns an unmanaged copy

COM Interop Rules and Facts

First, here are the most common causes of COM interop errors:

- The most common error when attempting to create a COM component is not having the component registered.

- The most common error when attempting to use .NET objects from COM clients is failure to place an assembly in an appropriate place.

The following are rules and facts about COM interop:

- Using COM+ components in ASP.NET may require security changes.

- COM properties that have by-reference parameters are not always supported by C#.

- When calling methods that have optional variant types, you must use `Type.Missing`, because C# does not support optional/default parameters.

- For optional nonvariant parameters, you must pass a default value.

- If you need to delete a COM object immediately, you can call `Marshal.ReleaseComObject(InteropServices)` several times while checking the return value until it is zero.

- COM variants `IUnknown*` and `IDispatch*` always look like `System.Object` in managed code.

- When using late binding, parameters are passed as variants. Therefore, you should use `ParameterModifier` when `Type.InvokeMember` is being used without metadata being present.

- The `void*` type used to represent a pointer to anything is always converted to `System.IntPtr`.

- Runtime Callable Wrapper (RCW) classes (classes imported as `ClassNameClass`) can be reliably cast only to interfaces that they implement.

- When casting an RCW to a coclass, you are casting the object to the default interface.

- Name conflicts are resolved by prefixing member names with the interface names and an underscore.

- You can always cast an RCW class to an interface to call any methods with their original names.

- In version 1.0 of the common language runtime (CLR), the type library importer does not properly handle type libraries containing a class that lists a source interface defined in a separate type.

- Never use `Marshal.SizeOf` to determine the "real size" of a managed type, because the results can be misleading.

- You can use the `sizeof` operator on any type that is blittable or a value type.

 CAUTION   People often confuse the built-in C# operator `sizeof` and the `Marshal.SizeOf` functionality. `sizeof` returns the managed size of the type in bytes. Marshal.SizeOf returns the unmanaged size of a type in bytes.

- The default importer behavior of `struct**` is to convert an `IntPtr`.

- In managed code, you cannot invoke members that use by-value user-defined type (UDT) parameters directly on `dispinterfaces`.

- Once a thread's apartment type is defined, you cannot change it in .NET.

NOTE In the *single-threaded apartment* (STA) model, [STAThread], one or more threads in a process use COM, and calls to COM objects are synchronized by COM. Interfaces are marshaled between threads. A degenerate case of the STA model, whcre only one thread in a given process uses COM, is called the *single-threading model.* In the *multithreaded apartment* (MTA) model, one or more threads use COM, and calls to COM objects associated with the MTA are made directly by all threads associated with the MTA, without any interposition of system code between caller and object. Because multiple simultaneous clients may be calling objects more or less simultaneously (simultaneously on multiprocessor systems), objects must synchronize their internal state by themselves. Interfaces are not marshaled between threads. Previous Microsoft documentation sometimes referred to the STA model simply as the *apartment model* and the MTA model as the *free-threaded model.*

- An InvalidCastException caused by a QueryInterface failure can happen when you are casting an RCW to a COM interface.

- When using .NET components as COM components, the InprocServer32 will always be set to mscoree.dll.

- Arrays of arrays are not supported in .NET clients that will be used by COM components.

- The default behavior for importing a SAFEARRAY varies depending on the tool used, Visual Studio or tlbimp.exe. If you use Visual Studio to import the executable, SAFEARRAYs become System.Array objects. This is also true when using the tlbimp.exe tool with the /sysarray switch.

- The Interop Marshaler does not support fixed-length arrays with more than one dimension.

RCW-Consuming COM Objects: Early Binding

When you are using a COM component in C#, you are actually using a *Runtime Callable Wrapper* (RCW). To consume COM components from .NET clients, you must import the type library information in a .NET assembly, and install the new assembly into the Global Assembly Cache (GAC) if it will be a shared assembly. In the C# code, use the using keyword to identify the module and the new keyword to create the new object.

Importing the Type Library Information

First, import type library information into a .NET assembly. This essentially creates the RCW. There are three ways to do this:

- Import the COM object via Visual Studio using the Add Reference feature.

- Use tlbimp.exe to create a new type library (.tlb), with the /sysarray switch.

- To import the information on the fly in memory, use the TypeLibConverter class in System.Runtime.InteropServices.

Installing the Assembly

If the new assembly is going to be a shared assembly, install it into the GAC. Otherwise, make sure the Interop_X.dll is in the same directory as the .NET client.

If you decide to place the new assembly in the GAC, you will need to make sure it has a *strong name* and has been signed using the sn.exe tool.

```
sn -k MyKey.snk
tlbimp /out:MyRCW.dll /keyfile:MyKey.snk MyCOM.dll
gacutil -I MyRCW.dll
```

It still goes without saying (even though I will say it) that the COM DLL must be registered!

Identifying the Module

In the C# code, make sure that you use the using keyword to followed by the case-sensitive name of the module you added a reference to, as follows:

```
using MyRCW
```

Creating and Instantiating the Object

Create and instantiate a new object with the new keyword by calling the default constructor. The end result of using an RCW is a class generated in the new assembly that will have the same name as the coclass, but with a Class extension, such as MyObjectClass. This is the class that you want to instantiate a type of when calling new.

```
ObjectClass MyObject = new ObjectClass()
```

The following example demonstrates how COM components can be consumed in .NET clients using early binding.

Code Example: Consuming COM Objects—Early Binding

```
using System;
using System.Runtime.InteropServices;
//Adds a Runtime Callable Wrapper (RCW) namespace
using SpeechLib;

namespace Client.Chapter_10___ COM_and_.NET_Interoperability
{
        class EarlyBinding
        {
            [STAThread]
            static void Main(string[] args)
            {
                //Creates an instance of a COM object using
                //early binding
                SpVoiceClass X = new SpVoiceClass();
                //Calls a method of the COM object
                X.Speak("Hello World", 0);
            }
        }
}
```

Consuming COM Objects: Late Binding

COM components can be consumed in .NET clients using late binding. To instantiate COM objects using late binding, you must use a two-step process.

First, you must get a type instance. This can be done in one of the following three ways:

```
Type X = Type.GetTypeFromProgID(Program ID);
```

```
Type X = Type.GetTypeFromCLSID(new Guid"Guid Number")
```

```
Type X = Type.GetType("string");
```

Next, create the object, as follows:

```
Object MyObject = Activator.CreateInstance(X)
```

The following example demonstrates how COM components can be consumed in .NET clients using late binding.

Code Example: Consuming COM Objects—Late Binding

```
using System;
using System.Reflection;


namespace Client.Chapter_10___COM_and_.NET_Interoperability
{
        class LateBinding
        {
                [STAThread]
                static void Main(string[] args)
                {
                    //Late binding example
                     Type t = Type.GetTypeFromProgID("SAPI.SpVoice");
                    //Creates an object
                     Object o = Activator.CreateInstance(t);
                     Object[] a = new Object[2];

                     a[0] = "Hello World";
                     a[1] = 0;
                    //Calls a method
                    t.InvokeMember("Speak", BindingFlags.InvokeMethod, null, o, a);
                }
        }
}
```

QueryInterface and Casting

QueryInterface is a method that is part of the IUnknown interface. In managed code, IUnknown is hidden from you, so you cannot call QueryInterface in C#. Instead of calling QueryInterface, you should simply cast the object that you have when you created the object to the appropriate interface, as shown in the following example.

NOTE   It is very important to realize that the familiar interfaces of IUnknown and IDispatch are hidden and no longer available to you to use in managed code.

Code Example: QueryInterface and Casting

```
using System;
using System.Runtime.InteropServices;
using SpeechLib;

namespace Client.Chapter_10___COM_and_.NET_Interoperability
{
    class QI
    {
        [STAThread]
        static void Main(string[] args)
        {
            SpVoiceClass X = new SpVoiceClass();
            X.Speak("Hello World", 0);
            //Casting does the work of QueryInterface
            ISpVoice Y = (ISpVoice)X;
        }
    }
}
```

CCW: Consuming .NET Objects from COM Clients

A *COM Callable Wrapper* (CCW) is used to wrap .NET components so they can be used from existing COM objects. There are four general rules that you must follow when using this approach:

- Only public types are available.

- Classes require the default constructor.

- No static members are allowed.

- Overloaded methods are appended with an underscore, followed by a number.

To consume a managed type from COM, first register the assembly's type library:

```
regasm /tlb:MyTlb.tlb MyApp.dll
```

Then install the assembly in the local directory of the client application or in the GAC:

```
gacutil -I MyApp.dll
```

The assembly must have a strong name generated with sn.exe.

If you do not wish to place the item in the GAC, you can use the /codebase switch of regasm to register the DLL location, as in the following example:

```
regasm /codebase C:\Cases\RemotingLifetime\Bin\Debug\MyApp.dll /tlb:MyApp.tlb
```

Next, import the type libraries in the new C++ application. You must import both mscorlib.tlb and your assembly .tlb file.

```
#import "mscorlib.tlb"
#import "..\LoanLib\LoanLib.tlb"
```

Finally, create the .NET object using normal COM creation means, such as CoCreateInstance.

The following example demonstrates consuming .NET objects from COM clients.

Code Example: Consuming .NET Objects from COM Clients

```
#include <objbase.h>
#include <iostream.h>
#include <windows.h>

#import "mscorlib.tlb"
#import "C:\Projects\COM Examples\NETTOCOM\bin\Debug\NETTOCOM.tlb" no_namespace
named_guids

using namespace NETTOCOM;

int main()
{
    CoInitialize(NULL);
    BSTR MyString = SysAllocString(L"Hello World");
    IMyInterface* pMy = NULL;

    HRESULT hr =  CoCreateInstance(__uuidof(MyClass),NULL,
             CLSCTX_INPROC_SERVER,__uuidof(IMyInterface),
                (void**)&pMy);

    if( SUCCEEDED(hr) )
    {
        pMy->PrintHelloWorld(MyString);
        pMy->Release();
    }
    CoUninitialize();
    return 0;
}
```

Subscribing and Publishing to Events

As a C# developer, you can still use and respond to events published by COM clients. There are two ways to do this: use the RAW method or use event abstraction. The latter method is much easier.

When you run tlbimp.exe or another tool that performs the same function, the following four items are generated in the Interop DLL:

- The SourceInterfaceName_Event interface, which is similar to the source interface, except it is .NET version of the interface describing the events.

- SourceInterfaceName_MethodNameEventHandler, which acts as the delegate when subscribing to the event.

- SourceInterfaceName_EventProvider is a private class that implements the interface created in SourceInterfaceName_Event. This handles the connection point requirements.

- SourceInterfaceName_SinkHelper is a private class that implements the source interface and is used in the call to IConnectionPoint.Advise.

By using the event abstraction method to subscribe to events, you have the added flexibility of being able to subscribe to a single event, rather than to all of the events described in the event interface, which was the normal practice when using IConnectionPoints.

The following examples demonstrate using event abstraction to subscribe to events in COM objects and publishing .NET objects to COM with events.

Code Example: Subscribing to Events in COM Objects

```csharp
using System;
using SHDocVw;

namespace Client.Chapter_10___COM_and_.NET_Interoperability
{
        class BrowserListener
        {
              private InternetExplorer ie;
              public BrowserListener()
              {
                      ie = new InternetExplorerClass();
                      ie.DocumentComplete +=
                       DWebBrowserEvents2_DocumentCompleteEventHandler(DocComp);
                      ie.TitleChange +=
                       new DWebBrowserEvents2_TitleChangeEventHandler(TitleMod);
                      ie.Visible = true;
                      ie.GoHome();
               }
             public void DocComp(object pDisp, ref object URL)
              {
                      Console.WriteLine("Document Complete: " + URL);
              }
              public void TitleMod(string Text)
              {
                      Console.WriteLine("Title Change: " + Text);
              }
              [STAThread]
              static void Main(string[] args)
              {
                      BrowserListener listener = new BrowserListener();
                      Console.WriteLine("*** Press Enter to quit ***");
                      Console.Read();
              }
        }
}
```

Code Example: Publishing .NET Objects to COM with Events

```csharp
using System;
using System.Threading;
using System.Runtime.InteropServices;
using System.Diagnostics;


namespace Client.Chapter_10___COM_and_.NET_Interoperability
{
        public delegate void CallbackDelegateHandler(bool myBool);

        [InterfaceType(ComInterfaceType.InterfaceIsIDispatch)]
        public interface ITest
        {
              [DispId(1)] void Callback(bool test);
        }

        [ComSourceInterfaces(typeof(ITest))]
        [ClassInterface(ClassInterfaceType.AutoDual)]
        public class Repro
        {
              public Repro()
              {

              }


        public event CallbackDelegateHandler Callback;
        public void Test()
        {
              Debug.WriteLine("Testing");
        }

        public void DoWork()
        {
              Thread MyThread = new Thread(new ThreadStart(ThreadProc));
              MyThread.Start();
        }
        public void ThreadProc()
        {
              Callback(true);
        }


    }
}
```

Using Platform Invoke to Call Native DLL Functions

To consume exported DLL functions from managed code, follow these steps:

1. Obtain the function names and signatures for the desired native code.

2. Create a class that will be used to wrap calls to the functions that you are calling. A good way to organize these is to have a separate class for every native DLL that you will be calling.

3. Prototype the code. In C#, use `DllImportAttribute` to identify the DLL and function. Mark the method with the `static` and `extern` modifiers. For example, for an exported function defined as follows:

   ```
   extern "C" _declspec(dllexport) int __stdcall MyTest(int MyInt)
   ```

4. The following is valid:

   ```
   using System.Runtime.InteropServices;
   DllImport("Test.dll")]
   public static extern int MyTest(int MyInt);
   ```

5. Call the method of the wrapped class you created in step 2. This will result in the native function being called in whatever executable it is placed.

Arrays are marshaled by value unless specifically passed by reference. This behavior can be controlled using the [In, Out] attributes. The following examples demonstrate using platform invoke (PInvoke) to call native DLL functions.

Code Example: Using PInvoke to Call Native DLL Functions

```csharp
using System;
using System.Runtime.InteropServices;

namespace Client.Chapter_10___COM_and_.NET_Interoperability
{
        public class Win32
        {
                //The DllImport statement allows you to call exported functions
                [DllImport("user32.dll", CharSet = CharSet.Auto)]
        public static extern int
            MessageBox(int hWnd, String text, String caption,  uint type);
        }
        class Class1
        {
            [STAThread]
            static void Main(string[] args)
            {
                //Calls an exported function
                Win32.MessageBox(0, "Hello World", "MyBox", 1);
            }
        }
}
```

Code Example: Call Native Functions: Array Parameter By Value

```
void ArrayOfInts(int* pArray, int psize);

using System;
using System.Runtime.InteropServices;

namespace Chapter10
{
    public class PassingArrayByValue
    {
        [DllImport( "My.dll" )]
        public static extern void ArrayOfInts(
                [In, Out] int[] array, int size );

        public static void Main()
        {
            int[] array1 = new int[10];
            for( int i = 0; i < array1.Length; i++ )
            {
                array1[ i ] = i;
            }
            PassingArrayByValue.ArrayOfInts(array1,
                                array1.Length);
        }
    }
}
```

Code Example: Call Native Functions: Array Parameter By Reference

```
void RefArrayOfInts(int** ppArray, int* pSize);


using System;
using System.Runtime.InteropServices;

namespace Chapter10
{

    public class PassingArrayByRef
    {
        [DllImport( "My.dll" )]
        public static extern void RefArrayOfInts(
            ref IntPtr   array, ref int size );
        public static void Main()
        {
            int[] array2 = new int[ 10 ];
            int size = array2.Length;
            for( int i = 0; i < array2.Length; i++ )
            {
                array2[ i ] = i;
            }
            IntPtr buffer = Marshal.AllocCoTaskMem(
                    Marshal.SizeOf( size ) * array2.Length );
            Marshal.Copy( array2, 0, buffer, array2.Length );

            PassingArrayByRef.RefArrayOfInts(
                    ref buffer, ref size );
            if( size > 0 )
            {
                int[] arrayRes = new int[ size ];
                Marshal.Copy( buffer, arrayRes, 0, size );
                Marshal.FreeCoTaskMem( buffer );
            }
        }
    }
}
```

Code Example: Call Native Functions: Multidimensional Arrays

```
void MultiOfInts(int pMatrix[][COL_DIM], int row);

using System;
using System.Runtime.InteropServices;

namespace Chapter10
{

    public class PassingMultiOfInts
    {
        [DllImport( "My.dll" )]
        public static extern void MultiOfInts(
                        [In, Out] int[,] pMulti,
                        int row );
        public static void Main()
        {

            const int DIM = 10;
            int[,] multi = new int[ DIM, DIM ];


            for( int i = 0; i < DIM; i++ )
            {
                for( int j = 0; j < DIM; j++ )
                {
                    multi[ i, j ] = j;
                }

            }
            PassingMultiOfInts.MultiOfInts( multi, DIM );
        }
    }
}
```

Code Example: Call Native Functions: String Arrays

```
void ArrayofStrings(char** ppStrings, int size);


using System;
using System.Runtime.InteropServices;

namespace Chapter10
{

    public class PassingArrayOfStrings
    {

        [DllImport( "My.dll" )]
        public static extern void ArrayOfStrings(
            [In, Out] String[] stringArray, int size );
        public static void Main()
        {
            string[] strArray = { "Jan", "Feb", "Mar", "Apr","May" };
            PassingArrayOfStrings.ArrayOfStrings(
            strArray, strArray.Length );
        }

    }
}
```

Code Example: Call Native Functions: Array of Struct1

```
void ArrayOfStructs(MyStruct* pStruct, int size);

typedef struct _MyStruct
{
   int x;
   int y;
} MYStruct;



using System;
using System.Runtime.InteropServices;

namespace Chapter10
{
     [ StructLayout( LayoutKind.Sequential )]
     public struct MyStruct
     {
         public int x;
         public int y;
         public MyStruct( int x, int y )
         {
            this.x = x;
            this.y = y;
         }
     }


     public class PassingArrayOfStructs
     {
         [DllImport( "My.dll" )]
         public static extern void ArrayOfStructs(
             [In, Out] MyStruct[] structArray, int size );

         public static void Main()
         {

            MyStruct[] points = { new MyStruct(1,1),
            new MyStruct(2,2), new MyStruct(3,3) };
            PassingArrayOfStructs.ArrayOfStructs(
            points, points.Length );
         }
     }
}
```

Code Example: Call Native Functions: Array of Struct2

```
Void ArrayOfStructs2(MyName* pStruct, int size);


typedef struct _MYName
{
   char* first;
   char* last;
} MYName;



using System;
using System.Runtime.InteropServices;

namespace Chapter10
{
    [ StructLayout( LayoutKind.Sequential, CharSet=CharSet.Ansi )]
    public struct MyName
    {
        public String first;
        public String last;
        public MyName( String first, String last )
        {
           this.first = first;
           this.last = last;
        }
    }
```

```
public class PassingArrayStructs2
{
    [DllImport( "My.dll" )]
    public static extern void ArrayOfStructs2(
        [In, Out] MyName[] nameArray, int size );

    public static void Main()
    {

        MyName[] MyList = { new MyName( "John", "Doe" ),
                            new MyName( "Jane", "Doe" ),
                            new MyName( "Jim",  "Doe" )};

        PassingArrayStructs2.ArrayOfStructs2(
            MyList, MyList.Length );
    }
}
}
```

Creating COM + Objects in .NET

Creating COM+ objects using .NET is easy. Follow these steps:

1. Write the class as shown in the code example following these steps. It is especially important to bring in the following namespaces:

```
using System;
using System.Runtime.InteropServices;
using System.EnterpriseServices;
using System.Reflection;
```

2. Your class must inherit `ServicedComponent`.

3. Sign your class using sn.exe, as follows:

```
sn.exe -k MyKey.snk
```

4. Modify the AssemblyInfo.cs file on the following attribute:

```
[assembly: AssemblyKeyFile("..\\..\\mykey.snk")]
```

5. Use regsvcs to register the DLL in COM+ as a library application. This means that it runs in the process of the process that instantiates it.

```
regsvcs /appname:SRX MyDLL.DLL
```

If you want to register the object as service application, you must open the application with the Component Services snap-in and change the application to a server application using the Activation tab.

The following example demonstrates creating COM+ objects in .NET.

Code Example: Creating COM+ Objects in .NET

```csharp
using System;
using System.EnterpriseServices;

namespace Client.Chapter_10___COM_and_.NET_Interoperability
{
        //Allows you to expose an object as a COM object
        public interface IObjCreator
        {
            void HelloWorld();
        }
        //By inheriting from ServicedComponent, you allow this object to be
        //run in COM+
        public class CObjCreator: ServicedComponent, IObjCreator
        {
            public void HelloWorld()
            {
                //Do something
            }
        }
}
```

Using Role-Based Security in Managed COM+ Applications

When using role-based security (RBS) with COM+ managed applications, you can pass only COM types to the COM+ server. The following example demonstrates using RBS with COM+ managed applications.

Code Example: Using RBS in Managed COM+ Applications

```
using System;
using System.EnterpriseServices;

[assembly: ApplicationName("SimpleRoles")]
[assembly: ApplicationActivation(ActivationOption.Server)]
[assembly: ApplicationAccessControl
(true, AccessChecksLevel=
AccessChecksLevelOption.ApplicationComponent)]
[assembly: SecurityRole("CompUsers", SetEveryoneAccess=true)]
[assembly: SecurityRole("Marshaler", SetEveryoneAccess=true)]

namespace Client.Chapter_10___Interop_Services
{
        public interface IMyArrayTests
        {
                int Test1Add(int Prop1, int Prop2);
                int Test2Add(int[] MyArray);
                void Test3Add(ref int[] MyArray);
        }

        [ComponentAccessControl]
        [SecureMethod]
        public class MyObj: ServicedComponent, IMyArrayTests
        {
                public MyObj(){ }

                [SecurityRole("CompUsers", true)]
                public int Test1Add(int Prop1, int Prop2)
                {
                        return (Prop1 + Prop2);
                }
```

```
[SecurityRole("CompUsers", true)]
public int Test2Add(int[] MyArray)
{
        return ((int)MyArray.GetValue(0) +
          (int)MyArray.GetValue(1));
}

[SecurityRole("CompUsers", true)]
public void Test3Add(ref int[] MyArray)
{
        MyArray.SetValue(((int)MyArray.GetValue(0) +
          (int)MyArray.GetValue(1)), 2);
        return;
}
    }
}
```

Advanced Customizing of Structures

There are three ways to define a .NET structure:

- With LayoutKind.Auto, the CLR chooses how to arrange the fields in the structure based on its own optimizations. You should not use this on any structure that will be used with unmanaged code.

- With LayoutKind.Explicit, the fields of the structure are arranged by using byte offsets.

- With LayoutKind.Sequential, the fields are arranged in the order they appear in the structure definition. Here is an example:

```
[StructLayout(LayoutKind.Sequential]
public struct MyUnion
{
        public long MyLong;
        public char MyChar;
        public string MyString;
}
```

Simulating Unions in .NET

Since .NET does not contain unions as a built-in feature, you are forced to use struct and modify it. A big limitation of this is that you cannot use reference types in the union. Here is an example:

```
[StructLayout(LayoutKind.Explicit]
public struct MyUnion
{
        public long MyLong;
        [FieldOffset(0)] public int MyInt;
        [FieldOffset(0)] public long MyLong;
        [FieldOffset(0)] public short MyShort;
}
```

Using the IntPtr Class

The IntPtr class allows you to store pointers in managed code. It is commonly used in scenarios where you are dealing with struct**, C-style arrays, by-reference value types that could be null, VARIANTs containing structures, and SAFEARRAYs containing VARIANTs containing structures. (The next section presents an example of passing an array of interface pointers.) The following example demonstrates using the IntPtr class.

Code Example: Using the IntPtr Class

```
using System;
using System.Runtime.InteropServices;

namespace Client.Chapter_10___ COM and .NET Interoperability
{
        public class TestClass
        {
                [STAThread]
                static void Main(string[] args)
                {
                        IntPtr ptr = IntPtr.Zero;

                        ptr = Marshal.AllocHGlobal(Marshal.SizeOf(typeof(int)));
                        Marshal.FreeHGlobal(ptr);
                }
        }
}
```

Using Arrays in COM Interop

Prepare to pull your hair out. Using arrays in COM interop is one of the biggest areas of problems.

From a COM perspective, there are five types of arrays:

- **Safe array:** A self-described array that can contain any type capable of being placed in a COM VARIANT. These arrays are typically converted to a System.Array type and vice versa.

- **Fixed-length array:** A basic array where you define the size of the array in the method definition. A major limitation of this type of array is that the Interop Marshaler supports only one-dimensional fixed-length arrays.

```
HRESULT Test([in] int MyArray[10]
```

- **Varying array:** Similar to a fixed-length array, but allows you to pass only a portion slice of an array. These arrays are also limited to only one dimension.

```
HRESULT VarArray [in, first_is(2),
last_is(6)]  short Array[1024])
HRESULT VarArray [in, first_is(2),

length_is(5)]  short Array[1024])
HRESULT VarArray([in] long cActual,
[in, length_is(cActual)]  short Array[1024])
```

- **Conformant array:** An array with a dynamic capacity.

```
HRESULT ConArray([in] long cElems,
[in, size_is(cElems)]  short Array[*])
HRESULT ConArray([in] long cElems,
[in, size_is(cElems)]  short Array[])
HRESULT ConArray([in] long cElems,
[in, size_is(cElems)]  short* Array)
```

- **Conformant varying array:** Combines the ability to pass a portion of the array while allowing for it to be dynamic.

```
HRESULT ConVarArray([in] cMax, [in] cActual,
[in, size_is(cMax), length_is(cActual)] short* Array)
HRESULT ConVarArray([in] cMax, [in] cActual,
[in, size_is(cMax), length_is(cActual)] short Array[*])
HRESULT ConVarArray([in] cMax, [in] cActual,
[in, size_is(cMax), length_is(cActual)] short Array[])
```

Passing an Array of Interface Pointers

The following example demonstrates the managed code for passing an array of pointers.

```
public class PassingAnArrayByExample
{
      //Create an array object that will hold X number of elements of Y objects.
      public Array T = Array.CreateInstance((typeof(MSXML2.IXMLDOMDocument)),20);

      public TestArrayLib.TestingClass MyObject = new TestArrayLib.TestingClass();
      public PassingAnArrayByExample()
      {
          for (int i=0; i<20 ;i++)
          {
              //Fill the array members with the objects desired,
              //so at this point we have an array of type
              //System.Array.
               SAFEARRAY(IDispatch))
              //These will be passed to the COM object as a SafeArray(IDispatch).
              //You can then pull out items and call QI to get the interface you
                want.
               T.SetValue((new MSXML2.DOMDocumentClass()),i);
               Console.WriteLine( T.GetValue(i) );
          }
      MyObject.Testme( ref T);
}
```

In unmanaged code, the IDL definition of the method is as follows:

```
[id(1), helpstring("method Testme")] HRESULT Testme([in,out]
SAFEARRAY(IDispatch*)* m);

STDMETHODIMP CTesting::Testme(SAFEARRAY** m)
{
IDispatch* pDispatch;long ElementNumber = 0;
HRESULT hr = 0;
//This will pull out by element of the array the object's IDispatch interface.
hr = SafeArrayGetElement(*m, &ElementNumber, &pDispatch);
return S_OK;
}
```

Passing an Entire C-Style Array to COM Code

The following example demonstrates the managed client code for passing an entire C-style array to COM code.

```
static void Main(string[] args)
{
        int Size = 5;
        byte[] Buffer = new byte[Size + 1];
        Buffer[0] = 65;
        Buffer[1] = 66;
        Buffer[2] = 67;
        COMTestClass Test = new COMTestClass();
        Test.SetMessage(Buffer, Buffer.Length);
         Console.WriteLine(Buffer[0]);
}
```

The unmanaged code is as follows:

```
STDMETHODIMP CCOMTest::SetMessage(BYTE* pBuffer, long size)
{
        *pBuffer = 68;
         return S_OK;
}
```

The IDL code looks like this:

```
[id(1), helpstring("method SetMessage")] HRESULT SetMessage
    ([in] BYTE* pBuffer, [in] long size);
```

You must modify the Microsoft Intermediate Language (MSIL) code generated by Visual Studio or tlbimp.exe because a C-style array parameter looks like a `ref` parameter, but it is actually treated as a by-value parameter. To modify the IL code, run the following:

```
ildasm /out:Interop.InteropTesterCOMLib.il Interop.InteropTesterCOMLib.dll
```

Then modify the method signature twice in the IL code. Open the IL code with Notepad and change the method signature from this:

```
instance void SetMessage([in] unsigned int8& pBuffer,
[in] int32 size) runtime managed internalcall
```

to this (you will need to do this twice in the IL code):

```
instance void SetMessage([in] unsigned int8[] marshal([+1]) pBuffer,
[in] int32 size) runtime managed internalcall
```

Save the results.

Then compile the IL code:

```
ilasm /DLL Interop.InteropTesterCOMLib.IL /RESOURCE=
Interop.InteropTesterCOMLib.res
```

Finally, add the new DLL as a reference.

The following example demonstrates setting security on a COM interface.

Code Example: Setting Security on a Specific COM Interface

```csharp
using System;
using System.Runtime.InteropServices;
using System.Reflection;

namespace Client.Chapter_10___COM_and_.NET_Interoperability
{
        public struct COAUTHIDENTITY
        {
                [MarshalAs(UnmanagedType.LPWStr)]
                public string User;
                public uint UserLength;
                [MarshalAs(UnmanagedType.LPWStr)]
                public string Domain;
                public uint DomainLength;
                [MarshalAs(UnmanagedType.LPWStr)]
                public string Password;
                public uint PasswordLength;
                public uint Flags;
        };
        class Class1
        {
                //Various constants
                const uint EOAC_NONE = 0;
                const uint SEC_WINNT_AUTH_IDENTITY_UNICODE = 2;
                const uint RPC_C_AUTHN_WINNT = 10;
                const uint RPC_C_AUTHZ_NONE = 0;
                const uint RPC_C_AUTHN_LEVEL_DEFAULT = 0;
                const uint RPC_C_IMP_LEVEL_IMPERSONATE = 3;
                [DllImport("Ole32.dll", CharSet = CharSet.Auto)]
                public static extern int CoSetProxyBlanket
                        (IntPtr pProxy, uint dwAuthnSvc, uint dwAuthzSvc,
                         uint
                         pServerPrincName, uint dwAuthLevel,
                         uint dwImpLevel, IntPtr pAuthInfo,
                         uint dwCapabilities);
                [STAThread]
```

```
static void Main(string[] args)
{
     int hr;
     Guid CLSID =
          new Guid("1ACD2158-6E0E-48B6-A01C-ACF1CAC48580");
     string machineName = "MyPCName";
     System.Type typeInfo =
          Type.GetTypeFromCLSID(CLSID,machineName,true);
     Console.WriteLine("Type.GetTypeFromCLSID successful");
     Console.ReadLine();

     object objDCOM = Activator.CreateInstance(typeInfo);
     Console.WriteLine("Activator.CreateInstance successful");
     Console.ReadLine();

     COAUTHIDENTITY Auth = new COAUTHIDENTITY();
     IntPtr pAuth = Marshal.AllocCoTaskMem(28);
     Auth.User = "myusername";
     Auth.UserLength = (uint)Auth.User.Length;
     Auth.Domain = "mydomain";
     Auth.DomainLength = (uint)Auth.Domain.Length;
     Auth.Password = "mypassword";
     Auth.PasswordLength = (uint)Auth.Password.Length;
     Auth.Flags = SEC_WINNT_AUTH_IDENTITY_UNICODE;
     Marshal.StructureToPtr(Auth, pAuth, false);

     hr = CoSetProxyBlanket
               (Marshal.GetIUnknownForObject(objDCOM), //pProxy
               RPC_C_AUTHN_WINNT, //dwAuthnSvc
               RPC_C_AUTHZ_NONE, //dwAuthzSvc
               0, // pServerPrincName
               RPC_C_AUTHN_LEVEL_DEFAULT, //dwAuthnLevel
               RPC_C_IMP_LEVEL_IMPERSONATE, //dwImpLevel
               pAuth, //pAuthInfo
               EOAC_NONE); //dwCapabilities
     Console.WriteLine(
               "CoSetProxyBlanket for IUnknown returned " + hr);
     if (hr != 0)
               return;
```

```
            hr = CoSetProxyBlanket
                    (Marshal.GetIDispatchForObject(objDCOM), //pProxy
                    RPC_C_AUTHN_WINNT, //dwAuthnSvc
                    RPC_C_AUTHZ_NONE, //dwAuthzSvc
                    0, // pServerPrincName
                    RPC_C_AUTHN_LEVEL_DEFAULT, //dwAuthnLevel
                    RPC_C_IMP_LEVEL_IMPERSONATE, //dwImpLevel
                    pAuth, //pAut
                    EOAC_NONE); //dwCapabilities

        Console.WriteLine(
                "CoSetProxyBlanket for IDispatch returned " + hr);
        if (hr != 0)
                return;

        object actualReturnValue =
        typeInfo.InvokeMember("TestMe",
        BindingFlags.Default|BindingFlags.InvokeMethod,
        null,objDCOM,null,null,null,null);
        Console.WriteLine("Done");
            }
        }
    }
```

Files and Streams

- Directory Management

- File Management: Creating, Opening, Deleting, Moving, and Copying Files

- Streams: Using `FileStream`, `StreamReader`, `StreamWriter`, `StringReader`, `StringWriter`, and `BinaryFormatter`

Directory Management

Both the Directory and DirectoryInfo class provide a means to create, move, and enumerate directories. However, the DirectoryInfo class is preferred, because it eliminates some security checks when reusing an object.

Code Example: Directory Management

```
using System;
using System.IO;

namespace Client.Chapter_11___Files_and_Streams
{
        public class DirectoryObject
        {
                static void Main(string[] args)
                {
                        DirectoryInfo MyRoot = new DirectoryInfo(@"c:\projects");
                        DirectoryInfo[] MySub;
                        DirectoryInfo TheFolder = null;
                        FileInfo[] MyFiles;
                        FileInfo TheFile = null;
                        FileStream MyStream;
                        MyRoot.CreateSubdirectory("MyFolder");
                        MySub = MyRoot.GetDirectories();
                        foreach (DirectoryInfo D in MySub)
                        {
                                if (D.Name == "MyFolder")
                                        TheFolder = D;
                        }
```

```
MyFiles = TheFolder.GetFiles();
foreach (FileInfo F in MyFiles)
{
        if (F.Name == "Testing.txt")
        {
            TheFile = F;
            MyStream =
        TheFile.Open(FileMode.Create,
            FileAccess.ReadWrite,
        FileShare.ReadWrite);
            int i = 0;
            byte b = 0;
            while (i != 000)
            {
                    MyStream.WriteByte(b);  i++; b++;
            }
        }
}
TheFile.Delete();
TheFolder.Delete();
        }
    }
}
```

File Management

Tables 11-1, 11-2, and 11-3 show file mode, file access, and file share information.

Table 11-1. File Modes

Mode	Description
Append	Opens the file if it exists and seeks to the end of the file, or creates a new file.
Create	Specifies that the operating system should create a new file. If the file already exists, it will be overwritten.
CreateNew	Specifies that the operating system should create a new file.
Open	Specifies that the operating system should open an existing file.
OpenOrCreate	Specifies that the operating system should open a file if it exists; otherwise, a new file should be created.
Truncate	Specifies that the operating system should open an existing file. Once opened, the file should be truncated so that its size is zero bytes.

Table 11-2. File Access

Access	Description
Read	Read access to the file. Data can be read from the file.
ReadWrite	Read and write access to the file. Data can be written to and read from the file.
Write	Write access to the file. Data can be written to the file.

Table 11-3. File Share Flags

Share	Description
Inheritable	Makes the file handle inheritable by child processes.
None	Declines sharing of the current file. Any request to open the file (by this process or another process) will fail until the file is closed.
Read	Allows subsequent opening of the file for reading. If this flag is not specified, any request to open the file for reading (by this process or another process) will fail until the file is closed. However, if this flag is specified, additional permissions might still be needed to access the file.
ReadWrite	Allows subsequent opening of the file for reading or writing. If this flag is not specified, any request to open the file for writing or reading (by this process or another process) will fail until the file is closed. However, if this flag is specified, additional permissions might still be needed to access the file.
Write	Allows subsequent opening of the file for writing. If this flag is not specified, any request to open the file for writing (by this process or another process) will fail until the file is closed. However, if this flag is specified, additional permissions might still be needed to access the file.

There are many ways to create a file. The two most common classes are File and FileInfo. Both classes provide a means to create, copy, delete, move, and open files. However, the FileInfo class is preferred because it eliminates redundant security checks when reusing an object. The FileSystemWatcher class provides a means to receive notification when the file system is modified with specific interest in attribute, size, last write, or other changes.

The following examples demonstrate creating, opening, deleting, moving, and copying files, as well as using the FileSystemWatcher class.

Code Example: Creating Files

```csharp
using System;
using System.IO;

namespace Client.Chapter_11___Files_and_Streams
{
        public class CreatingFiles
        {
                public CreatingFiles()
                {
                        FileInfo MyFile = new FileInfo(@"c:\Projects\Testing.txt");
                        MyFile.Create();
                }
        }
}
```

Code Example: Opening Existing Files

```csharp
using System;
using System.IO;

namespace Chapter11
{
        public class OpenExistingFile
        {
                public OpenExistingFile()
                {
                        //Opens a file
                        FileInfo MyFile = new FileInfo(@"c:\Projects\Testing.txt");
                         FileStream MyStream;
                         MyStream = MyFile.Open(
                            FileMode.Open,FileAccess.Read, FileShare.None);
                }
        }
}
```

Code Example: Deleting Files

```
using System;
using System.IO;
namespace Client.Chapter_11___Files_and_Streams
{
        public class DeletingFiles
        {
                static void Main(string[] args)
                {
                    FileInfo MyFile = new FileInfo(@"c:\Projects\Testing.txt");
                      MyFile.Create();
                      MyFile.Delete();
                  }
          }
}
```

Code Example: Moving Files

```
using System;
using System.IO;
namespace Client.Chapter_11___Files_and_Streams
{
        public class MovingAFile
        {
                static void Main(string[] args)
                {
                    FileInfo MyFile = new FileInfo(@"c:\Projects\Testing.txt");
                      MyFile.Create();
                      MyFile.MoveTo(@"c:\Projects\MyFolder\Moved Testing.txt");
                      MyFile.MoveTo(@"C:|projects\MyFolder");
                 }
        }
}
```

Code Example: Copying Files

```csharp
using System;
using System.IO;

namespace Client.Chapter_11___Files_and_Streams
{
    public class CopyingAFile
    {
        static void Main(string[] args)
        {
            FileInfo MyFile = new FileInfo(@"c:\Projects\Testing.txt");
            MyFile.Create();
            MyFile.CopyTo(@"c:\Projects\MyFolder\Moved Testing.txt");
            //Or
            MyFile.CopyTo(
                @"c:\Projects\MyFolder\Moved Testing.txt", true);
        }
    }
}
```

Code Example: FileSystemWatcher

```csharp
using System;
using System.IO;

namespace Client.Chapter_11___Files_and_Streams
{
        public class Test
        {
                public static void Main(string[] args)
                {
                        FileSystemWatcher watcher = new FileSystemWatcher();
                        watcher.Path = @"c:\Test";
                        watcher.NotifyFilter   =
                                                NotifyFilters.LastAccess |
                                                NotifyFilters.LastWrite |
                                                NotifyFilters.FileName |
                                                NotifyFilters.DirectoryName;
                        watcher.Filter = "*.txt";
                        watcher.Changed += new FileSystemEventHandler(OnChanged);
                        watcher.Created += new FileSystemEventHandler(OnChanged);
                        watcher.Deleted += new FileSystemEventHandler(OnChanged);
                        watcher.Renamed += new RenamedEventHandler(OnRenamed);
                        watcher.EnableRaisingEvents = true;

                }

                public static void OnChanged(object source,
                                        FileSystemEventArgs e)
                {
                    Console.WriteLine("Event Fired");
                }
                public static void OnRenamed(object source, RenamedEventArgs e)
                {
                    Console.WriteLine("Event Fired");
                }

        }
}
```

Streams

Streams are used for transferring data from your application to an external source or to transfer data from an external source to your application. Streams provide a way to read and write bytes to and from a back store, which could be a file, memory, or another source.

There are many types of streams that you can choose. Table 11-4 describes the main stream classes provided by .NET that you can use in C#.

Table 11-4. Common Streams

Stream Type	Description
System.IO.MemoryStream	A stream that uses memory for backing
System.Net.Sockets.NetworkStream	A stream used for network transmission
BufferedStream	A stream that reads and writes using buffers
FileStream	A stream used to read and write to a binary file
CryptoStream	A stream that links data streams to cryptographic transformations

All the .NET classes that represent streams inherit from the base class of System.IO.Stream. Table 11-5 describes the common stream reader and writer classes. All stream classes provide the following methods and properties: Read, Write, Seek, CanRead, CanWrite, and CanSeek. They also have the Flush and Close methods. The Flush method is important because it pushes the stream from memory to the actual back store. The Close method calls Flush.

Table 11-5. Common Readers and Writers

Class	Description
StringReader/StringWriter	Used like sprintf to modify strings into different types
StreamReader/StreamWriter	Allows you to read and write to and from a text file
TextReader/TextWriter	Provides character input and output
BinaryReader/BinaryWriter	Reads and writes primitive types as binary values in a specific encoding to and from a stream

The following examples demonstrate the use of FileStream, StreamReader, StreamWriter, and StringReader. The final example shows the use of the BinaryFormatter class, which allows you to serialize and deserialize a stream into binary format. The example shows a simple solution that takes a class and serializes it to binary format inside a file.

Code Example: FileStream

```
using System;
using System.IO;

namespace Client.Chapter_11___Files_and_Streams
{
        public class UsingFileStreams
        {
                static void Main(string[] args)
                {
                        //Creates a file with read-write access
                        //that allows others to read.
                        FileStream MyFileStream1 =
                        new FileStream(@"c:\Projects\Testing.txt",
                            FileMode.Create);
                         FileInfo MyFiles = new FileInfo(@"c:\Projects\Testing.txt");
                          FileStream MyFileStream2 = MyFiles.OpenRead();
                         //Or any of the following
                        MyFileStream2 = MyFiles.OpenWrite();
                        MyFileStream2 = MyFiles.Open(FileMode.Append,
                            FileAccess.Read, FileShare.None);
                        MyFileStream2 = MyFiles.Create();
                         //You can read file streams on a per-byte
                         //basis or as an array of bytes.
                        int MyBytes = MyFileStream1.ReadByte();
                         //Or
                        int NumberOfBytes = 200;
                        byte[] MyByteArray = new Byte[NumberOfBytes];
                        int BytesRead = MyFileStream1.Read(MyByteArray,
                            0, NumberOfBytes);
                        //Data can be written to FileStreams as well through bytes
                         //or arrays of bytes.
                        byte MyWriteByte = 100;
                        MyFileStream1.WriteByte(MyWriteByte);
                         //Or via an array
                        int NumberOfBytesToWrite = 256;
                        byte[] MyWriteByteArray = new Byte[NumberOfBytesToWrite];
```

```
            for (int i = 0; i < 256; i++)
            {
                MyWriteByteArray[i] = (byte)i;
                i++;
            }
            MyFileStream1.Write(MyWriteByteArray,
                0, NumberOfBytesToWrite);
            MyFileStream1.Close();
            MyFileStream2.Close();
        }
    }
}
```

Code Example: StreamReader

```csharp
using System;
using System.IO;
namespace Client.Chapter_11___Files_and_Streams
{
        public class StreamReaderAndWriter
        {
                static void Main(string[] args)
                {
                        StreamReader MyStreamReader =
                            new StreamReader(@"c:\Projects\Testing.txt");
                         //If you need to control share permissions when
                         //creating a file, use FileStream with StreamReader.
                        FileStream MyFileStream =
                         new FileStream(@"c:\Projects\Testing.txt", FileMode.Open,
                        FileAccess.Read, FileShare.None);
                        StreamReader MyStreamReader2 =
                            new StreamReader(MyFileStream);
                        MyFileStream.Close();
                        MyStreamReader2.Close();
                         //The easiest way to read a stream is to
                         //use the ReadLine method.
                        //This method reads until it gets to the end of a line, but
                         //it does not copy the carriage return line feed /n/r.
                        string MyStringReader = MyStreamReader.ReadLine();
                        //You can also read the whole file by using the following.
                        string MyStringReadToEOF = MyStreamReader.ReadToEnd();
                         //The other route is to read one character at a time.
                        int[] MyArrayOfCharacters = new int[100];
                        for (int i = 0; i < 99; i++)
                        {
                            MyArrayOfCharacters[i] = MyStreamReader.Read();
                        }
                        MyStreamReader.Close();
                }
        }
}
```

Code Example: StreamWriter

```
using System;
using System.IO;
namespace Client.Chapter_11___Files_and_Streams
{
        public class UsingStreamWriter
        {
                static void Main(string[] args)
                {
                        //StreamWriter can be used only to write
                        //to files or other streams.
                        StreamWriter MyStreamWriter =
                                new StreamWriter(@"c:\Projects\Testing.txt");
                        //You can also use FileStream with StreamWriter
                        //to provide a greater degree of control
                        //in how the file is opened.
                        FileStream MyFileStream =
                                new FileStream(@"c:\Projects\Testing.txt",
                                FileMode.CreateNew, FileAccess.Write,
                                FileShare.None);
                        StreamWriter MyStreamWriter2 =
                                new StreamWriter(MyFileStream);
                        MyFileStream.Close();
                        MyStreamWriter2.Close();
                        //You can write sequentially to a file using this technique.
                        FileInfo MyFile = new FileInfo(@"c:\Projects\Testing.txt");
                        StreamWriter MyStreamWriter3 = MyFile.CreateText();
                        MyStreamWriter3.Close();
                        //There are four overloaded ways to use StreamWriter.Write().
                        //Writes a stream to a file
                        string MyString = "Hello World";
                        MyStreamWriter.Write(MyString);
                        //Writes single characters to a stream
                        char MyChar = 'A';
                        MyStreamWriter.Write(MyChar);
```

```
        //Writes an array of characters
char[] MyCharArray = new char[100];
for (int i = 0; i < 99; i++)
{
        MyCharArray[i] = (char)i;
}
MyStreamWriter.Write(MyCharArray);
 //Or you can write a portion of an array
MyStreamWriter.Write(MyCharArray, 25, 30);
MyStreamWriter.Close();
    }
}
}
```

Code Example: StringReader

```csharp
using System;
using System.IO;

namespace Client.Chapter_11___Files_and_Streams
{
        public class UsingStringReader
        {
                static void Main(string[] args)
                {
                        //Create a string to read characters from.
                        String MyString = "Hello World";
                        //Size the array to hold all the characters of the string,
                        //so that they are all accessible.
                        char[] MyChar = new char[12];
                        //Create a StringReader and attach it to the string.
                        StringReader MyStringReader = new StringReader(MyString);
                        //Read 5 characters from the array that holds
                        //the string, starting from the first array member.
                        MyStringReader.Read(MyChar, 0, 5);
                        //Display the output.
                        Console.WriteLine(MyChar);
                        //Close the StringReader.
                        MyStringReader.Close();
                }
        }
}
```

Code Example: BinaryFormatter

```
using System;
using System.IO;
using System.Runtime.Serialization.Formatters.Binary;

namespace Client.Chapter_11___Files_and_Streams
{
        class Class1
        {
                [STAThread]
                static void Main(string[] args)
                {
                        Point p1 = new Point();
                        p1.xpoint = 0x1111;
                        p1.ypoint = 0x2222;
                          //Opens a file and serializes the object into it.
                        Stream stream = File.Open("onepoint.bin", FileMode.Create);
                        BinaryFormatter bformatter = new BinaryFormatter();
                        bformatter.Serialize(stream, p1);
                        stream.Close();
                          //Read the data from a file and deserialize it.
                        Stream openStream =
                            File.Open("onepoint.bin", FileMode.Open);
                        Point deserializedPoint = new Point();
                        deserializedPoint =
                            (Point)bformatter.Deserialize(openStream);
                }
         }
        [Serializable()]
        class Point
        {
                public int xpoint;
                public int ypoint;
        }
}
```

CHAPTER 12

Active Directory

- Accessing Active Directory

- Connecting and Binding to Active Directory

- Traversing Objects in Active Directory

- Reading Attributes of an Object

- Writing New Objects to Active Directory

- Writing and Modifying Attributes of an Object

- Changing Passwords

- Deleting Objects from Active Directory

- Searching Active Directory

- Directory Caching

Accessing Active Directory

The System.DirectoryServices namespace allows you to access Active Directory. There are three main classes that are used to access the directory:

- The DirectoryEntry class represents an object in Active Directory. Property contains a collection of attributes for the objects that are stored in a PropertyCollection. PropertyValueCollection is used to store the value of each attribute in the PropertyCollection.

- The DirectoryEntries class is a collection of DirectoryEntry objects. The Children property contains a list of child objects of this object in a DirectoryEntries collection.

- The DirectorySearcher class can be used to search the directory for objects with specific attributes. It includes SortOption, SearchScope, SortDirection, SearchResults, SearchResultCollection, ResultPropertyCollection, and ResultPropertyValueCollection.

Connecting and Binding to Active Directory

For simple access, you can use the DirectoryEntry class to create Directory objects that allow you to bind to Active Directory. The following examples demonstrate how to bind to Active Directory as a specific user and how to bind to Active Directory as the logged-on user.

Code Example: Binding to Active Directory As a Specific User

```csharp
using System;
using System.DirectoryServices;

namespace Chapter12
{
        public class DirectoryBinding
        {
                public DirectoryBinding()
                {
                        DirectoryEntry MyDirectoryObject = new DirectoryEntry();

                        MyDirectoryObject.Path = "LDAP://HMSRevenge/rootDSE";
                        MyDirectoryObject.Username = @"Test\gregmcb";
                        MyDirectoryObject.Password = @"MyPassword";
                }
        }
}
```

Code Example: Binding to Active Directory As the Logged-on User

```csharp
using System;
using System.DirectoryServices;
namespace Chapter12
{
        public class DirectoryBinding
        {
                public DirectoryBinding()
                {
                        DirectoryEntry MyDirectoryObject =
                            new DirectoryEntry("LDAP://HMSRevenge/rootDSE");

                }
        }
}
```

Traversing Objects in Active Directory

The following example demonstrates how to access child objects of an Active Directory object. This is useful in situations where you have a parent organizational unit (OU) and you wish to iterate through the members of the OU.

Code Example: Traversing Objects in Active Directory

```
using System;
using System.DirectoryServices;

namespace Chapter12
{
        public class DirectoryBinding
        {
                public DirectoryBinding()
                {
                        DirectoryEntry MyDirectoryObject = new DirectoryEntry();

                        MyDirectoryObject.Path = "LDAP://HMSRevenge/rootDSE";
                        MyDirectoryObject.Username = @"redmond\gregmcb";
                        MyDirectoryObject.Password = @"MyPassword";
                        //Gets the child objects and returns
                        //them into a collection
                        DirectoryEntries MyChildObjects =
                            MyDirectoryObject.Children;



                }
        }
}
```

Reading Attributes of an Object

You can use the DirectoryEntry class's PropertyCollection and PropertyValueCollection collections to get an object's attributes. The following example demonstrates how to read and print the attributes of an Active Directory object.

Code Example: Reading Object Attributes

```csharp
using System;
using System.DirectoryServices;

namespace Chapter12
{

    public class DirectoryBinding
    {
        public DirectoryBinding()
        {
            DirectoryEntry MyDirectoryObject = new DirectoryEntry();
            //Port 389 is LDAP port
            MyDirectoryObject.Path =
                "LDAP://HMSRevenge:389/OU=Users,DC=Test,DC=COM";
            MyDirectoryObject.Username = @"Test\gregmcb";
            MyDirectoryObject.Password = @"MyPassword";
            //Gets the attributes of an object
            PropertyCollection MyAttributes =
                    MyDirectoryObject.Properties;
            foreach(string MyAttributeName in
                        MyAttributes.PropertyNames)
            {
                //Gets the values of an object
                PropertyValueCollection MyAttributeValues =
                    MyAttributes[MyAttributeName];
                foreach(string MyValue in MyAttributeValues)
                {
                        Console.WriteLine(MyAttributeName +
                        " = " + MyValue);
                }
            }
        }
    }
}
```

```
using System;
using System.DirectoryServices;

namespace Chapter12
{
        public class ReadingKnownDirectoryObjects
        {
                public ReadingKnownDirectoryObjects()
                {
                        DirectoryEntry MyObject = new DirectoryEntry();
                        MyObject.Path =
                            "LDAP://HMSRevenge/OU=Users,DC=Test,DC=com";
                        foreach(string MyValue in MyObject.Properties["email"])
                                Console.WriteLine("Email" + " : " + MyValue);
                }
        }
}
```

Writing New Objects to Active Directory

Using the DirectoryEntries class and collection, you can add objects to the Active Directory. This following example demonstrates creating a new User object in the Active Directory.

 CAUTION   When writing new objects to Active Directory, it is important to remember that you are working in the client's memory and that the changes are not propagated to the server until you call CommitChanges.

Code Example: Writing Objects to Active Directory

```
using System;
using System.DirectoryServices;

namespace Chapter12
{
        public class AddingObjectsToTheDirectory
        {
                public AddingObjectsToTheDirectory()
                {
                        DirectoryEntry MyObject = new DirectoryEntry();
                        MyObject.Path =
                            "LDAP://HMSRevenge/OU=Users,DC=Test,DC=com";
                        DirectoryEntries users = MyObject.Children;
                        //Creates a new user object
                        DirectoryEntry NewUser =
                            users.Add("Greg MacBeth", "user");
                        //Modifies the properties of an object
                        NewUser.Properties["company"].Add
                            ("Microsoft Corporation");
                        NewUser.Properties["employeeID"].Add("1001");
                        NewUser.Properties["userPassword"].Add("Password");
                        NewUser.CommitChanges();
                }
        }
}
```

Writing and Modifying Attributes of an Object

Along with adding objects and setting their properties, you may also want to set the attributes for new Active Directory objects or modify the attributes of existing objects. The following examples demonstrate how to write new attributes to an object and modify an object's attributes.

Code Example: Writing Attributes to an Object

```
using System;
using System.DirectoryServices;

namespace Chapter12
{
        public class AddingObjectsToTheDirectory
        {
                public AddingObjectsToTheDirectory()
                {
                        DirectoryEntry MyObject = new DirectoryEntry();
                        MyObject.Path =
                            "LDAP://HMSRevenge/OU=Users,DC=Test,DC=com";
                        DirectoryEntries users = MyObject.Children;
                        DirectoryEntry NewUser = users.Add("Greg MacBeth", "user");
                        NewUser.Properties["company"].Add("Microsoft Corporation");
                        NewUser.Properties["employeeID"].Add("1001");
                        NewUser.Properties["userPassword"].Add("Password");
                        //Writes values to an object
                        NewUser.CommitChanges();
                }
        }
}
```

Code Example: Modifying Object Attributes

```
using System;
using System.DirectoryServices;

namespace Chapter12
{
        public class ModifyingExistingObjectAttributes
        {
                public ModifyingExistingObjectAttributes()
                {
                        DirectoryEntry MyDirectoryObject = new DirectoryEntry();

                        MyDirectoryObject.Path =
                          "LDAP://HMSRevenge/CN=gregmcb,OU=users,DC=Test,DC=com";
                        MyDirectoryObject.Username = @"Test\gregmcb";
                        MyDirectoryObject.Password = @"MyPassword";
                        if(MyDirectoryObject.Properties[("company")].Value ==
                            "Old Company Name. inc.")
                        {
                            MyDirectoryObject.Properties[("company")][0] =
                                    "Microsoft Corporation";
                        }
                        MyDirectoryObject.CommitChanges();
                }
        }
}
```

Changing Passwords

Using the ChangePassword property, you can easily give a user a different password. The following example shows how to change a user's password.

 NOTE   You do not need to call CommitChanges on ChangePassword calls, because this information is not stored in the cache.

Code Example: Changing Passwords

```
using System;
using System.DirectoryServices;
using ActiveDs;

namespace ChangePassword
{

    class Class1
    {

        [STAThread]
        static void Main(string[] args)
        {
            string Path =
                "LDAP://XYZ.com/CN=Welby,OU=gregmcb,DC=XYZ, DC=com";
            string User = "XYZ\\gregmcb";
            string Password = "gregmcb";
            DirectoryEntry Entry =
                new DirectoryEntry(Path, User, Password);

            //This code allows you to retrieve native COM pointers
            //for interfaces such as IADSUser, IADS, and more.
            IADsUser IUsr = (IADsUser) Entry.NativeObject;
            IUsr.ChangePassword("Yes", "welby");

            Entry.Close();
        }
    }
}
```

Deleting Objects from Active Directory

You can easily remove an object from Active Directory by specifying the object and using the Remove method. This following example shows how to delete a User object from Active Directory.

Code Example: Deleting Objects from Active Directory

```csharp
using System;
using System.DirectoryServices;

namespace Chapter12
{
        public class DeletingObjects
        {
                public DeletingObjects()
                {
                        DirectoryEntry MyObject = new DirectoryEntry();
                        MyObject.Path =
                            "LDAP://HMSRevenge/OU=Users,DC=Test,DC=com";
                        DirectoryEntries users = MyObject.Children;
                        foreach(DirectoryEntry D in users)
                        {
                            if(D.Properties["email"].Value.
                                    ToString() == "gregmcb")
                            {
                                //Removes an object
                                users.Remove(D);
                            }
                        }

                        MyObject.CommitChanges();
                }
        }
}
```

Searching the Directory

Using the DirectorySearcher class, you can find specific Active Directory objects. The following is an example of searching the Active Directory for the user account Administrator.

Code Example: Searching Active Directory

```
using System;
using System.DirectoryServices;
using System.Windows.Forms;

namespace UnumTest
{
public class CloseClass
{

    static void Main(string[] args)
    {
        try
        {
            DirectoryEntry oRoot = new DirectoryEntry("LDAP://RootDSE");
            string searchOU =
                (string)oRoot.Properties["defaultnamingcontext"].Value;
            DirectoryEntry de =
                new DirectoryEntry("LDAP://CN=Users," + searchOU);
            Console.WriteLine(oRoot.Name);
            oRoot.Close();

            DirectorySearcher search = new DirectorySearcher(de);
            search.Filter = "(CN=Administrator)";
            search.PropertiesToLoad.Add("distinguishedName");
            SearchResultCollection results = search.FindAll();
```

```
            string strRet="Not Found";
            foreach(SearchResult result in results)
            {
                  DirectoryEntry data = result.GetDirectoryEntry();
                  strRet =
                  (string)data.Properties["distinguishedName"].Value;
                  Console.WriteLine(strRet);
                  data.Close();
            }
            de.Close();
            results.Dispose()
            //Required or you may leak TCP connections
        }
        catch(Exception e)
        {
            Console.WriteLine( e.Message);
        }
     }
   }
 }
```

Directory Caching

By default, ADSI/System.DirectoryServices uses caching when you call the first
method or use the first property of an object. You can disable this by setting
DirectoryEntry.UsePropertyCache to false, as shown in the following example.
The other workaround is for you to call DirectoryEntry.RefreshCache(), which
will reload the cache.

CAUTION   When you set the cache to false, you no longer work in the
client's memory. Changes are immediately propagated to the server.

Code Example: Directory Cache

```
using System;
using System.DirectoryServices;

namespace Chapter12
{

        public class DirectoryBinding
        {
                public DirectoryBinding()
                {
                        DirectoryEntry MyDirectoryObject = new DirectoryEntry();

                        MyDirectoryObject.Path = "LDAP://HMSRevenge/rootDSE";
                        MyDirectoryObject.Username = @"redmond\gregmcb";
                        MyDirectoryObject.Password = @"MyPassword";
                        MyDirectoryObject.UsePropertyCache = false;
                        DirectoryEntries MyChildObjects =
                           MyDirectoryObject.Children;

                        PropertyCollection MyAttributes =
                           MyDirectoryObject.Properties;
                        foreach(string MyAttributeName in
                                MyAttributes.PropertyNames)
                        {
                                PropertyValueCollection MyAttributeValues =
                                    MyAttributes[MyAttributeName];
                                foreach(string MyValue in MyAttributeValues)
                                {
                                        Console.WriteLine(MyAttributeName +
                                            " = " + MyValue);
                                }
                        }
                }
        }
}
```

ADO.NET

- Basic ADO.NET Concepts

- Creating Database Connections

- Using `DataSets`

- Using `DataReaders`

- Using ADO.NET Events

- Creating Data Tables and Populating Them

- Working with Data in a Database

- Using `DataViews` to Control the Display of a `DataGrid`

- ADO.NET Changes from 1.0 to 1.1 of the Framework

Basic ADO.NET Concepts

There are two ways to use a database: connected and disconnected. The connected method makes use of the XXXConnection, XXXCommand, and XXXDataReader classes. The disconnected state uses the XXXDataAdapter class in conjunction with the same three classes used by the connected method, as well as a DataSet.

ADO.NET has two basic components:

- DataTable: A tabular representation of a data table containing rows and columns.

- DataSet: A client representation of the data collected from a data source (known as a *recordset* in ADO). A DataSet is made up of a collection of DataTables. A DataSet can contain multiple tables from multiple sources.

Data providers allow access to specific kinds of databases. These include SQL (SqlClient), OLE DB (Oledb), and ODBC (Odbc) databases. The data providers are made up of a consistent set of classes based on the classes shown in Table 13-1. Table 13-2 shows the common System.Data classes used to work with data tables.

Table 13-1. Main Database Access Classes

Class	Description
Connection	Used to connect to the data sources.
Command	Used for command execution. For example, the ExecuteReader method returns a DataReader, the ExecuteScalar method returns a single value, and ExecuteNonQuery is used when no data will be returned (such as in an UPDATE statement).
DataReader	Forwards read-only connection results.
DataAdapter	Used to populate or update a data set. This acts as a bridge between the data set and the data source. SelectCommand retrieves data, InsertCommand adds a new record, UpdateCommand updates an existing record, and DeleteCommand deletes a record.

NOTE   Table 13-1 shows generic names for the classes. The actual implementations of these classes are named after their data provider. For example, the SQL Connection class is called `SqlConnection`, and the OLE DB Connection class is called `OledbConnection`.

Table 13-2. System.Data Common Classes

Class	Description
Constraint	Represents a constraint that can be applied to DataColumn objects
ConstraintCollection	DataTable collection of constraint objects
DataColumn	DataTable column schema
DataColumnCollection	Collection of DataColumn objects
DataRelation	Represents a parent-child relationship between two tables
DataRelationCollection	Collection of DataRelation objects
DataRow	Represents a row of data in a table
DataRowCollection	Collection of DataRow objects
DataRowView	Contains properties of a view of a data row
DataSet	Represents an in-memory version of one or more tables
DataTable	Represents an in-memory version of a table
DataView	Represents a view of a DataTable
DataViewManager	Contains a default view of a DataTable

Creating Database Connections

As noted earlier, you use the Connection class for the specific data provider to connect to a database. The following examples demonstrate creating SQL, ODBC, and OLE DB connections.

Code Example: Creating a SqlClient Connection

```
using System;
using System.Data.SqlClient;

namespace Client.Chapter_13___ADO.NET
{
        class CreatingSQLConnections
        {
                static void Main(string[] args)
                {
                        SqlConnection MyConnection =
                           new SqlConnection("Data Source=(local);"
                           + "Initial  Catalog" + "MyDatabase;"
                           + "User ID=sa;Password=");
                        //Creates and opens a connection to the database
                        MyConnection.Open();
                }
        }
}
```

Code Example: Creating an ODBC Connection

```
using System;
using System.Data.Odbc;

namespace Client.Chapter_13___ADO.NET
{
        class CreatingConnectionToODBC
        {
                static void Main(string[] args)
                {
                        OdbcConnection MyConnection = new OdbcConnection(
                          "DRIVER={MySQL};SERVER=TESTSRV;DATABASE="
                          + "MyDatabase;UID=root;PWD=\"\"");
                        MyConnection.Open();
                }
        }
}
```

Code Example: Creating an OleDb Connection Using an Access Database

```csharp
using System;
using System.Data.OleDb;


namespace Client.Chapter_13___ADO.NET
{
        class ConnectingToAccess
        {
                static void Main(string[] args)
                {
                        OleDbConnection MyConnection = new OleDbConnection (
                          @"Provider=Microsoft.Jet.OLEDB.4.0;"
                            + " Data Source = c:\MyAccessDB.mdb");
                        MyConnection.Open();
                }
        }
}
```

Code Example: Creating an OleDb Connection Using Another OLE DB-Compliant Database (Such As Oracle)

```csharp
using System;
using System.Data.OleDb;


namespace MyOleDbClient
{
        class Client
        {
                static void Main(string[] args)
                {
                        OleDbConnection MyConnection = new OleDbConnection (
                        @"Provider=MSDAORA; Data Source ="
                          + " orcl.csharp.com;User ID=Me;" + "Password=pass");
                        MyConnection.Open();
                }
        }
}
```

Using DataSets

DataSets are similar to traditional ADO recordsets. They are the client's representation of the database and are used to manipulate data on the client. In ADO.NET, DataSets are always disconnected, which means that they are not concerned with the actual source of the data. In this environment, you use a DataAdapter to connect the DataSet to the actual data source.

The traditional use of a DataSet follows these steps:

1. Create a DataAdapter.

2. Create a DataSet.

3. Use DataAdapter.Fill to populate the DataSet.

A DataSet contains a Tables property, which returns a collection of tables (DataTableCollection). This allows a DataSet to have data consisting of more than one connection from more than one source.

Using Multiple-Table DataSets Through DataTables

A DataTable represents a single table in a DataSet. This is new in that DataSets can now contain multiple tables from multiple sources. The following example demonstrates using multiple-table DataSets.

Code Example: Using Mutiple-Table DataSets

```
using System;
using System.Data;
using System.Data.OleDb;

namespace Client.Chapter_13___ADO.NET
{
        class UsingMultiTabledDatasets
        {
              static void Main(string[] args)
              {
                    OleDbConnection MyConnection =
                      new OleDbConnection(@"Provider=Microsoft.Jet.OLEDB.4.0;"
                      + " Data Source = c:\MyAccessDB.mdb");
                    OleDbDataAdapter MyAdapter =
                      new OleDbDataAdapter("SELECT Column1, Column2, Column3"
                      + " FROM MyTable", MyConnection);
                    DataSet MyDataSet = new DataSet();

                    MyAdapter.Fill(MyDataSet, "MyTable");
                    foreach (DataTable MyTable in MyDataSet.Tables)
                    {
                          foreach (DataColumn MyColumn in MyTable.Columns)
                          {
                               foreach (DataRow MyRow in MyTable.Rows)
                               {
                               }
                          }
                    }
              }
        }
}
```

Updating a Data Source Quickly and Simply

As noted earlier, you must use a DataAdapter to connect a DataSet to a data source. To update a data source, you need to create a new DataAdapter. The following example demonstrates how to update a data source.

Code Example: Updating a Data Source

```
using System;
using System.Data;
using System.Data.OleDb;

namespace Client.Chapter_13___ADO.NET
{
        class UpdatingADataSource
        {
            static void Main(string[] args)
            {
                    OleDbConnection MyConnection =
                    new OleDbConnection(@"Provider=Microsoft.Jet.OLEDB.4.0;"
                        + " Data Source = c:\MyAccessDB.mdb");
                    OleDbDataAdapter MyAdapter =
                    new OleDbDataAdapter("SELECT Column1, Column2, Column3"
                        + " FROM MyTable", MyConnection);
                    DataSet MyDataSet = new DataSet();
                    MyAdapter.Fill(MyDataSet, "MyTable");
                    MyDataSet.Tables[0].Rows[3]["Column3"] = "Test";
                    OleDbCommandBuilder MyBuilder =
                        new OleDbCommandBuilder(MyAdapter);
                    MyAdapter.Update(MyDataSet.Tables[0]);
            }
        }
}
```

Using Persisted DataSets

The standard persistence format of a DataSet is XML, and thus a DataSet can be persisted to an XML file, as follows:

```
MyDataSet.WriteXml("@c:\MyDatSet.xml");

using System;
using System.Data;
using System.Data.SqlClient;

namespace Client.Chapter_13___ADO.NET
{
        class UsingDatasets
        {
              static void Main(string[] args)
              {
                      SqlConnection MyConnection =
                        new SqlConnection(@"Data Source=(local); Initial Catalog"
                        + "= CaseManager; Integrated Security=true");
                      SqlDataAdapter MyAdapter =
                       new SqlDataAdapter("SELECT * FROM CaseInfo", MyConnection);
                      DataSet MyDataSet = new DataSet();
                      MyAdapter.Fill(MyDataSet, "MyTable");
                      MyDataSet.WriteXml(@"c:\MyDatSet.xml");
              }
        }
}
```

The following examples demonstrate persisting a data set to an XML file and reading XML into a data set.

Code Example: Persisting a DataSet to an XML File

```
using System;
using System.Data;
using System.Data.OleDb;

namespace Client.Chapter_13___ADO.NET
{
        class PersistingADatasetToAnXMLFile
        {
                static void Main(string[] args)
                {
                        OleDbConnection MyConnection =
                        new OleDbConnection(@"Provider=Microsoft.Jet.OLEDB.4.0;"
                                + " Data Source = c:\MyAccessDB.mdb");
                        OleDbDataAdapter MyAdapter =
                        new OleDbDataAdapter("SELECT Column1, Column2, Column3"
                                + " FROM MyTable", MyConnection);
                        DataSet MyDataSet = new DataSet();
                        MyAdapter.Fill(MyDataSet, "MyTable");
                        MyDataSet.WriteXml(@"c:\MyDatSet.xml");
                }
        }
}
```

Code Example: Reading XML into a DataSet

```
using System;
using System.IO;
using System.Data;

namespace Client.Chapter_13___ADO.NET
{
        class ReadingAnXMLFileIntoADataset
        {
            static void Main(string[] args)
            {
                    string MyXMLDoc = @"<?xml version='1.0'>?"
                                    + @"<title> MyExample</title>";
                    StringReader MyStringReader = new StringReader(MyXMLDoc);
                    DataSet MyDataSet = new DataSet();
                    MyDataSet.ReadXml(MyStringReader);
            }
        }
}
```

Creating a Strong-Typed DataSet Using the IDE

To create a strong-typed DataSet, using Visual Studio, follow these steps:

1. Create a new project.

2. Use drag-and-drop to create a DataAdapter. Complete the dialog boxes to establish a connection.

3. Access the database using a stored procedure or a SQL query.

4. Use the Generate DataSet dialog box to create the DataSet. This dialog box can be accessed via the Data menu.

5. Save the XSD and .cs files that are generated.

6. Copy the TableMappings from the Windows Form's InitializeComponents method to the Clipboard.

7. Create or open the desired project.

8. Add the XSD and DataSet.cs files you saved in step 5.

9. Paste the TableMappings into the Form's constructor.

10. Write your DataAccess code.

11. Declare the DataSet by referencing the XSD file that you generated.

Using DataReader

DataReaders allow you to access a database in a fast and efficient fashion by providing read-only and forward-only access. The beauty of DataReaders is that cursor types and lock types are no longer required. The following example demonstrates using a DataReader.

Code Example: Using a DataReader

```
using System;
using System.Data;
using System.Data.SqlClient;

namespace Client.Chapter_13___ADO.NET
{
        class UsingADataReader
        {
            static void Main(string[] args)
            {
                    SqlConnection MyConnection =
                    new SqlConnection(@"Data Source=(local);"
                      + "Initial Catalog = CaseManager;"
                      + "Integrated Security=true");
                    MyConnection.Open();
                    SqlCommand MyCommand =
                       new SqlCommand("SELECT * FROM CaseInfo", MyConnection);
                    SqlDataReader MyDataReader =
                     MyCommand.ExecuteReader(CommandBehavior.CloseConnection);
                    while (MyDataReader.Read())
                    {
                            Console.WriteLine(MyDataReader[0] + " "
                                            + MyDataReader[1]);
                    }
                    MyConnection.Close();
            }
        }
}
```

Using ADO.NET Events

ADO.NET events can be used to notify subscribers of significant actions that have occurred in a database. The following example demonstrates using ADO.NET events.

Code Example: Using ADO.NET Events

```
using System;
using System.Data;
using System.Data.SqlClient;

namespace Client.Chapter_13___ADO.NET
{
    class UsingADONETEvents
    {
        static void Main(string[] args)
        {
            SqlConnection MyConnection =
            new SqlConnection(@"Data Source=(local);"
             + "Initial Catalog = CaseManager;"
             + "Integrated Security=true");
            MyConnection.StateChange +=
              new StateChangeEventHandler(OnStateChange);
            MyConnection.Open(); //Trigger Open event
            MyConnection.Close();
        }
        //This method gets called when the state changes
         public static void OnStateChange(object sender,
                    System.Data.StateChangeEventArgs e)
        {
            Console.WriteLine("Connection State Chnaged: {0}",
                             ((SqlConnection)sender).State);
        }
    }
}
```

Creating Data Tables and Populating Them

A DataTable contains a DataColumnCollection, which holds DataColumn objects, and a DataRowCollection, which contains DataRow objects. DataColumns are equivalent to fields, and DataRows represent a single row of data. The following example demonstrates creating and populating DataTables.

Code Example: Creating and Populating DataTables

```
using System;
using System.Data;
using System.Data.SqlClient;

namespace Client.Chapter_13___ADO.NET
{
        class CreatingDataTablesandPopulatingThem
        {
                static void Main(string[] args)
                {
                        SqlConnection MyConnection =
                        new SqlConnection(@"Data Source=(local);"
                          + "Initial Catalog = CaseManager;"
                          + "Integrated Security=true");
                        SqlDataAdapter MyAdapter =
                        new SqlDataAdapter("SELECT * FROM CaseInfo", MyConnection);
                        DataSet MyDataSet = new DataSet();
                        //Create a new DataTable
                        DataTable MyTable2 = MyDataSet.Tables.Add("My2ndTable");
                        //Adding columns and rows
                        DataColumn myColumn = new DataColumn();
                        myColumn.DataType = System.Type.GetType("System.Decimal");
                        myColumn.AllowDBNull = false;
                        myColumn.Caption = "Price";
                        myColumn.ColumnName = "Price";
                        myColumn.DefaultValue = 25;
                        //Add the column to the table.
                        MyTable2.Columns.Add(myColumn);
```

```
//Add 10 rows and set values.
DataRow myRow;
for (int i = 0; i < 10; i++)
{
    myRow = MyTable2.NewRow();
    myRow[0] = i + 1;
  //Be sure to add the new row to the DataRowCollection.
    MyTable2.Rows.Add(myRow);
}
SqlCommandBuilder Builder =
  new SqlCommandBuilder(MyAdapter);
MyAdapter.Update(MyDataSet, "My2ndTable");
        }
      }
    }
```

Working with Data in a Database

To work with databases, there are several SQL commands you must know:

- SELECT chooses the fields/columns in the database. The following example returns columns 1 through 3 from the table called MyTable.

  ```
  SELECT Column1, Column2, Column3 FROM MyTable
  ```

- FROM defines the table. The following example returns all fields from the table named MyTable.

  ```
  SELECT * FROM MyTable
  ```

- WHERE adds conditions to a statement. The following example returns all the columns/fields from the table called MyTable where Column2 is equal to "Smith".

  ```
  SELECT * FROM MyTable WHERE Column2 = "Smith"
  ```

- INSERT INTO adds a new row. The following example inserts a new row into the table called MyTable with values.

  ```
  INSERT INTO MyTable( Column1, Column2, Column3) VALUES(1, Greg, MacBeth)
  ```

- DELETE FROM deletes a row. The following example deletes all rows from the table called MyTable where Column2 is equal to "Smith".

  ```
  DELETE FROM MyTable WHERE Column2 = "Smith"
  ```

- UPDATE modifies a row in a table. The following example goes through the table called MyTable and sets Column2 to "Lee" only when Column1 = "Robert".

  ```
  UPDATE MyTable SET Column2 = "Lee" WHERE Column1 = "Robert"
  ```

You can also use CommandBuilder to insert, update, and delete data in databases. The following examples demonstrate how to perform these tasks with SQL statements and with CommandBuilder, as well as how to use transactions, find rows in a database, use DataTableMappings, and call a stored procedure.

Code Example: Inserting Data into a Database Using SQL Statements

```
using System;
using System.Data;
using System.Data.SqlClient;

namespace Client.Chapter_13___ADO.NET
{

        class InsertingDataUsingSQLStatements
        {
            static void Main(string[] args)
            {
                    SqlConnection MyConnection =
                      new SqlConnection(@"Data Source=(local);"
                      + "Initial Catalog = CaseManager;"
                      + "Integrated Security=true");
                    MyConnection.Open();
                    String MyString = @"INSERT INTO Test(ID, Contact, Email)"
                      + @"VALUES(2, 'Greg', 'MacBeth')";
                    SqlCommand MyCmd = new SqlCommand(MyString, MyConnection);
                    MyCmd.ExecuteScalar();
                    MyConnection.Close();

            }
        }
}
```

Code Example: Inserting Data into a Database Using CommandBuilder

```
using System;
using System.Data;
using System.Data.SqlClient;

namespace Client.Chapter_13___ADO.NET
{
        class InsertingDataUsingCommandBuilder
        {
                static void Main(string[] args)
                {
                        SqlConnection MyConnection =
                          new SqlConnection(@"Data Source=(local);"
                          + "Initial Catalog = CaseManager;"
                          + "Integrated Security=true");
                        SqlDataAdapter MyDataAdapter =
                          new SqlDataAdapter("SELECT ID, Contact, Email FROM Test",
                          MyConnection);

                        SqlCommandBuilder MyCmd =
                          new SqlCommandBuilder(MyDataAdapter);
                        DataSet MyDataSet = new DataSet();
                        MyDataAdapter.Fill(MyDataSet);
                        DataRow MyRow = MyDataSet.Tables[0].NewRow();
                        MyRow["ID"] = 200;
                        MyRow["Contact"] = "Greg";
                        MyRow["Email"] = "MacBeth";
                        MyDataSet.Tables[0].Rows.Add(MyRow);
                        MyDataAdapter.Update(MyDataSet);
                }
        }
}
```

Code Example: Updating Data in a Database Using SQL Statements

```
using System;
using System.Data;
using System.Data.SqlClient;

namespace Client.Chapter_13___ADO.NET
{
        class UpdatingDataUsingSqlStatements
        {
            static void Main(string[] args)
            {
                    SqlConnection MyConnection =
                      new SqlConnection(@"Data Source=(local);"
                      + "Initial Catalog = CaseManager;"
                      + "Integrated Security=true");
                    MyConnection.Open();
                    String MyString = "UPDATE Test SET Contact = 'Lee'";
                    SqlCommand MyCmd = new SqlCommand(MyString, MyConnection);
                    MyCmd.ExecuteScalar();
                    MyConnection.Close();
            }
        }
}
```

Code Example: Using Transactions

```csharp
using System;
using System.Data;
using System.Data.SqlClient;

namespace Client.Chapter_13___ADO.NET
{
        class UpdatingDataUsingTransactions
        {
                static void Main(string[] args)
                {
                        SqlConnection MyConnection =
                          new SqlConnection(@"Data Source=(local);"
                          + "Initial Catalog = CaseManager;"
                          + "Integrated Security=true");
                        MyConnection.Open();
                        String MyString = "INSERT INTO Test(ID, Contact, Email)"
                          + @"VALUES(1, 'Greg', 'Mac')";
                        SqlTransaction MyTransaction =
                          MyConnection.BeginTransaction();
                        SqlCommand MyCmd =
                          new SqlCommand(MyString, MyConnection, MyTransaction);
                        MyCmd.ExecuteScalar();
                        MyTransaction.Commit();
                        MyConnection.Close();
                }
        }
}
```

NOTE This is a useful shortcut that allows you to avoid using the SQL statements when you are working with just one table.

Code Example: Updating Data in a Database Using CommandBuilder

```
using System;
using System.Data;
using System.Data.SqlClient;

namespace Client.Chapter_13___ADO.NET
{
    class UpdatingDataUsingCommandBuilder
    {
        static void Main(string[] args)
        {
            SqlConnection MyConnection =
              new SqlConnection(@"Data Source=(local);"
              + "Initial Catalog = CaseManager; "
              + "Integrated Security=true");
            SqlDataAdapter MyDataAdapter =
              new SqlDataAdapter("SELECT ID, Contact,"
               + "Email FROM Test", MyConnection);
            DataSet MyDataSet = new DataSet();
            MyDataAdapter.Fill(MyDataSet);
            MyDataSet.Tables[0].Rows[0][0] = 55;
            SqlCommandBuilder MyCmd =
              new SqlCommandBuilder(MyDataAdapter);
            MyDataAdapter.Update(MyDataSet);
        }
    }
}
```

Code Example: Deleting Data from a Database Using SQL Statements

```
using System;
using System.Data;
using System.Data.SqlClient;

namespace Client.Chapter_13___ADO.NET
{
        class DeletingDataUsingSQLStatements
        {
              static void Main(string[] args)
              {
                    SqlConnection MyConnection =
                      new SqlConnection(@"Data Source=(local);"
                      + @"Initial Catalog = CaseManager; "
                      + "Integrated Security=true");
                    MyConnection.Open();
                    String MyString = "DELETE Test";
                    SqlCommand MyCmd = new SqlCommand(MyString, MyConnection);
                    MyCmd.ExecuteScalar();
                    MyConnection.Close();
              }
        }
}
```

Code Example: Deleting Data from a Database Using a CommandBuilder

```
using System;
using System.Data;
using System.Data.SqlClient;

namespace Client.Chapter_13___ADO.NET
{
        class DeletingDataUsingCommandBuilder
        {
                static void Main(string[] args)
                {
                        SqlConnection MyConnection =
                          new SqlConnection(@"Data Source=(local);"
                          + "Initial Catalog = CaseManager;"
                          + "Integrated Security=true");
                        SqlDataAdapter MyDataAdapter =
                          new SqlDataAdapter("SELECT * FROM Test", MyConnection);
                        SqlCommandBuilder MyCmd =
                          new SqlCommandBuilder(MyDataAdapter);
                        DataSet MyDataSet = new DataSet();
                        MyDataAdapter.Fill(MyDataSet);
                        DataColumn[] MyKey = new DataColumn[1];
                        MyKey[0] = MyDataSet.Tables[0].Columns[0];
                        MyDataSet.Tables[0].PrimaryKey = MyKey;
                        DataRow FindMyRow = MyDataSet.Tables[0].Rows.Find(1);

                        FindMyRow.Delete();
                        MyDataAdapter.Update(MyDataSet);
                }
        }
}
```

Code Example: Finding Rows in a Database

```
using System;
using System.Data;
using System.Data.SqlClient;

namespace Client.Chapter_13___ADO.NET
{
        class FindingRowsInData
        {
                public static void Main()
                {
                        SqlConnection MyConnection =
                          new SqlConnection(@"Data Source=(local);"
                          + "Initial Catalog = CaseManager;"
                          + "Integrated Security=true");
                        SqlDataAdapter MyDataAdapter =
                        new SqlDataAdapter("SELECT * FROM Test", MyConnection);
                        SqlCommandBuilder MyCmd =
                          new SqlCommandBuilder(MyDataAdapter);
                        DataSet MyDataSet = new DataSet();
                        MyDataAdapter.Fill(MyDataSet);
                        DataColumn[] MyKey = new DataColumn[1];
                        MyKey[0] = MyDataSet.Tables[0].Columns[0];
                        MyDataSet.Tables[0].PrimaryKey = MyKey;
                        DataRow FindMyRow = MyDataSet.Tables[0].Rows.Find(1);
                }
        }
}
```

Code Example: Using DataTableMappings

```
using System;
using System.Data;
using System.Data.Common;
using System.Data.SqlClient;

namespace Client.Chapter_13___ADO.NET
{
        class UsingDataTableMappings
        {
                static void Main(string[] args)
                {
                        SqlConnection SConn =
                          new SqlConnection("Data Source=(local);" +
                          "Initial Catalog = CaseManager;" +
                          "Integrated Security=true");
                        SqlDataAdapter da =
                          new SqlDataAdapter("SELECT ID, Contact,"
                          + "Email FROM CaseInfo", SConn);
                        DataSet ds = new DataSet();
                        DataTableMapping custMap =
                          da.TableMappings.Add("CaseInfo", "MyDatabase");
                        custMap.ColumnMappings.Add("ID", "CaseNumber");
                        custMap.ColumnMappings.Add("Contact", "MyContact");
                        custMap.ColumnMappings.Add("Email", "Email Address");
                        da.Fill(ds);
                }
        }
}
```

Code Example: Calling a Stored Procedure

```csharp
using System;
using System.Data;
using System.Data.SqlClient;

namespace Client.Chapter_13___ADO.NET
{
        class Client
        {
            static void Main(string[] args)
            {
                    SqlConnection cn = new SqlConnection(
                      @"Data Source=(local); Initial  Catalog = MyDatabase;" +
                      "User ID=sa;Password=");
                    SqlCommand cmd = new SqlCommand("MyStoredProcedure", cn);
                    cmd.CommandType = CommandType.StoredProcedure;
                    SqlParameter param =
                      new SqlParameter("@ReturnValue", SqlDbType.Int);
                    cmd.Parameters.Add(param);
                    cmd.Parameters.Add("MyFirstParameter", SqlDbType.Int);
                    cmd.Parameters.Add("MySecondParameter",
                      SqlDbType.Int).Direction =
                      ParameterDirection.Output;
                      SqlDataAdapter da = new SqlDataAdapter(cmd);
            }
        }
}
```

Here is how the stored procedure in this example was created:

```sql
CREATE PROCEDURE MyStoredProcedure(
                              @MyFirstParameter   int,
                              @MySecondParameter int OUTPUT)
AS
SELECT @MySecondParameter =
(SELECT Count FROM MyDB where ID LIKE @MyFirstParameter)
RETURN 1
```

Using DataViews to Control the Display of a DataGrid

The DataGrid ItemDataBound event can be used to define the view of data that is to be displayed in a DataGrid. The following is an example of implementing this.

Code Example: Using DataViews to Control the Display of a DataGrid

```csharp
private void UseDataViewToControlGrid(object sender,

              System.Web.UI.WebControls.DataGridItemEventArgs e)
{
      if(e.Item.ItemType == ListItemType.Header)
      {
            e.Item.Cells[0].Text = "Age";
            e.Item.Cells[1].Text = "Labor";
            e.Item.Cells[2].Text = "Case Number";
            e.Item.Cells[3].Text = "Status";
            e.Item.Cells[4].Text = "Owner";
            e.Item.Cells[5].Text = "Severity";
            e.Item.Cells[6].Text = "Title";
      }

      if( (e.Item.ItemType == ListItemType.Item)
          || ( e.Item.ItemType ==
          ListItemType.AlternatingItem))
      {
            //Fix up the age and color code it
            DataRowView dr = (DataRowView)e.Item.DataItem;
            int DaysOpen = Convert.ToInt32(dr[0].ToString());
            DaysOpen = ((DaysOpen/60)/24);
            if(DaysOpen > 30)
                e.Item.Cells[0].BackColor = Color.Red;
            if(DaysOpen < 30 && DaysOpen > 7)
                e.Item.Cells[0].BackColor = Color.Yellow;
            e.Item.Cells[0].Text = Convert.ToString(DaysOpen);
            //Color code the severity
            if(e.Item.Cells[5].Text.StartsWith("A"))
                e.Item.Cells[5].BackColor = Color.Red;
            if(e.Item.Cells[5].Text.StartsWith("B"))
                e.Item.Cells[5].BackColor = Color.Yellow;
      }
}
```

ADO.NET Changes from 1.0 to 1.1 of the Framework

The following are some of the differences between versions 1.0 and 1.1 of the
framework that relate to ADO.NET:

- The following methods return a new exception when a transaction is dead-locked: Execute, ExecuteScalar, and Execute.NonQuery. The end result is that SQL Server will close a session involved in the deadlock and allow the other session to continue.

- OleDbConnection.OnStateChangeEvent is no longer fired when an invalid connection string is used.

- OleDbConnection.Open will no longer allow blank passwords.

- In version 1.0, DataSets with a value of "" (empty string) were treated as DBNULL. In version 1.1, they are treated as "" by default.

- OleDbCommand.ExecuteReader no longer throws an exception when CommandBehavior.SingleRow is used and no rows are returned.

- SqlClient in a partially trusted environment will work only with version 1.1.

- SqlClient.EnlistDistributedTransactions was added to allow a SqlClient to manually enlist in a distributed transaction.

Networking and WWW Connections

- Socket Connections

- DNS Name Resolution

- Web Clients and Web Requests

- Displaying Web Pages Using the WebBrowser Control

Socket Connections

For networking, you need to create socket connections for clients and listen for socket connections. The following examples demonstrate creating and listening for socket connections.

Code Example: Creating a Socket Connection/Client

```
using System;
using System.Net;
using System.Net.Sockets;
using System.Text;

namespace Client.Chapter_14___Networking_and_WWW_Connections
{
        class CreatingSocketConnections
        {

                [STAThread]
                static void Main(string[] args)
                {
                        TcpClient MyClient = new TcpClient();
                        MyClient.Connect("localhost", 10000);
                        NetworkStream MyNetStream = MyClient.GetStream();
                        if(MyNetStream.CanWrite && MyNetStream.CanRead)
                        {
                            //Does a simple write.
                             byte[] sendBytes =
                                Encoding.ASCII.GetBytes("Is anybody there");
                             MyNetStream.Write(sendBytes, 0, sendBytes.Length);
                            //Reads the NetworkStream into a byte buffer.
                             byte[] bytes = new byte[MyClient.ReceiveBufferSize];
                             MyNetStream.Read(bytes, 0,
                                (int) MyClient.ReceiveBufferSize);
                            //Returns the data received from the
                            //host to the console.
                             string returndata = Encoding.ASCII.GetString(bytes);
                             Console.WriteLine("This is what the host " +
                                 "returned to you: " + returndata);
                        }
```

```
else if (!MyNetStream.CanRead)
{
      Console.WriteLine(
        "You cannot write data to this stream");
      MyClient.Close();
}
else if (!MyNetStream.CanWrite)
{
      Console.WriteLine(
        "You cannot read data from this stream");
      MyClient.Close();
}
        }
    }
}
```

Code Example: Listening for Socket Connections

```csharp
using System;
using System.Net;
using System.Text;
using System.Net.Sockets;

namespace Client.Chapter_14___Networking_and_WWW_Connections
{
        class ListeningForSockets
        {
            [STAThread]
            static void Main(string[] args)
            {
                    int PortNumber = 10000;
                    TcpListener MyListener = new TcpListener(PortNumber);
                    MyListener.Start();
                    //Console.WriteLine("Waiting For Connection ");
                    TcpClient MyClient = MyListener.AcceptTcpClient();
                    Console.WriteLine("Connection Accepted");
                    NetworkStream MyNetStream = MyClient.GetStream();
                    String Response = "Connection Has been accepted";
                    byte[] SendTheseBytes = Encoding.ASCII.GetBytes(Response);
                    MyNetStream.Write(SendTheseBytes, 0, SendTheseBytes.Length);
                    MyClient.Close();
                    MyListener.Stop();
            }
        }
}
```

DNS Name Resolution

To handle Domain Name System (DNS) name resolution, use the Dns class Resolve method. The following example demonstrates how to implement this.

Code Example: DNS Name Resolution

```
using System;
using System.Net;

namespace Client.Chapter_14___Networking_and_WWW_Connections
{
        class Class1
        {
             [STAThread]
             static void Main(string[] args)
             {
                    IPHostEntry MyHost = Dns.Resolve(args[0]);
                    foreach (IPAddress MyIP in MyHost.AddressList)
                    {
                           Console.WriteLine(MyIP.Address);
                    }
             }
        }
}
```

Web Clients and Web Requests

For your WWW systems, you will need to set up a Web client, as well as a procedure for making Web requests and getting responses. The following examples demonstrate a Web client and Web request procedure.

Code Example: WebClient

```
using System;
using System.Net;
using System.Text;
using System.IO;

namespace Client.Chapter_14___Networking_and_WWW_Connections
{
        class MyWebClient
        {
            [STAThread]
            static void Main(string[] args)
            {
                 WebClient MyClient = new WebClient();
                Stream MyStream = MyClient.OpenRead("http://www.MyWeb.com");
                 StreamReader MyReader = new StreamReader(MyStream);
                 Console.WriteLine(MyReader.ReadLine());
                 MyStream.Close();
            }
        }
}
```

Code Example: Web Request

```
using System;
using System.Net;
using System.IO;

namespace Client.Chapter_14___Networking_and_WWW_Connections
{
        class Class1
        {
                [STAThread]
                static void Main(string[] args)
                {
                        WebRequest MyRequest =
                          WebRequest.Create("http://www.MyWeb.com");
                        WebResponse MyResponse = MyRequest.GetResponse();
                        Stream MyStream = MyResponse.GetResponseStream();
                        StreamReader MyReader = new StreamReader(MyStream);
                        string MyWebLine;
                        while ((MyWebLine = MyReader.ReadLine()) != null)
                        {
                                Console.WriteLine(MyWebLine);
                        }
                        MyStream.Close();
                }
        }
}
```

Displaying Web Pages Using the WebBrowser Control

The WebBrowser control in Internet Explorer provides an easy way to display Web pages. To add the WebBrowser control to the toolbox, right-click it and selecting Customize Toolbox. On the COM tab of the Customize dialog box, select the Microsoft WebBrowser control. The following example demonstrates how to display Web pages with this control.

Code Example: Displaying Web Pages Using the WebBrowser Control

```
using System;
using System.Net;

namespace DisplayingWebPages
{
        class Class1
        {
            [STAThread]
            static void Main(string[] args)
            {
                    int Zero = 0;
                    object MyZeroed = Zero;
                    String MyString = " ";
                    object My2ndObject = MyString;
                    //Displays a Web page control
                    axWebBrowser1.Navigate("http://www.MyWeb.com",
                                        ref MySeroed,
                                        ref My2ndObject,
                                        ref My2ndObject,
                                        ref My2ndObject);

            }
        }
}
```

Networking and WWW Changes from 1.0 to 1.1 of the Framework

The following are some of the differences between versions 1.0 and 1.1 of the framework that relate to networking and WWW connections:

- Support for IP version 6 has been added.

- You can now limit the size of reply headers in `HttpWebRequest`. The default is 64KB, but this programmatically modifiable.

- `ConnectStream` `Read` and `Write` methods now obey timeout values.

CHAPTER 15
Threading

- Threading Basics

- Creating Threads

- Destroying Threads

- Using Background Threads

- Controlling Thread Execution

- Synchronizing Threads

- Using Thread Pools

- Making Asynchronous Calls

Threading Basics

The framework's Thread class provides the means for working with threads. Table 15-1 shows how Win32 relates to threading in the framework.

Table 15-1. Threading in Win32 and the Framework

Win32	Framework
CreateThread	new Thread (new ThreadStart(XXXX))
TerminateThread	Thread.Abort
SuspendThread	Thread.Suspend
ResumeThread	Thread.Resume
Sleep	Thread.Sleep
WaitForSingleObject on a thread handle	Thread.Join
ExitThread	No equivalent
GetCurrentThread	Thread.CurrentThread
SetThreadPriority	Thread.Priority
No equivalent	Thread.Name
No equivalent	Thread.IsBackground
CoInitializeEx	Thread.Apartment

Table 15-2 shows some synchronization object comparisons. You can also use the Synchronization attribute to synchronize access to an entire class if the class inherits from ContextBoundObject. Additionally, you can use MethodImplAttribute(MethodImplOptions.Synchronized) to synchronize an entire method.

Table 15-2. Synchronization Object Comparisons

Win32	Framework
InterlockedXXXX	InterlockedClass
CriticalSection	lock or Monitor class
Event	AutoResetEvent or ManualResetEvent
Mutex	Mutex

Creating Threads

Creating threads is easy to do in C#. So, the real question is this: Why do you want to go to the trouble of using multiple threads? The answer lies in the following statement.

Any time you need to do concurrent operations, the true solution is threading. Yes, it has some caveats, but the end results makes threading worth the effort.

Another great feature of multithreading in C# is that it does not require you to rely only on static thread procedures (as in the following example). You can start new threads using a static method or instance method. You can actually use an instance-based class, and pass the whole class to be worked on by another thread by calling a method on another instance-based class in the ThreadStart delegate.

NOTE   When a thread is created in managed code, it defaults to being a foreground thread. When a thread is created in unmanaged code and transitions into managed code, it is considered a background thread. This is important because in a managed application when there are no foreground threads, the process will end.

Code Example: Creating Threads

```csharp
using System;
using System.Threading;

namespace Client.Chapter_15___Threading
{
        class CreatingThreads
        {
                static void Main(string[] args)
                {
                        Thread MyNewThread =
                          new Thread(new ThreadStart(ThreadProc));
                        MyNewThread.Start();
                        MyNewThread.Join();
                }
                protected static void ThreadProc()
                {
                        for (int i = 0; i > 100; i++)
                        {
                            Console.WriteLine(i);
                        }
                }
        }
}
```

Destroying Threads

Threads can be destroyed using one of two methods: Abort, which will cause
the thread to terminate, or Interrupt. The only difference between these two
methods of the Thread class are that the Interrupt method throws an exception
of ThreadInterruptException, which can be caught by the underlying thread
procedure, or the thread will be terminated. The Abort method throws
ThreadAbortException, which can be caught and handled but requires you to call
Thread.ResetAbort to prevent ThreadAbortException from being rethrown. The
Thread.ResetAbort method should be called in the catch(ThreadAbortException)
clause.

The following example demonstrates destroying threads.

Code Example: Destroying Threads

```
using System;
using System.Threading;

namespace Client.Chapter_15___Threading
{
        class DestroyingThreads
        {
                static int MyCount = 0;
                static void Main(string[] args)
                {
                        MyClassThread me = new MyClassThread();
                        Thread MyNewThread =
                            new Thread(new ThreadStart(me.MyThread));
                        MyNewThread.Start();
                        if (MyCount == 0)
                                MyNewThread.Abort();
                }
        }
        class MyClassThread
        {
                public void MyThread()
                {
                }
        }
}
```

Using Background Threads

Background threads are used to do an application's chores that do not have the same priority as the task performed by the main thread. To make a thread a background thread, just set the new thread's IsBackground property to true.

 CAUTION If you set a thread's IsBackground property to false, the thread will prevent the process from terminating, even if the main method returns, until this thread's ThreadProc returns.

The only unfortunate effect of using background threads is that you need to deal with interthread communication. One reason you must do this is that background threads cannot communicate directly with GUI elements. To set up communication between a background thread and GUI elements, first create a thread as described in the previous section, and then define your new ThreadProc as follows:

```
public void ThreadProc()
{
        MethodInvoker me = new MethodInvoker(this.UpdateGUI);
        while(true)
        {
                counter++; //counter is an instance-based member of this class
                this.BeginInvoke(me);
        }
}
```

This simple code snippet will allow you to increment a counter on a background thread for an instance of an object, and then call a handler method on the originating thread.

```
public void UpdateGUI()
{
        label1.Text = counter.ToString();
}
```

For this to work, the counter member must be a class instance member. This way, both the GUI and the background thread can use it. Essentially, this is a callback to the originating thread.

Controlling Thread Execution

You can use Thread.Sleep to place a thread in a wait state. You can then wake the thread by calling Thread.Interrupt. You can force a thread to wait by calling Thread.Suspend, and then continue execution of that thread via Thread.Resume.

 CAUTION   Thread.Suspend and Thread.Resume are *not recommended* for use in production code!

There are two ResetEvent classes: AutoResetEvent and ManualResetEvent. They perform the same function with one exception: AutoResetEvent is automatically set to signal after the waiting thread has been released.

The following examples demonstrate how to use waiting threads.

Code Example: Thread Sleep, Interrupt, Resume, and Suspend

```
using System;
using System.Threading;

namespace Client.Chapter_15___Threading
{
        public class ThreadTest
        {
                public static int Main()
                {
                        Thread X = new Thread(new ThreadStart(SecondThread));
                        X.Start();
                        //Cause the second thread to resume
                        X.Interrupt();
                        //Place the second thread in a suspended state
                        X.Suspend();
                        //Do some work and restart the thread
                        X.Resume();
                        //Force this thread to wait until the second
                        //thread is finished
                        X.Join();
                        return 0;
                }
        }
```

```
public static void SecondThread()
{
    Console.WriteLine("Running second thread");
    //Place the second thread to sleep infinitely
    try
    {
        Thread.Sleep(Timeout.Infinite);
    }
    catch (ThreadInterruptedException e)
    {
        Console.WriteLine("Thread Interrupted");
    }
    catch(ThreadAbortException e)
    {
        Thread.ResetAbort();
    }
}
}
}
```

Code Example: Using the WaitHandle Classes to Wait on Threads

```csharp
using System;
using System.Threading;

namespace Client.Chapter_15___Threading
{
        public class ManagingThreads
        {
                public AutoResetEvent A = new AutoResetEvent(false);
                public AutoResetEvent[] B = new AutoResetEvent[3];
                public static int Main()
                {
                        ManagingThreads M = new ManagingThreads();
                        M.InitEvents();
                        Thread T = new Thread(new ThreadStart(M.MyNewThread));

                        T.Start();
                        //T.Join();   //Blocks this thread until T Stops
                        Console.WriteLine("Waiting!");
                        M.A.WaitOne();
                        WaitHandle.WaitAll(M.B);
                        return 0;
                }
                public void InitEvents()
                {
                        for (int i = 0; i < 3; i++)
                        {
                                B[i] = new AutoResetEvent(false);
                        }
                }
                public void MyNewThread()
                {
                        Console.WriteLine("MyNewThread Called");
                        A.Set();
                        B[0].Set();
                        B[1].Set();
                        B[2].Set();
                }
        }
}
```

Code Example: Using Timers

```csharp
using System;
using System.Threading;

namespace Client.Chapter_15___Threading
{
    public class TimerDemo
    {
        public static AutoResetEvent A = new AutoResetEvent(false);
        public static int index = 0;
        public static int Main()
        {
            Timer T =
                new Timer(new TimerCallback(TimerDemo.DoUpdates),
                            null, 5000, 10000);
            A.WaitOne();
            Console.WriteLine("Main Thread event signaled");
            T.Dispose();
            return 0;
        }
        public static void DoUpdates(object state)
        {
            Console.WriteLine("DoUpdates");
            if (index == 5)
                    A.Set();
            index++;
            Console.WriteLine(index);
        }
    }
}
```

Synchronizing Threads

In C#, we can use critical sections to prevent simultaneous access to a piece of code. This is done with the lock statement or by using the Monitor class. When code is encountered inside a lock statement, it actually uses the Monitor class under the hood.

The following examples demonstrate synchronizing threads using the lock keyword, the Monitor class, and mutexes.

Code Example: Synchronizing Threads Using lock

```
using System;
using System.Threading;

namespace Client.Chapter_15___Threading
{
    class MyThreadingClass
    {
        static void Main(string[] args)
        {
            My2ndClass me = new My2ndClass();
            Thread[] MyThreads = new Thread[10];
            for (int I = 0; I > 100; I++)
            {
                MyThreads[I] =
                  new Thread(new ThreadStart(me.MyThreadProc));
                MyThreads[I].Start();
            }
        }
    }
    class My2ndClass
    {
        private int counter;
        public void MyThreadProc()
        {
            IncCounter();
        }
        private void IncCounter()
        {
            lock (this)
            {
                counter++;
            }
        }
    }
}
```

Code Example: Synchronizing Threads Using the Monitor Class

```
using System;
using System.Collections;
using System.Threading;

namespace Client.Chapter_15___Threading
{
        class ThreadingClassMonitor
        {
                public static Thread ThreadOne =
                    new Thread(new ThreadStart(MonitorExample));
                public static ArrayList MyList = new ArrayList();
                public ThreadingClassMonitor()
                {
                        MyList.Add("Test1");
                        MyList.Add("Test2");
                }
                static void Main(string[] args)
                {
                        ThreadOne.Start();
                }
                protected static void MonitorExample()
                {
                        Monitor.Enter(MyList);
                        MyList.Add("Test3");
                        Monitor.Exit(MyList);
                }
        }
}
```

Code Example: Synchronizing Threads with Mutex

```
using System;
using System.Collections;
using System.Threading;

namespace Client.Chapter_15___Threading
{
        class ThreadingClassMutex
        {
                public static Thread ThreadOne =
                    new Thread(new ThreadStart(MutexExample));
                public static ArrayList MyList = new ArrayList();
                private static Mutex MyMutex = new Mutex(false, "MyMutex");
                public ThreadingClassMutex()
                {
                        MyList.Add("Test1");
                        MyList.Add("Test2");
                }
                static void Main(string[] args)
                {
                        ThreadOne.Start();
                }
                protected static void MutexExample()
                {
                        MyMutex.WaitOne();
                        MyList.Add("Test3");
                        MyMutex.ReleaseMutex();
                }
        }
}
```

Using Thread Pools

The thread pool is created the first time you create an instance of the `ThreadPool` class. The thread pool has a default limit of 25 threads per available processor. Each thread uses the default stack size and runs at the default priority. Each process can have only one operating system thread pool.

NOTE   For each process, you have a single `ThreadPool`.

.NET implements `ThreadPools` via the `ThreadPoolMgr` class. This class has five thread types, of which only two may be used in managed code: completion port threads and worker threads. A completion port thread executes a callback after an item is queued via `QueueUserWorkItem`. If the thread pool manager determines that there are not enough completion port threads to fulfill the request, it will be queued and acted on by a worker thread. The worker thread will dequeue the item and execute the action. Another thread, called the gate thread monitor, is created to control the behavior of the thread pool. The gate thread monitor is responsible for controlling the lifetime and number of worker threads.

This whole process can be controlled via configuration files or programmatically. The following is an example of controlling this behavior in ASP.NET. This can be done for an individual application or for all applications via the Machine.config file.

```
<processModel>
requestLimit—Specifies the number of requests that can be served
requestQueueLimit—Specifies the number of requests that can be queued
maxWorkerThreads—Specifies the number of worker threads per CPU in the ThreadPool.
Defaults to 25
maxIoThreads—Specifies the upper limit of IO threads per CPU. Defaults to 25
</processModel>
```

When you are using threading with Windows controls, you need to be aware that controls can execute methods only on the thread that created them. Therefore, every control provides `Invoke(synchronous)`, `BeginInvoke`, and `EndInvoke` methods that can be used to marshal data back to the originating thread.

In ASP.NET threading, with Internet Information Server (IIS) 6, HTTP requests are handled via a kernel mode driver, Http.sys. They are then sent to the worker process, where they are handled by worker threads.

NOTE   With IIS 5, the thread pool was used to service rquests. Generally, HTTP requests were sent to the inetinfo process, which would then use the IO completion port via a named pipe connection to the worker process to post requests. Most of the time, the request would be handled on the IO threads that accepted the requests, but under times of load, some worker threads could be used to process requests. This behavior has changed in IIS 6 in that requests are handled by worker threads.

The following example demonstrates using thread pools and ResetEvent classes.

Code Example: Using ThreadPools and ResetEvent Classes

```
using System;
using System.Threading;

namespace Client.Chapter_15___Threading
{
        class MyMainClass
        {
                public static ManualResetEvent MyManualEvent =
                    new ManualResetEvent(false);
            public static AutoResetEvent MyAutoEvent = new AutoResetEvent(false);
            static void Main(string[] args)
            {
                    ThreadPool.QueueUserWorkItem(
                        new WaitCallback(DoBackgroundWorkManual));
                    MyManualEvent.WaitOne();
                MyManualEvent.Reset();  //Sets the event back to nonsignaled
                    ThreadPool.QueueUserWorkItem(
                        new WaitCallback(DoBackgroundWorkAuto));
                    MyAutoEvent.WaitOne();
            }
            public static void DoBackgroundWorkManual(Object state)
            {
                    Console.WriteLine("Thread 1");
                    //Do stuff
                    //Then release control back to the main thread
                    MyManualEvent.Set(); //Signals the event
            }
```

```
public static void DoBackgroundWorkAuto(Object state)
{
    Console.WriteLine("Thread 1");
    //Do stuff
    MyAutoEvent.Set();
}
}
}
```

Making Asynchronous Calls

By default, all delegates support synchronous calls. This is built in, so you do not
need to do anything special. To make asynchronous calls, you use the `BeginInvoke`
method of the delegate. It is important to realize that all asynchronous calls are
handled by the `ThreadPool`, so you do not have the option of canceling these calls.

The following examples demonstrate making asynchronous calls and an
asynchronous wait timeout.

Code Example: Asynchronous Calls Using Callback

```
using System;
using System.Threading;
using System.Runtime.Remoting.Messaging;

namespace Client.Chapter_15___Threading
{
        class MyMainClass
        {
                delegate int MyDelegate(string s, ref int a, ref int b);
                static void Main(string[] args)
                {
                        MyDelegate X = new MyDelegate(DoSomething);
                        int a = 0;
                        int b = 0;
                        //Make async call that calls a callback when finished
                        AsyncCallback cb = new AsyncCallback(DoSomething2);
                        IAsyncResult ar =
                        X.BeginInvoke("Hello", ref a, ref b, cb, null);
                        Console.ReadLine();
                }
                //My async method
                static int DoSomething(string s, ref int a, ref int b)
                {
                        a = 10;
                        b = 100;
                        Console.WriteLine("Fired! DoSomething1");
                        return 0;
                }
        }
```

```
//My callback method when finished running DoSomething
static void DoSomething2(IAsyncResult ar)
{
    int a = 0;
    int b = 0;
    Console.WriteLine("Fired! DoSomething2");
    //Get the delegate
    MyDelegate X = (MyDelegate)((AsyncResult)ar).AsyncDelegate;
    //Get results
    X.EndInvoke(ref a, ref b, ar);
    Console.WriteLine(a);
    Console.WriteLine(b);
}
}
}
```

Code Example: Asynchronous Wait Timeout

```
using System;
using System.Runtime.Remoting.Messaging;

namespace Client.Chapter_15___Threading
{
        class MyMainClass
        {
                delegate int MyDelegate(string s, ref int a, ref int b);
                static void Main(string[] args)
                {
                        MyDelegate X = new MyDelegate(DoSomething);
                        int a = 0;
                        int b = 0;
                        IAsyncResult ar = X.BeginInvoke("Hello", ref a, ref b,
                        null, null);
                        ar.AsyncWaitHandle.WaitOne(10000, false);
                        if (ar.IsCompleted)
                        {
                            int c = 0;
                            int d = 0;
                          //Get results
                           X.EndInvoke(ref c, ref d, ar);
                           Console.WriteLine(c);
                           Console.WriteLine(d);
                        }
                }
            //My async method
             static int DoSomething(string s, ref int a, ref int b)
             {
                        a = 10;
                        b = 100;
                        Console.WriteLine("Fired! DoSomething1");
                        return 0;
             }
        }
}
```

CHAPTER 16
Debugging

- Tracing

- Creating an Event Log and Writing Logs

- Measuring Elapsed Time: A Simple Profiler and StopWatch (new to Whidbey)

- Using Asserts

- Using Breakpoints

- Power Debugging the CIL

- Debugging with Cordbg

- Debugging Assembly X386

- Debugging with Windbg

- Debugging with SOS

- Writing Data to Performance Monitor

- Debugging Memory Leaks

- Debugging Contention Problems in ASP.NET

- Enabling Debug Probes for Interop Services (new to Whidbey)

Tracing

There are two types of tracing that you can do with the System.Diagnostics namespace. You can use the Trace class to place Trace statements in both the retail and debug builds, without requiring a recompilation. The Debug class exists only in the debug build of an application, but the overall goal and results are the same as using the Trace class.

 TIP A healthy dose of tracing and debug logging in your application will save you many hours of support work and debugging. The Microsoft Exchange team included extended amounts of tracing in the transport components of Exchange 2000. This saved thousands of hours in troubleshooting and debugging.

By default, tracing information is sent to the debugger, but you have the following choices for listeners: debugger (DefaultTraceListener), file or console (TextWriterTraceListener), or event log (EventLogTraceListener).

You can enable tracing using one of these methods:

- Define the compilation constant TRACE and set it to true.

- Use the BooleanSwitch class.

- Use the TraceSwitch class and configuration file. This provides a multilevel switch to control tracing and debug output without recompiling your code.

```
TraceSwitch MySwitch = new TraceSwitch(
    "MySwitch", MySwitch.Level=TraceLevel.Info);
```

```
<system.diagnostics>
        <switches>
                <add name="My Switch" value =0
        </switches>
</system.diagnostics>
```

The following examples demonstrate tracing methods.

NOTE When tracing to a file, event log, the debugger, or console, you can use the Debug class instead of the Trace class if you want to do the tracing only in debug mode.

Code Example: Tracing to a File

```
using System;
using System.IO;
using System.Diagnostics;

namespace Client.Chapter_16___Debugging
{
        class TracingToAFile
        {
            [STAThread]
            static void Main(string[] args)
            {
                    FileStream Log =
                        new FileStream("Log.txt", FileMode.OpenOrCreate);
                    Trace.Listeners.Add(new TextWriterTraceListener(Log));
                    Trace.WriteLine("My Trace String To Log File");
                    Trace.Flush();
                    Log.Close();
            }
        }
}
```

Code Example: Tracing to the Event Log

```csharp
using System;
using System.IO;
using System.Diagnostics;

namespace Client.Chapter_16___Debugging
{
        class TracingToEventLog
        {
                [STAThread]
                static void Main(string[] args)
                {
                        //You can change the listener with the following code
                        EventLogTraceListener EventListener =
                            new EventLogTraceListener("MyApp");
                        Trace.Listeners.Add(EventListener);
                        Trace.WriteLine("My Trace String To Console");
                }
        }
}
```

Code Example: Tracing to the Debugger

```
using System;
using System.IO;
using System.Diagnostics;

namespace Client.Chapter_16___Debugging
{
        class TracingToDebugger
        {
                [STAThread]
                static void Main(string[] args)
                {
                        Trace.WriteLine("My Trace String");
                        Trace.Flush();
                }
        }
}
```

Code Example: Tracing to the Console

```
using System;
using System.IO;
using System.Diagnostics;

namespace Client.Chapter_16___Debugging
{
        class Class1
        {
                [STAThread]
                static void Main(string[] args)
                {
                        Trace.Listeners.Add(
                            new TextWriterTraceListener(Console.Out));
                        Trace.WriteLine("My Trace to the console");
                }
        }
}
```

Code Example: Using BooleanSwitch

```csharp
using System;
using System.IO;
using System.Diagnostics;

namespace Client.Chapter_16___Debugging
{
        class UsingBooleanSwitch
        {
                static BooleanSwitch MySwitch =
                    new BooleanSwitch("MyData", "MyModule");
                [STAThread]
                static void Main(string[] args)
                {
                        MySwitch.Enabled = true;
                        if (MySwitch.Enabled)
                                Console.WriteLine("Error happened!");
                }
        }
}
```

Code Example: Using TraceSwitch and Config Files

```
using System;
using System.Diagnostics;

namespace Client.Chapter_16___Debugging
{
        class TracingExample
        {
                static void Main(string[] args)
                {
                        TraceSwitch General =
                            new TraceSwitch("General", "Application Switch");
                        Trace.WriteLineIf(General.TraceError,
                            "General - Error Tracing Enabled");
                        Trace.WriteLineIf(General.TraceWarning,
                            "General - Warning Tracing Enabled");
                        Trace.WriteLineIf(General.TraceInfo,
                            "General - Info Tracing Enabled");
                        Trace.WriteLineIf(General.TraceVerbose,
                            "General - Verbose Tracing Enabled");
                        TraceSwitch MyComponent =
                            new TraceSwitch("MyComponent", "Application Switch");
                        Trace.WriteLineIf(MyComponent.TraceError,
                            "MyComponent - Error Tracing Enabled");
                        Trace.WriteLineIf(MyComponent.TraceWarning,
                            "MyComponent - Warning Tracing Enabled");
                        Trace.WriteLineIf(MyComponent.TraceInfo,
                            "MyComponent - Info Tracing Enabled");
                        Trace.WriteLineIf(MyComponent.TraceVerbose,
                            "MyComponent - Verbose Tracing Enabled");
                }
        }
}
```

The configuration file settings are as follows:

```xml
<?xml version="1.0" encoding="utf-8" ?>
<configuration>
      <system.diagnostics>
          <switches>
          <add name="General" value="1" />
          <add name="MyComponent" value="3" />
          </switches>
      </system.diagnostics>
</configuration>
```

The values settings in the configuration file are as follows:

Off	0
Error	1
Warnings & Error	2
Info, Warning & Error	3
Verbose	4

Creating and Writing to an Event Log

You can also use the following code to write directly to the event log without using Trace methods.

```
EventLog Log = new EventLog();
if (!EventLog.SourceExists("Remoting"))
        EventLog.CreateEventSource("Remoting", "Application");
Log.Source = "Remoting";
Log.WriteEntry(System.Security.Principal.WindowsIdentity.GetCurrent().Name);
```

The following example shows how to create and write to an event log.

Code Example: Creating and Writing to an Event Log

```
using System;
using System.Diagnostics;

namespace EventLogging
{
        class Class1
        {

                [STAThread]
                static void Main(string[] args)
                {
                     //Creates a new event log in Event Viewer
                      EventLog E = new EventLog("ApplicationLog");
                      E.Source = "MyApplication";
                     //Writes an entry in the log
                      E.WriteEntry("My Logged Event");
                      E.WriteEntry("My2ndEvent",EventLogEntryType.Error, 5555, 2);
                }
        }
}
```

Measuring Elapsed Time

For debugging and troubleshooting, as well as optimizing code, you may want to measure the amount of time it takes for specific operations to occur. Two methods for measuring an operation's time are presented here.

A Simple Profiler

You can use the DateTime class to measure the time it takes for a specific operation to complete, as shown in the following example. This is the easiest way to measure an operation in version 1.1 or in version 1.0, where the StopWatch class (discussed in the next section) is not available.

Code Example: A Simple Profiler

```
using System;
using System.Diagnostics;

namespace Client.Chapter_16___Debugging
{
        class PoorMansProfiler
        {
            [STAThread]
            static void Main(string[] args)
            {
                    DateTime Start = DateTime.Now;
                    //Call methods or do work needing to be measured
                    DateTime End = DateTime.Now;
                    TimeSpan CallTime = End - Start;
                    Console.WriteLine("Call Time(MS): " +
                    CallTime.Milliseconds.ToString());
            }
        }
}
```

Using StopWatch

StopWatch, a new object added to the 2.0 version of the framework, can be used
to measure the time for operations in your code. This object resides in the
System.Diagnostics namespace. It is a simple wrapper to the
QueryPerformanceCounter and QueryPerformanceFrequency APIs.

The following example demonstrates using StopWatch.

Code Example: Using StopWatch

```
using System;
using System.Diagnostics;

namespace Client.Chapter_16___Debugging
{
        class PoorMansProfiler
        {
                [STAThread]
                static void Main(string[] args)
                {
                    //Simple sample
                     Stopwatch stopWatch = Stopwatch.StartNew();
                     System.Threading.Thread.Sleep(milliseconds);
                     Console.WriteLine(stopWatch.Elapsed);
                }
        }
}
```

```csharp
using System;
using System.Diagnostics;
namespace Client.Chapter_16___Debugging
{
        class PoorMansProfiler
        {
                [STAThread]
                static void Main(string[] args)
                {
                    //Interval measurement
                    Stopwatch stopWatch = new Stopwatch();
                    foreach(Order o in orders)
                    {
                        stopWatch.Start();
                            //Do work
                        stopWatch.Stop();
                    }
                    //Prints time span elapsed
                    Console.WriteLine(stopWatch.Elapsed);
                    stopWatch.Reset();
                }
        }
}
```

Using Asserts

Asserts can be used to present a dialog box when a condition is false, as defined in the Assert statement. The following example demonstrates using asserts.

Code Example: Using Asserts

```
using System;
using System.IO;
using System.Diagnostics;

namespace Client.Chapter_16___Debugging
{
        class Class1
        {
              [STAThread]
              static void Main(string[] args)
              {
                    int i = 0;
                    Trace.Assert((i == 1), "My Trace Assertion");
                    Debug.Assert((i == 1), "My Debug Assertion");
              }
        }
}
```

Using Breakpoints

Breakpoints are used to stop the execution of an application at a specific point in the code to determine the state of the application. There are four ways to use breakpoints:

- Break immediately when the breakpoint is reached.

- Break on the evaluation of a Boolean statement.

- Break when a breakpoint has been reached a specific amount of times.

- Break when a breakpoint is hit and a variable has changed since the last breakpoint was hit.

When debugging an application, you often want to examine the value of objects and variables. Visual Studio .NET offers the following windows to do this:

- **Autos:** Shows variables that are part of a given method.

- **Locals:** Shows all the variables that are in scope.

- **Watch:** Allows you to add specific variables and create your own list.

TIP At the very heart of debugging is setting good breakpoints. The more specific and accurate you are in setting breakpoints, the easier and faster you will debug.

Power Debugging the CIL

You can control many debugging features by manipulating the Registry. The
`HKLM\Software\Microsoft\.NETFramework\DbgJITDebugLaunchSetting` key sets debug
notifications, as follows:

0   Message box is displayed
1   No message box; bottom stack dump taken
2   Control passed to default debugger

The `HKLM\Software\Microsoft\.NETFramework\DbgManagedDebugger` key defines
the default debugger path to `debugger\cordbg.exe !a %d`.

In addition to using the Registry, you can view MSIL for an assembly by using
Ildasm. This tool allows you to view the IL code and send the code to a text file for
modification by using the following syntax:

```
ildasm module.dll /out:module.il
```

Then you can open the .il file with Notepad, modify the IL code, and reassemble it
by using Ilasm.

```
ilasm /dll module.il
```

In addition, there are other tools that you can use to conceal your code from
having this type of operation done to it. These tools are called *obfuscators*. There
are many third-party vendors who sell these tools. The following are some Web
sites of obfuscator vendors:

```
http://www.remotesoft.com
http://www.wiseowl.com
http://www.preemptive.com/dotfuscator
http://www.lesser-software.com
http://www.desaware.com
```

Table 16-1 lists the directives for debugging the CIL, and Table 16-2 lists
the opcodes.

Table 16-1. Debugging Directives

Name	Description
.addon	Allows for client event registration
.assembly	Used to reference assemblies and define information about assemblies
.class	Defines types
.corflags	Documents the portable execution information
.custom	Adds attributes information
.data	Defines a data segment
.entrypoint	Defines the first method called on entry into an assembly
.event	Defines an event
.export	Defines the name for an exported method
.field	Defines a field of a class
.file	References a file
.fire	Defines a method that can raise an event
.get	Retrieves a property value
.hash	Creates or shows the algorithm used for a hash
.locale	Defines the culture
.locals	Defines local variables
.maxstack	Defines the maximum number of values on the stack
.method	Adds a method to a class
.mresource	Adds resource information
.namespace	Groups code into a logical entity
.override	Defines a method that overrides a base method
.pack	States field boundary size
.permission	Defines security information
.permissionset	Defines security information on multiple resources
.property	Defines a class property
.publickey	States the public key used to sign the assembly
.publickeytoken	Contains 8 bytes of the reference key assembly

Table 16-1. Debugging Directives (Continued)

Name	Description
.removeon	Unregisters an event
.set	Sets the value on a property
.size	Defines a block of memory in a class
.subsystem	Defines user interaction preference
.try	Enters a try block
.ver	States the current version or desired version
.ventry	States the slot a method should be in a vtable
.vtfixup	Defines a vtable for exported methods

Table 16-2. Debugging Opcodes

Name	Description
Add	Adds two values on the stack and pushes the results on the stack
And	Performs a logical AND and pushes the results on the stack
Arglist	Gets variable argument list for a vararg method
Beq	Breaks to a code label if the two top values on the stack are true
Bge	Breaks to a code label if the second-most top value is greater than or equal to the value on top of the stack
Bgt	Breaks to a code label if the second-most top value on the stack is greater than the top value
Ble	Breaks to a code label if the second-most top value is less than or equal to the top stack value
Blt	Breaks to a code label if the second-most top value is less than the top stack value
Bne.un	Breaks to a code label if the two top values are not equal
Box	Turns a value type into a reference type
Br	Breaks to a code label unconditionally
Brfalse	Breaks to a code label if the top stack value is false
Brtrue	Breaks to a code label if the top value is true

Table 16-2. Debugging Opcodes (Continued)

Name	Description
Call	Calls an instance method and does not throw an exception if the value is on the stack
Calli	Calls a method via a function pointer
Callvirt	Calls an instance method and throws an exception if the reference is not on the stack
Castclass	Checks to a see if a reference type is a specific type and pushes the result on the stack; throws an exception on failure
Ceq	Compares two values for equality and pushes the results on the stack
Cgt	Compares the two top values on the stack to see if the second-most top value is larger
Ckfinite	Checks for divide-by-zero conditions
Clt	Compares the two top values on the stack to see if the second value is smaller
Conv	Converts a value to the appended type
Cpblk	Copies data from one memory location to another
Cpobj	Takes the value at one address and copies it to the another address
Div	Divides the two top values on the stack and pushes the result
Dup	Duplicates the current value on the stack
Endfault	Signals the end of a catch block
Endfinally	Signals the end of a finally block
Initblk	Initializes a block of memory
Isinst	Checks to see if a reference is of a specific type and pushes the results on the stack; returns null on failure
Jmp	Calls a method with the same argument values as the current method and then terminates the current method execution
Ldarg	Loads an argument value on the stack
Ldc	Loads a loads a specific value on the stack
Ldelem	Retrieves an element in an array and pushes it on the stack

Table 16-2. Debugging Opcodes (Continued)

Name	Description
Ldelma	Gets the address of an element in an array and pushes it on the stack
Ldfld	Loads an instance field's value on the stack
Ldftn	Loads a function pointer on the stack
Ldind	Retrieves a value given an address; the type is defined after the opcode
Ldlen	Pushes the length of an array on the stack
Ldloc	Loads a variable's value on the stack
Ldloca	Loads a variable's address on the stack
Ldnull	Loads a null reference on the stack
Ldobj	Gets values from an address on the stack and pushes the result on the stack
Ldsfld	Loads the value of a static field or an instance field on the stack
Ldstr	Loads a string on the stack
Ldvirftn	Loads a function pointer on the stack
Leave	Leaves a try block
Mul	Multiplies two values on the stack and pushes the result
Newarr	Creates a new array
Newobj	Creates a new instance of an object
Nop	Does nothing; no opcode
Not	Performs the NOT binary operation on the topmost stack value and pushes the result
Or	Performs an OR binary operation on two stack values and pushes the results
Rem	Divides two values on the stack and pushes the remainder on the stack
Ret	Ends execution of a method and returns the topmost value on the stack
Shl	Performs a shift left operation
Shr	Performs a shift right operation

Table 16-2. Debugging Opcodes (Continued)

Name	Description
Sizeof	Calculates the size of a value type and pushes the result on the stack
Stelem	Takes a value on the stack and places it in an array
Stdfld	Stores the value of an instance field on the stack
Stind	Stores a value in a local variable given an address
Stloc	Stores a value on the stack
Stobj	Stores a value on the stack in the value defined by an address
Stsfld	Stores a value on the stack in either a static field or an instance field
Sub	Subtracts two values on the stack and pushes the result
Switch	Defines a jump table
Tail	Calls a method, and then terminates the current method
Throw	Throws an exception
Unaligned	States that the next address is unaligned
Unbox	Turns a reference type into a value type

Debugging with Cordbg

Cordbg is the .NET Framework Runtime Debugger. Table 16-3 lists the Cordbg commands, and Table 16-4 lists the mode arguments. Cordbg can be started from the Visual Studio command prompt.

Table 16-3. Cordbg Commands

Name	Description
show	Shows source code lines before and after the current line of execution (the command with the asterisk will be the current command)
print	Shows the local variables values
next [count]	Steps to the next line of code, skipping over method calls; count is the number of code lines to skip
so [count]	Same as next
step [count]	Steps through the lines of code entering into any method calls
si [count]	Same as step
in [count]	Same as step
nsingle [count]	Steps through the code, skipping method calls
ssingle [count]	Steps through code, stepping into method calls
out [count]	Steps out of the current method
se	Sets the next line of code to execute
disassemble	Shows disassembly information
registers	Shows registers
dump	Dumps a memory address
break	Sets a breakpoint (break module!class::method)
remove	Removes a breakpoint
go	Starts execution
kill	Shuts down an application
<	Reads a batch file (< Mybatch.txt)
>	Writes to a file

Table 16-4. CORDBG Mode Arguments

Name	Description
appDomainLoads	Displays application domain and assembly load information
classLoads	Displays class load events
dumpMemoryInBytes	Displays memory as bytes or DWORDs
enhanceDiag	Displays enhanced diagnostic information
hexDisplay	Displays numbers in hex or decimal format
ilNatPrint	Displays offsets in MSIL offsets or native format
iSAll	Steps through all interceptors
iSClinit	Steps through class initializers
iSExceptF	Steps through exception filters
iSInt	Steps through user interceptors
iSPolicy	Steps through context policies
iSSec	Steps through security interceptors
jitOptimizations	Specifies if JIT creates easy-to-debug code
loggingMessages	Displays managed code log messages
moduleLoads	Displays module load events
separateConsole	Specifies if the process being debugged gets its own console
showArgs	Displays method arguments in a stack trace
showModules	Displays module names in a stack trace
showStaticsOnPrint	Displays static fields for objects
showSuperClassOnPrint	Displays contents of base classes on print
uSAll	Steps through unmapped stop locations
uSEpi	Steps through method epilogues
uSPro	Steps through method prologues
uSUnmanaged	Steps through unmanaged code

Debugging Assembly X386

Tables 16-5 through 16-7 list assembly X386 debugging instructions, registers, and calling conventions.

Table 16-5. Assembly X386 Debugging Instructions

Instruction	Description
PUSH	Places an item on the stack and increments the stack pointer.
POP	Removes an item from the stack and places it in the register identified in the operand as well as decrementing the stack pointer.
MOV	Moves a value of from the source to the destination.
SUB	Subtracts the source from the destination.
ADD	Adds the source to the destination.
RET	Takes the current value of the stack pointer and places it into the instruction pointer. Also for functions called via stdcall, there will be a value indicating how many bytes to subtract from the current stack pointer to clean up the parameters passed to the function.
CALL	Pushes the return address on the stack (which is the address that will be executed when the function called returns) and places the address stored in the operand in the EIP register. For example, CALL 0X006682568 calls a function in the same module. CALL [0x00401234] calls a function in another module. CALL [EAX + 24] calls a function via a vtable.
AND	Logical AND.
OR	Logical OR.
NOT	Complement operation (opposite).
INC	Increments the operand by one.
DEC	Decrements the operand by one.
SHL	Multiplies by two.
SHR	Divides by two.
DIV	Performs unsigned division.
MUL	Performs unsigned multiplication.
IDIV	Performs signed division.
IMUL	Performs signed multiplication.

Table 16-5. Assembly X386 Debugging Instructions (Continued)

Instruction	Description
MOVSX	Moves with sign-extend. This operation copies smaller values to larger values and dictates the way the upper bits are filled.
MOVZX	Moves with zero-extend. This operation copies smaller values to larger values and dictates the way the upper bits are filled.
LEA	Loads the destination register with the address of the source operand. Used to load locals or parameters into registers. The & statement in an assignment would use this.
CMP	Compares the source to the destination operands; for example if(a == b).
TEST	Performs a bitwise AND; for example, if (a & b).
JMP	Appears at the end of a loop or on an exit or goto statement.
JE	Jumps if equal.
JL	Jumps if less than.
JG	Jumps if greater than.
JNE	Jumps if not equal.
JGE	Jumps if greater than or equal to.
JLE	Jumps if less than or equal.
JNZ	Jumps if not zero.
JZ	Jumps if zero.
LOOP	Used in loop statements, and ECX is the counter (for, while, do...while).
MOVS	memcpy that moves ESI into EDI. Used to move strings.
SCAS	Scans string; used to compare the value of EDI with the value stored in EAX.
STOS	Stores string; used to store the value of EAX in EDI.
CMPS	Compares string (memcmp)
XOR	Zeros out the value of the operand.

Table 16-6. Assembly X386 Debugging Registers

32-bit Register	16	0-7	8-15	Description
EAX	AX	AL	AH	Stores return values
EBX	BX	BL	BH	
ECX	CX	CL	CH	This pointer, loop counter, `fastcall` parameter
EDX	DX	DL	DH	
ESI	SI			Source compare or string
EDI	DI			Destination compare or string
ESP	SP			Stack pointer
EBP	BP			Base pointer
EIP				Instruction pointer

Table 16-7. Assembly X386 Debugging Calling Conventions

Convention	Argument Passing	Stack Cleanup	Name	Notes
`cdecl`	Right to left	Caller—RET	_Foo	Default for C & C++
`stdcall`	Right to left	Called—RET X	_Foo@12	@ followed by number of bytes passed as arguments
`fastcall`	First two DWORDs are stored in ECX and EDX; rest are passed right to left	Called—RET X	@Foo@12	@ followed by number of bytes passed as arguments
`thiscall`	Right to left, the `this` pointer is stored in ECX	Called—RET X	None	Used by member functions

For cdecl, you will see the operation ret with no value. This will force the code to return to an address that is an add operation (add esp, X), where *X* is the number of bytes subtracted in the prologue code. For stdcall, fastcall, and thiscall, you will see a ret X, where *X* is the number of bytes to remove from the stack.

Here is some typical prologue code:

```
push        EBP
mov         EBP, ESP
sub          ESP, 8
```

Here is some typical epilogue code:

```
mov         ESP, EBP
pop          EBP
ret
```

Debugging with Windbg

Windbg is the Windows Debugger tool. It can be found at http://www.microsoft.com/ ddk/debugging/default.asp. Table 16-8 lists the Windbg commands.

Table 16-8. Windbg Commands

Command	Description
kvn	Dumps stack
r	Dumps registers
u	Unassembles
~[#]s	Changes thread to #
dt [type] address	Dumps *type*
dv	Dumps locals and parameters
bp (address or module!name)	Sets breakpoint
bc	Clears breakpoint
bd	Disables breakpoint
be	Enables breakpoint
x module!function	Returns function address
sxe ld:module.dll	Breaks on module load
dc	Dumps characters
da	Dumps ASCII
du	Dumps Unicode
!lmi	Loads module information
ln	Lists nearest method
lm	Lists modules
lmv	Lists modules verbose
!heap	Gets Win32 heap information
!sympath	Sets symbols path
!srcpath	Sets source path
!locks	Shows critical sections for process
!gle	Gets last error

Table 16-8. Windbg Commands (Continued)

Command	Description
!peb	Dumps process block
!teb	Dumps thread block
.dump /f [path.dmp]	Forces a fill memory dump
.server tcp:port=5000	Debug server
tcp:server=name,port=5000	Debug client
!logo	Sets up API logging
!loge	Enables logging
!logm x module.dll	Excludes module logging
!logm I ntdll.dll	Logs NTDLL calls

Debugging with SOS Commands

Another useful debugging tool is SOS. SOS is part of the .NET Framework in version 1.1 and later. For version 1.0 of the framework, the SOS.dll debugger extension can be found at the following URL:

```
http://www.microsoft.com/downloads/release.asp?ReleaseID=44274.
```

In Visual Studio 2003, SOS can be loaded directly using the command window and the following command:

```
.load sos.dll
```

Table 16-9 lists the SOS commands.

Table 16-9. SOS Commands

COMState	Lists COM state for each thread
ClrStack	Provides true managed stack trace, source, and line numbers; additional parameters are -p[arams] -l[ocals] -r[egs] -a[ll]
DumpClass <addr>	Dumps EE class information
DumpDomain [<addr>]	Lists assemblies and modules in a domain
DumpHeap [-stat] [-min 100] [-max 2000] [-mt 0x3000000] [-type <partial type name>] [-fix] [start [end]]	Dumps GC heap contents
DumpMD <addr>	Dumps method description information
DumpMT [-MD] <addr>	Dumps method table information
DumpModule <addr>	Dumps EE module information
DumpObj <addr>	Dumps an object on GC heap
DumpStack [-EE] [-smart] [top stack [bottom stack]	EE shows only managed stack items
DumpStackObjects [top stack [bottom stack]	Dumps managed objects on the stack
DumpVC <mt> <addr>	Dumps a value class object
EEHeap [-gc] [-win32] [-loader]	Lists GC/loader heap information
EEStack [-short] [-EE]	Lists all stacks EE knows
EEVersion	Lists mscoree.dll version

Table 16-9. SOS Commands (Continued)

COMState	Lists COM state for each thread
FinalizeQueue [-detail]	Works queue for finalize thread
GCInfo [<MD>] [IP]	Dumps GC encoding information for a managed method
GCRoot <addr>	Finds roots on stack/handle for object
IP2MD <addr>	Finds method description from IP
Name2EE <module name> <item name>	Finds memory address of EE data given a class/method name
ObjSize [<addr>]	Finds number of bytes that a root or all roots keep alive on GC heap
ProcInfo [-env] [-time] [-mem]	Displays the process information
RWLock [-all] <addr>	Lists information for a Read/Write lock
SyncBlk [-all|#]	Lists synchronize block
ThreadPool	Displays CLR thread pool state
Threads	Lists managed threads
Token2EE <module name> <mdToken>	Finds memory address of EE data for metadata token
u [<MD>] [IP]	Unassembles managed code

The following sections provide examples of using many of the SOS commands listed in Table 16-9.

!COMState

The !COMState command returns the COM apartment state for each thread in
the process.

```
!comstate
ID     TEB    APT        APTId CallerTID Context
3040   be0    7ffde000 Ukn
2096   830    7ffdc000 Ukn
2468   9a4    7ffdb000 MTA        0         0 00168e60
756    2f4    7ffda000 Ukn
2560   a00    7ffd9000 MTA        0         0 00168e60
```

!ClrStack

The !ClrStack command dumps the managed stack for the thread.

```
0:003> !clrstack -smart
Thread 3
ESP       EIP
06e3fbc8  7ffe0304 [FRAME: GCFrame]
06e3fc7c  7ffe0304 [FRAME: HelperMethodFrame]
06e3fca8  06d30242 [DEFAULT] [hasThis] Void Test.Ch14.Deadlock.Method1()
  at [+0x62] [+0x2e] c:\class\test\ch14\deadlock.cs:39
06e3fed4  791da717 [FRAME: GCFrame]
```

!DumpClass

The !DumpClass <addr> command dumps the managed class information.

```
!dumpclass 79c0d20c
Class Name : System.Collections.Hashtable
mdToken : 020000f9 (Fusion.DLL)
Parent Class : 79bf83c8
ClassLoader : 0014e970
Method Table : 79c0d0cc
Vtable Slots : 1c
Total Method Slots : 38
Class Attributes : 102001 :
Flags : 3000821
NumInstanceFields: b
NumStaticFields: 1
ThreadStaticOffset: 0
ThreadStaticsSize: 0
ContextStaticOffset: 0
ContextStaticsSize: 0
FieldDesc*: 79c0d270
MT    Field    Offset
   Type       Attr        Value Name
79c0d0cc  4000395       4
   CLASS    instance           buckets
79c0d0cc  4000396       1c
   System.Int32    instance           count
79c0d0cc  4000397       20
   System.Int32    instance           occupancy
79c0d0cc  4000398       24
   System.Int32    instance           loadsize
79c0d0cc  4000399       28
   System.Single    instance           loadFactor
79c0d0cc  400039a       2c
   System.Int32    instance           version
79c0d0cc  400039b       8
   CLASS    instance           keys
79c0d0cc  400039c       c
   CLASS    instance           values
79c0d0cc  400039d       10
   CLASS    instance           _hcp
79c0d0cc  400039e       14
   CLASS    instance           _comparer
```

```
79c0d0cc  400039f       18
   CLASS   instance            m_siInfo
79c0d0cc  4000394        0
   CLASS     shared   static   primes
```

The address required for this can be acquired by using !DumpMT on the class.

```
!dumpmt 79c0d0cc
EEClass : 79c0d20c
Module : 79be2000
Name: System.Collections.Hashtable
mdToken: 020000f9  (c:\windows\microsoft.net\framework\v1.1.4322\mscorlib.dll)
MethodTable Flags : 2040000
Number of IFaces in IFaceMap : 6
Interface Map : 79c0d1dc
Slots in VTable : 56
```

!DumpDomain

The !DumpDomain <addr> command shows the assemblies and modules in the domain. (You can get the application domain addresses by using the !Threads command.)

```
0:000> !dumpdomain
--------------------------------------
System Domain: 793e6fc8
LowFrequencyHeap: 793e702c
HighFrequencyHeap: 793e7080
StubHeap: 793e70d4
Name:
Assembly: 00157a10 [mscorlib]
ClassLoader: 00157ae8
  Module Name
79b66000 c:\windows\microsoft.net\framework\v1.1.4322\mscorlib.dll
--------------------------------------
Shared Domain: 793e83f8
LowFrequencyHeap: 793e845c
HighFrequencyHeap: 793e84b0
StubHeap: 793e8504
Assembly: 00157a10 [mscorlib]
ClassLoader: 00157ae8
  Module Name
79b66000 c:\windows\microsoft.net\framework\v1.1.4322\mscorlib.dll
--------------------------------------
Domain 1: 146320
LowFrequencyHeap: 00146384
HighFrequencyHeap: 001463d8
StubHeap: 0014642c
Name: Test.exe
Assembly: 001605d0 [Test]
ClassLoader: 001606a8
  Module Name
00160178 C:\class\Test\bin\Debug\Test.exe
```

!DumpHeap

The !DumpHeap [-stat] [-min 100] [-max 2000] [-mt 0x30000000] [-fix] [start [end]] command displays the contents of the managed heap. The options are as follows:

-stat	Show only statistics
-min <#>	Show only objects that are larger than # bytes
-max <#>	Show only objects that are smaller than # bytes
-mt <addr>	Show only objects with a particular method table

!dumpheap -stat

```
Last good object: 04a43268
total 143 objects
Statistics
      MT    Count TotalSize Class Name
79bcf944        1        12 System.Runtime.Remoting.
   Messaging.CallContextSecurityData
79b87458        1        12 System.IO.Stream/NullStream
  3e50cc        1        16 Test.Ch14.Deadlock
79bba67c        1        20 System.Text.UTF8Encoding/UTF8Encoder
79bba3c4        1        20 System.IO.TextWriter/NullTextWriter
79bba114        1        20 System.Text.CodePageEncoding
79b8b7b4        1        20 System.Collections.ArrayList
79b87efc        1        20 System.Text.UTF8Encoding
79b830a4        1        20 System.AppDomainSetup
79bcea2c        1        28
    System.Runtime.Remoting.Messaging.LogicalCallContext
79b80b44        1        32 System.SharedStatics
79be58d4        2        40 System.IO.__ConsoleStream
79b7f4f4        2        40 System.Text.StringBuilder
  3e5174        2        40 Test.Ch14.Resources
79b802dc        1        64 System.StackOverflowException
79b801a4        1        64 System.OutOfMemoryException
79b81bec        1        80 System.AppDomain
  14d5d0        5      6124     Free
  93209c        4      6312 System.Object[]
Total 143 objects
```

```
large objects
Address  MT Size
90d9350  79b4f3f8 87492 System.String
90c3df8  79b4f3f8 87360 System.String
90ae928  79b4f3f8 87224 System.String
total XX large objects
```

You can also scan the managed heap for a specific object by using
`!DumpHeap -mt <MT address>`.

```
0:005> !dumpheap -mt 3e50cc
 Address       MT      Size
04a41ad0 003e50cc        16
Bad MethodTable for Obj at 04a432a4
Last good object: 04a43268
total 1 objects
Statistics
      MT   Count TotalSize Class Name
  3e50cc       1        16 Test.Ch14.Deadlock
Total 1 objects
```

!DumpMD

The !DumpMD <addr> command shows method description information.

```
0:005> !dumpmd 79b7c530
Method Name : [DEFAULT] [hasThis] Void System.Object.Finalize()
MethodTable 79b7c364
Module: 79b66000
mdToken: 0600000a (c:\windows\microsoft.net\framework\v1.1.4322\mscorlib.dll)
Flags : 8000
IL RVA : 00007a00
```

The following examples show how to set a breakpoint in managed code, both in code that has been jitted and in code that has not been jitted.

Code Example: Setting a Breakpoint in Managed Code That Has Been Jitted

```
!name2ee test.Exe Test.Ch14.ThreadPoolDemo.Main
----------------------------------------
MethodDesc: 3e5290
Name: [DEFAULT] I4 Test.Ch14.ThreadPoolDemo.Main()
!dumpmd 3e5290
Method Name : [DEFAULT] I4 Test.Ch14.ThreadPoolDemo.Main()
MethodTable 3e52c8
Module: 15d230
mdToken: 06000001 (c:\class\Test\bin\Debug\Test.exe)
Flags : 10
Method VA : 06db0078
Set the breakpoint on the Method VA of 06db0078
```

Code Example: Setting a Breakpoint in Managed Code That Has Not Been Jitted

```
!name2ee test.Exe Test.Ch14.ThreadPoolDemo.Main
---------------------------------------
MethodDesc: 3e5290
Name: [DEFAULT] I4 Test.Ch14.ThreadPoolDemo.Main()
!dumpmd 3e5290
Method Name : [DEFAULT] I4 Test.Ch14.ThreadPoolDemo.Main()
MethodTable 3e52c8
Module: 15d230
mdToken: 06000001 (c:\class\Test\bin\Debug\Test.exe)
Flags : 10
Method RVA : 0078
ba w4 3e5290+4
!dumpmd 3e5290
Method Name : [DEFAULT] I4 Test.Ch14.ThreadPoolDemo.Main()
MethodTable 3e52c8
Module: 15d230
mdToken: 06000001 (c:\class\Test\bin\Debug\Test.exe)
Flags : 10
Method VA : 06db0078
Bp 06db0078
```

!DumpMT

The !DumpMT [-MD] <addr> command dumps the managed class information. If you use the –MD switch, as in the following example, you will also get the methods that the object hosts. You can get more information on the methods by using !DumpMD <addr>.

```
0:005> !dumpmt -MD 3e5174
EEClass : 06c037d0
Module : 00160178
Name: Test.Ch14.Resources
mdToken: 02000002  (C:\class\Test\bin\Debug\Test.exe)
MethodTable Flags : c0000
Number of IFaces in IFaceMap : 0
Interface Map : 003e51b4
Slots in VTable : 5
----------------------------------------
MethodDesc Table
  Entry  MethodDesc  JIT    Name
79b7c4eb 79b7c4f0   None   [DEFAULT] [hasThis] String System.Object.ToString()
79b7c473 79b7c478   None   [DEFAULT] [hasThis]
    Boolean System.Object.Equals(Object)
79b7c48b 79b7c490   None   [DEFAULT] [hasThis] I4 System.Object.GetHashCode()
79b7c52b 79b7c530   None   [DEFAULT] [hasThis] Void System.Object.Finalize()
003e515b 003e5160   None   [DEFAULT] [hasThis] Void Test.Ch14.Resources..ctor()
```

!DumpModule

The !DumpModule <addr> command shows EE module information.

```
0:000> !dumpmodule 00160178
Name C:\class\Test\bin\Debug\Test.exe
dwFlags 00003280
Attribute PEFile Edit&Continue
Assembly 001605d0
LoaderHeap* 001601f8
TypeDefToMethodTableMap* 06bf0010
TypeRefToMethodTableMap* 06bf001c
MethodDefToDescMap* 06bf0038
FieldDefToDescMap* 06bf0050
MemberRefToDescMap* 06bf0068
FileReferencesMap* 06bf0090
AssemblyReferencesMap* 06bf0094
MetaData starts at 00402260 (0x428 bytes)
```

!DumpObj

The !DumpObj <addr> command shows an object on the GC heap.

```
0:000> !dumpobj 04a41ad0
Name: Test.Ch14.Deadlock
MethodTable 0x003e50cc
EEClass 0x06c032e8
Size 16(0x10) bytes
mdToken: 02000003  (C:\class\Test\bin\Debug\Test.exe)
FieldDesc*: 003e5058
      MT    Field   Offset            Type      Attr      Value Name
003e50cc  4000004        4           CLASS   instance 04a41ae0 Resource1
003e50cc  4000005        8           CLASS   instance 04a41b48 Resource2
```

!DumpStack

The !DumpStack [-EE] [-smart] [<top stack> [<bottom stack>]] command shows managed stack items.

```
0:000> !dumpstackobjects
0012f690 06db0118 (MethodDesc 0x3e5280 +0xc0 TheTraceSwitch.TracingExample.Main)
```

!DumpStackObjects

The !DumpStackObjects [<top stack>[<bottom stack>]] command dumps all the
managed objects on the stack.

```
!dumpstackobjects
ESP/REG  Object    Name
0012f2fc 04aaa810 System.Diagnostics.TraceSwitch
0012f320 04aaa810 System.Diagnostics.TraceSwitch
0012f328 04a52bf4 System.Diagnostics.TraceSwitch
0012f37c 04aaa7e8 System.String      logfilename
0012f380 04aaa7e8 System.String      logfilename
0012f3bc 04aaa810 System.Diagnostics.TraceSwitch
0012f460 04aaa810 System.Diagnostics.TraceSwitch
0012f464 04a52bf4 System.Diagnostics.TraceSwitch
0012f468 04aaa810 System.Diagnostics.TraceSwitch
0012f470 04aaa810 System.Diagnostics.TraceSwitch
0012f474 04a528e4 System.String      Application Switch
0012f6a4 04a4a43c System.Object[]
0012f6d8 04a4a43c System.Object[]
0012f928 04a4a43c System.Object[]
0012f92c 04a4a43c System.Object[]
```

!EEVersion

The !EEVersion command shows the version of mscoree.dll in use.

!eeversion
```
1.1.4322.573 retail
Workstation build
```

!FinalizeQueue

Each generation has its own finalization queue. Objects are placed into this queue if they contain a finalizer(~*ClassName*) method. When a garbage collection cycle for a generation is started, a graph of available objects is made. When an object is found to be no longer available, it is compared to the finalization queue. If a corresponding object is found, the object is placed on the FReachable queue, which is defined as "Ready For Finalization." Objects in the FReachable queue have their finalizer called, and then they are made no longer strongly referenced, which can be seen by using !GCRoot [MT]. If results show HANDLE(STRONG), then the object is considered strongly rooted.

The !FinalizeQueue [-detail] command shows information about finalizable objects.

```
!finalizequeue
SyncBlock to be cleaned up: 0
----------------------------------
generation 0 has 0 finalizable objects (001559e8->001559e8)
generation 1 has 0 finalizable objects (001559e8->001559e8)
generation 2 has 0 finalizable objects (001559e8->001559e8)
Ready for finalization 0 objects (001559e8->001559e8)
Statistics
      MT    Count TotalSize Class Name
   3e512c       1        16 Test.Ch10.FSTest
Total 1 objects
```

!EEHeap

The !EEHeap -gc command shows the address of each heap.

```
!eeheap -gc
generation 0 starts at 0x1b8eb280
generation 1 starts at 0x1b831028
generation 2 starts at 0x05061028
 segment    begin allocated      size
05060000 05061028  0605ffbc 0x00ffef94(16773012)    //Generation 2 Heap
19410000 19411028  1a3873ec 0x00f763c4(16212932)
15010000 15011028  15e65b04 0x00e54adc(15026908)
17010000 17011028  17f7c1ac 0x00f6b184(16167300)
1b830000 1b831028  1b9341f8 001031d0(1061328)      //Generation 0 and 1 Heaps
Large object heap starts at 0x06061028
 segment    begin allocated      size
06060000 06061028  06d7f8e8 0x00d1e8c0(13756608)   //Large Object Heap
16010000 16011028  1682b560 0x0081a538(8496440)
18010000 18011028  18fe4288 0x00fd3260(16593504)
Total Size  0x63441e0(104088032)
------------------------------
GC Heap Size  0x63441e0(104088032)
```

!GCRoot

The !GCRoot <addr> command shows the roots on the stack and handle for an object.

```
0:003> !gcroot 04a41ad0
Scan Thread 0 (a0c)
Scan Thread 1 (eac)
Scan Thread 3 (150)
ESP:6e3fcbc:Root:04a41ad0(Test.Ch14.Deadlock)
ESP:6e3fd04:Root:04a41b5c(System.Threading.ThreadStart)->04a41ad0(
    Test.Ch14.Deadlock)
ESP:6e3ff00:Root:04a41b5c(System.Threading.ThreadStart)->04a41ad0(
    Test.Ch14.Deadlock)
ESP:6e3ff08:Root:04a41b5c(System.Threading.ThreadStart)->04a41ad0(
    Test.Ch14.Deadlock)
Scan Thread 4 (cfc)
ESP:6f3fcbc:Root:04a41ad0(Test.Ch14.Deadlock)->04a41ad0(Test.Ch14.Deadlock)
ESP:6f3fd04:Root:04a41f9c(System.Threading.ThreadStart)->04a41ad0(
    Test.Ch14.Deadlock)
ESP:6f3ff00:Root:04a41f9c(System.Threading.ThreadStart)->04a41ad0(
    Test.Ch14.Deadlock)
ESP:6f3ff08:Root:04a41f9c(System.Threading.ThreadStart)->04a41ad0(
    Test.Ch14.Deadlock)
Scan HandleTable 148240
Scan HandleTable 149650
```

!Name2EE

The !Name2EE <module name> <item name> command shows the memory address of
EE data given a class and method name.

```
0:003> !name2ee Test.exe Test.Ch14.Deadlock.Main
--------------------------------------
MethodDesc: 3e5088
Name: [DEFAULT] I4 Test.Ch14.Deadlock.Main()
```

!ObjSize

The !ObjSize [<addr>] command shows the number of bytes that a root (or all roots) keep alive on the GC heap.

```
0:001> !ObjSize 010a50e0
    sizeof(010a50e0) = 28 ( 0x1c) bytes (Behavior1.Behavior1)
```

!SyncBlk

The !SyncBlk [-all|<#>] command shows synchronization blocks.

```
!syncblk -all
Index SyncBlock MonitorHeld Recursion   Thread   ThreadID   Object Waiting
    1 00000000                                               04a42678
    2 00167d84           0          0        0      none     04a4a4e4
      System.Threading.Thread
    3 00167db0           0          0        0      none     04a4a558
      System.Threading.Thread
    4 00167ddc           3          1   1679f0    274 628    04a4a44c
      Test.Ch14.Resources
    5 00167e08           3          1   167bb8    8082056    04a4a4b4
      Test.Ch14.Resources
-----------------------------
Total           6
ComCallWrapper  0
ComPlusWrapper  0
ComClassFactory 0
Free            0
```

!ThreadPool

The !ThreadPool command does many things for you. It tells you the current processor utilization, as well as the number of items in the queue. In addition, it shows statistics about the thread pool and I/O threads.

```
!ThreadPool
CPU utilization 44%
Worker Thread: Total: 2 Running: 2 Idle: 0 MaxLimit: 25 MinLimit: 1
Work Request in Queue: 7
QueueUserWorkItemCallback DelegateInfo@0016ce40
QueueUserWorkItemCallback DelegateInfo@0016d098
QueueUserWorkItemCallback DelegateInfo@0016d618
QueueUserWorkItemCallback DelegateInfo@0016d990
QueueUserWorkItemCallback DelegateInfo@0016d900
QueueUserWorkItemCallback DelegateInfo@0016d870
QueueUserWorkItemCallback DelegateInfo@0015da98
----------------------------------------
Number of Timers: 0
----------------------------------------
Completion Port Thread: Total: 0 Free: 0 MaxFree: 2
CurrentLimit: 0 MaxLimit: 1000 MinLimit: 1
```

!Threads

The !Threads command shows managed threads.

!Threads
```
ThreadCount: 4
UnstartedThread: 0
BackgroundThread: 3
PendingThread: 0
DeadThread: 0
                          PreEmptive   GC Alloc
      ID ThreadOBJ    State     GC        Context       Domain
   Lock Count APT Exception
3040    be0 0014cc38         28 Enabled   00000000:00000000 00146f10
   1 Ukn
2096    830 001571b0       1228 Enabled   00000000:00000000 00146f10
   0 Ukn (Finalizer)
2468    9a4 0016c980    1800228 Enabled   00000000:00000000 00146f10
   2 MTA (Threadpool Worker)
2560    a00 0016dee8    3800228 Enabled   00000000:00000000 00146f10
   0 MTA (Threadpool Worker)
```

Writing Data to Performance Monitor

Performance Monitor counters allow you to measure specific metrics in your application at runtime, with the help of the Performance Monitor snap-in provided by the operating system. The following example shows how to write data to Performance Monitor.

Code Example: Writing Data to Performance Monitor

```
using System;
using System.Diagnostics;



//Reg path for Perf counters
//HKEY_LOCAL_MACHINE\SYSTEM\ControlSet001\Services\Remoting
namespace RemObj
{
    public class ClientRemotingPerfCounters
    {
        public static PerformanceCounter CallTime;
        public static PerformanceCounter Calls;
        public static PerformanceCounter CallsReturned;
        public static PerformanceCounter CurrentCallers;



        public bool CreateCategory()
        {
            if ( !PerformanceCounterCategory.Exists("Remoting - Client") )
            {
                CounterCreationDataCollection CCDC =
                    new CounterCreationDataCollection();

                //Add the Response counter
                CounterCreationData ResponseTime = new CounterCreationData();
                ResponseTime.CounterType =
                    PerformanceCounterType.NumberOfItems32;
                ResponseTime.CounterName = "Response Time";
                CCDC.Add(ResponseTime);
```

```
                    //Add the Remoting Calls counter
                    CounterCreationData RemotingCalls = new CounterCreationData();
                    RemotingCalls.CounterType =
                      PerformanceCounterType.NumberOfItems32;
                    RemotingCalls.CounterName = "Remoting Calls";
                    CCDC.Add(RemotingCalls);

                    //Add the Remoting Calls Returned counter
                    CounterCreationData RemotingCallsReturned =
                      new CounterCreationData();
                    RemotingCallsReturned.CounterType =
                      PerformanceCounterType.NumberOfItems32;
                    RemotingCallsReturned.CounterName = "Remoting Calls Returned";
                    CCDC.Add(RemotingCallsReturned);

                    //Add the Remoting Current Callers counter
                    CounterCreationData RemotingCurrentCallers =
                      new CounterCreationData();
                    RemotingCurrentCallers.CounterType =
                      PerformanceCounterType.NumberOfItems32;
                    RemotingCurrentCallers.CounterName =
                      "Remoting Current Callers";
                    CCDC.Add(RemotingCurrentCallers);

                    //Create the category
                    PerformanceCounterCategory.Create("Remoting - Client",
                        "gregmcb - Remoting Perf Counters", CCDC);


                    return(true);
                }
                else
                {
                    Console.WriteLine("Category exists - Remoting - Client");
                    return(false);
                }
            }
        }
```

```csharp
public void CreateCounters()
{
    //Create the counters
    CallTime = new PerformanceCounter("Remoting - Client",
        "Response Time", false);
    Calls = new PerformanceCounter("Remoting - Client",
        "Remoting Calls", false);

    CallsReturned = new PerformanceCounter("Remoting - Client",
        "Remoting Calls Returned", false);

    CurrentCallers = new PerformanceCounter("Remoting - Client",
        "Remoting Current Callers", false);
}

public void InitValues()
{
    CallTime.RawValue=0;
    Calls.RawValue=0;
    CallsReturned.RawValue = 0;
    CurrentCallers.RawValue = 0;
}
}
}
```

Debugging Memory Leaks

Use the following procedure to debug memory leaks:

1. Use Performance Monitor to determine if the leak is managed or native. To do this, you want to examine the values of Process:PrivateBytes and .NET CLR Memory:# of Bytes in All Heaps. If PrivateBytes and # of Bytes in All Heaps grow consistently, you are dealing with a managed leak.

2. If you are debugging IIS, you will need to modify the Registry and cause ASP.NET to call `DebugBreak` rather than recycle the process. You do this by setting `HKLM\Software\Microsft\ASP.NET\DebugOnHighMem` to a value of 1 and `UnderDebugger` to a value of 2. This will allow you to run ADPlus in crash mode because `DebugBreak` will be called instead of the ASP.NET `wp` process being recycled at 60 percent memory consumption, which is the default setting. If you are not debugging ASP.NET wp.exe, you do not need to do this! Run ADPlus with the following syntax:

    ```
    adplus.vbs -pn aspnet_wp.exe -crash
    ```

    If you are not debugging a problem in ASP.NET wp.exe, you should run ADPlus with this command:

    ```
    adplus.vbs -pn MyProcess.exe -hang
    ```

    This will produce a snapshot of memory that you can debug.

3. Use a debugger like Windbg.exe, with the SOS.dll debugger extension. Load the dump in the debugger and load the SOS extension by using this command:

    ```
    !load sos.dll
    !FindTable
    ```

4. Determine the size of the managed heap by issuing the command `!eeheap -gc`.

5. Determine which objects are taking up space on the heap by running `!dumpheap -stat`. This will tell you how many copies of each object are on the heap.

6. Use the !gcroot <ObjAddress> command to see if an object is rooted (referenced). The object address is easily available if the object is in the Large Object Heap. If it is in the Small Object Heap, you must use the !name2ee module.exe [full path to object] command to get the method table. Then use !dumpheap -mt [Method Table] to get the address of the instances of the object on the heap.

7. Use the !objsize <ObjAddress> command to determine the size of an object.

8. Use the !dumpobj<ObjAddress> command to see the contents of the object.

Debugging Contention Problems in ASP.NET

Use the following procedure to debug contention problems in ASP.NET:

1. Since ASP.NET wp.exe has a built-in deadlock detection, you may need to increase the default three-minute limit by adjusting responseDeadlockInterval in the <processModel> section of Machine.config. You can also disable this functionality by modifying the responseRestartDeadlockInterval to infinite.

2. If you are running 1.0 +325947 version or 1.1, you can configure a Registry modification DebugOnDeadlock, which will call DebugBreak when deadlock detection is invoked.

3. Install the debuggers from http://www.microsoft.com/ddk/debugging/default.asp.

4. Run adplus.vbs -pn aspnet_wp.exe -crash. This will produce a dump file when a deadlock occurs. You can then interpret the debug file using Windbg.exe and SOS.dll.

5. It is best to look at threads that are in a wait state. You want to determine which threads are in this state and why they are in this state. You also want to make sure that the thread pool is not exhausted.

 NOTE Threads that have mscorwks!ThreadpoolMgr::WorkerThreadStart are worker threads.

Enabling Customer Debug Probes for Interop Services

The debug probes are mainly focused toward Interop Services debugging. The logging goes to `OutputDebugString`. To enable this logging, you must add entries in Machine.config and App.config.

In the Machine.config file, add the following:

```
<runtime>
        <developerSettings
                CDP.AllowDebugProbes="true"
                CDP.AllowDebugBreak="true"
        />
</runtime>
```

In your App.config file, add the following:

```
<runtime>
        <developerSettings
                          CDP.Apartment="true"
                          CDP.BufferOverrun="true"
                          CDP.CollectedDelegate="true"
                          CDP.DisconnectedContext="true"
                          CDP.NotMarshalable="true"
                          CDP.InvalidIUnknown="true"
                          CDP.ObjNotKeptAlive="true"
                          CDP.PInvokeCallConvMismatch="true"
                          CDP.Marshaling="true"

        />
</runtime>
```

Adam Nathan has written a tool called CLRSpy, which can be very helpful in setting up logging for Interop Services debugging. It can be found at `http://www.gotdotnet.com`.

There is also a GUI tool called GUI Spy, which you can use to set these settings. It can be downloaded from the following URL:

```
http://www.gotdotnet.com/Community/UserSamples/
  Details.aspx?SampleGuid=C7B955C7-231A-406C-9FA5-AD09EF3BB37F
```

The following sections describe the debug probes.

BufferOverrun

The . BufferOverrun probe triggers a garbage collection after a call from managed to unmanaged code.

Unmanaged code can corrupt the state of the runtime. This frequently happens as a result of a stack buffer overrun during a call from managed to unmanaged code. If a pointer the GC is responsible for has been corrupted, when the GC compresses the heap, it will attempt to dereference the corrupted pointer, likely resulting in an access violation. The . BufferOverrun probe attempts to reduce the time between the corruption of the GC pointer and the access violation.

CollectedDelegate

The . CollectedDelegate probe prevents the collection of stubs created when a delegate is marshaled as a function pointer. This way, if unmanaged code attempts to place a callback on a function pointer to a collected delegate, the call can be intercepted by this probe. This probe will raise a debug break if these breaks are enabled.

When delegates are marshaled to unmanaged code as function pointers, the runtime is unable to keep track of when the unmanaged code is finished with the function pointer. This is because the unmanaged code has no way to report its references to the GC. If the managed code neglects to keep a reference to the delegate for the lifetime of the function pointer, a garbage collection could collect the delegate and invalidate the function pointer, causing calls on that function pointer to fail.

DisconnectedContext

The . DisconnectedContext probe fires if the runtime cannot place a call in the correct apartment because the apartment thread is dead.

NotMarshalable

The . NotMarshalable probe reports if an IMarshal provided by a COM object fails when the runtime attempts to marshal the object.

InvalidIUnknown

The . InvalidIUnknown probe reports if a call to QueryInterface fails.

ObjNotKeptAlive

The . ObjNotKeptAlive probe forces a garbage collection just before a call from managed to unmanaged code is made, in an effort to collect all COM objects whose counts have fallen to zero.

If unmanaged code neglects to reference count a COM object correctly, the count could drop to zero prematurely. In this case, the object will delete itself and the next access to the object will fail. These bugs are difficult to track down because it's not clear which AddRef does not have a corresponding release. This problem is even harder to track down when the COM object is an exported managed object, because these objects are not deleted when their reference count drops to zero, but rather during the next garbage collection.

PInvokeCallConvMismatch

On x86, the = . PInvokeCallConvMismatch probe compares the EBP register before and after a PInvoke call to determine if the unmanaged function executed the calling convention specified by the DllImport custom attribute. This probe will raise a debug break if the calling conventions do not match.

The common calling conventions—stdcall, cdecl, and thiscall—specify if the callee or the caller should remove the arguments from the stack and whether the this pointer should be passed on the stack or in ECX. If the caller and callee do not agree on the calling convention, the stack could become corrupted.

Marshaling

The . Marshaling probe logs which unmanaged type a managed object is marshaled as when an unmanaged function is called from managed code. The filter can be used to limit which functions have their marshaling logged.

When the runtime tries to marshal an object, it first looks to see if the object implements IMarshal and then, if not, looks for a registered stub. If the runtime cannot marshal the object, for whatever reason, it simply breaks COM protocol and places the call using whatever thread requested the Remote Procedure Call (RPC). The . Marshaling probe reports when that protocol is broken in the case of IMarshal failing.

Apartment

The . Apartment probe causes the runtime to check to see if the apartment state of a thread has changed without the runtime being aware of the change.

COM identifies a thread as STA or MTA by storing a bit of information in the thread local storage for the thread. COM clients set that bit when they call CoInitialize and CoUninitialize. The runtime also identifies a thread as STA or MTA by storing a bit of information in a private data structure. Currently, COM does not provide notification when a thread's state changes from MTA to STA, and hence those two bits of information can become inconsistent.

CHAPTER 17
Remoting

- Remoting Basics

- Configuration Files and Attributes

- Creating a Hosting Process: Console Application, IIS Host, and Service

- Creating Remoted Objects

- Server Programmatic Design for Remoting

- Server Configuration File Design for Remoting

- Client Programmatic Design for Remoting

- Client Configuration File Design for Remoting

- Managing Object Lifetimes

- Using Client-Side Sponsors

- Calling Remoted Methods Asynchronously

- Using Call Context

- Using Sinks: Dynamically and Programmatically

- Remoting and Threading Issues

- Using Custom Serialization

Remoting Basics

Remoting, in short, is the replacement technology for Distributed COM (DCOM) in intranet solutions. It allows you to communicate among application domains, processes, and machines. So the question at this point is this: What do you get with Remoting that you didn't get with DCOM? The answer lies in one word: control!

Remoting provides control by allowing you to determine how objects are created, which protocol you will use as a transport, how messages are transferred between the client and server, and the lifetime of objects. That is a lot of control!

Your control of how objects are created specifically refers to whether objects are client-activated or server-activated. This allows you to control the lifetime of the object and who will control the object.

For protocols, you have maximum control in that you may use TCP, HTTP, IPC, or any custom protocol that you choose to write via the open-programming structure of sinks.

Finally, you control the formatting of the messages that are transferred from the client to the server. You have a choice of SOAP, binary formatting, or a custom format that you design.

Now that you have a clear picture of what Remoting is, you may be wondering when Remoting is necessary. Remoting is most effective in an intranet environment where performance is a priority.

Remoting Components

There are three parts to Remoting:

- **Hosting process:** Hosts the remoted object and opens a channel that clients may connect to. This could be your executable, IIS, or a service.

- **Client process:** Calls and uses the remoted object.

- **Remoted object:** A DLL that implements the remote object.

Remoted Object Access

When deciding how the remoted object will be made available to clients, you should consider the choices carefully. Each of the following options requires specific design considerations.

- **Shared DLL:** The object is implemented in this shared assembly.

- **Shared interface:** The interface of the remoted object is defined in this assembly, and the implementation is in another assembly.

- **Shared abstract base class:** The base class is defined in this assembly, and another assembly contains the base class in a new derived class.

- **SoapSuds:** This tool is used to connect to a running instance of a remoted object and generates a new assembly with the metadata needed to use the remoted object in a client.

Remoted Object Types

Remoting provides for `MarshalByValue` objects and `MarshalByRefObject` objects.

`MarshalByValue` objects are created on the client, and all calls to these objects run in the same context as the calling client. This means that these types of objects are not really remoted objects. These objects must be marked with the `[Serializable]` attribute or inherit from the `ISerializable` interface, so they will be serialized to a specific format and sent in their entirety to the client.

`MarshalByRefObject` objects are true remoted objects. When you create an instance of one of these objects, a proxy will be created on the client, and all calls will be forwarded to that proxy. The proxy will then create a serialized message that is passed to the server to be processed and run on the server. Any `out` parameters or return values are then serialized back and returned to the client. There are three types of `MarshalByRefObject` objects:

- **Server Activated Object (SAO),** `SingleCall`: These objects are created on calling a method of the remoted object, and then the object is destroyed when that method returns.

- **Server Activated Object (SAO),** `Singleton`: These objects are created once on the server, and the single instance that is created services all client requests.

- **Client Activated Objects (CAO):** These objects contain state information and are maintained by their lifetime values and reference counts.

Remoting Configuration Files and Configuration Attributes

The following is a standard configuration file for Remoting:

```
<configuration>
          <system.runtime.remoting>
                    <application>
                              <lifetime />
                              <channels
                                             <channel>
                              <serverProviders>
                              <formatter/>
                              <provider/>
                              </serviceProviders>
                              <clientProviders>
                               <formatter/>
                               <provider/>
                               </clientProviders>
                               </channels>
                               <service>
                                          <wellknown/>
                                           <activated/>
                               </service>
                               <client>
                                          <wellknown/>
                                          <activated/>
                               </client>
                    </application>
          </system.runtime.remoting>
</configuration>
```

Configuration attributes include lifetime, channel, formatter, wellknown service and client, and activated server and client attributes.

Remoting Lifetime Attributes

Table 17-1 shows the lifetime attributes you can use to configure Remoting.

Table 17-1. Lifetime Attributes

Attribute	Description
leaseTime	The initial lease time for objects. The default is 5 minutes.
sponsorshipTimeout	Time to wait for a sponsor's reply. The default is 2 minutes.
renewOnCallTime	Time to add to an object's Time to Live (TTL) when a method is called. The default is 2 minutes.
leaseManagerPollTime	The interval in which an object's TTL will be checked. The default is 10 seconds.

Channel Attributes

Table 17-2 shows the common channel attributes you can use to configure Remoting channels. Tables 17-3 and 17-4 show the HTTP channel and TCP channel attributes, respectively.

Table 17-2. Common Channel Attributes

Attribute	Description
Ref	References a predefined channel, such as tcp or http.
Type	References a custom channel when one of the predefined channels is not used.
Port	Server-side port number.

Table 17-3. HTTP Channel Attributes

Attribute	Description
Name	Name of the channel.
Priority	Indicates the priority of the channel. The higher the integer, the greater the possibility that the channel will be used. The default is 1.
clientConnectionLimit	Number of connections that can be simultaneously opened. The default is 2.
proxyName	Name of the proxy server.
proxyPort	Port number for the proxy server.
SuppressChannelData	Determines if the channel will contribute to the channel data. The default is false.
useIpAddress	Determines if the channel will use the IP address or hostname. The default is true (to use the IP address).
Listen	Specifies if activation can hook into the listener service. The default is true.
bindTo	IP address on which the server will listen. Used on computers with more than one IP address.
machineName	Sets the machine name used with the current channel. This overrides the useIpAddress attribute.

Table 17-4. TCP Channel Attributes

Attribute	Description
rejectRemoteRequests	Determines if the channel will accept requests from remote servers.
socketCachePolicy	Sets how the socket cache works.
retryCount	Sets the number of retry attempts. The default is 1.

Formatter Attributes

For Remoting, you can use several formatter attributes, as listed in Table 17-5.

Table 17-5. Formatter Attributes

Attribute	Description
Ref	Sets the sink used to format messages, such soap, binary, or wsdl.
Type	Used when specifying a custom formatter.
includeVersions	Determines if version information is included in the formatted data. The default is true.
strictBinding	Specifies whether the exact version will be used when deserializing data. The default is false.
typeFilterLevel	Sets security on the filter.

Wellknown Service and Client Attributes

There is one wellknown client attribute: url sets the path to the server. The three wellknown service attributes are listed in Table 17-6.

Table 17-6. Wellknown Service Attributes

Attribute	Description
Type	Stores type information about the object being remoted
Mode	Specifies SingleCall or Singleton objects
objectUri	Sets the endpoint for remoted calls

Activated Server and Client Attributes

There is one activated server attribute and one activated client attribute. Both have the Type attribute, which specifies the type being remoted.

Creating a Hosting Process

The hosting process hosts the remoted object and opens a channel for client connections. The following sections describe how to create hosting processing code for a console application, IIS, and a service.

Hosting Process for a Console Application

The following example demonstrates using a simple console application to host a Remoting object.

 CAUTION   In version 1.0 of the framework, there was a security hole that was removed in 1.1. The default serialization was reduced from High to Low. This is why I add a property called typeFilterLevel to all of my formatters. If you do not do this when using version 1.1 or higher, you will get an exception.

Code Example: Simple Hosting Process Code, Console Application

```
using System.Runtime.Remoting;
using System.Collections;
using System.Runtime.Remoting.Channels;
using System.Runtime.Remoting.Channels.Tcp;
using System.Windows.Forms;
using RemoteObject;

namespace Server
{

    class RemotingServer
    {
        [STAMain]
        static void Main(string[] args)
        {
            Console.WriteLine("Configuring Host . . .");
            IDictionary props = new Hashtable();
            props["typeFilterLevel"] = "Full";
            BinaryServerFormatterSinkProvider BinFormatter =
              new BinaryServerFormatterSinkProvider(props, null);
            TcpServerChannel channel =
              new TcpServerChannel("TCP Channel", 9999, BinFormatter);
```

```
ChannelServices.RegisterChannel(channel);
WellKnownServiceTypeEntry remObj =
  new WellKnownServiceTypeEntry(typeof(MyObject),
 "Server/MyObject",WellKnownObjectMode.SingleCall);
RemotingConfiguration.RegisterWellKnownServiceType(remObj);
Application.Run();

        }
    }
}
```

IIS Hosting

Follow these steps to create an IIS hosting process:

1. Create a remoted object and add a reference to System.Runtime.Remoting, as shown in the "IIS Hosting, Remoted Object Creation" code example following these steps.

2. Create a new directory called HelloWorldWeb, under Inetpub\wwwroot\ or anywhere on the hard disk.

3. Create a bin directory underneath the HelloWorldWeb directory.

4. Copy the HelloWorldObject.dll to the bin directory.

5. Create a new file called Web.config using Notepad.exe and copy the configuration file shown in the "IIS Hosting, Configuration File" example following these steps. Save the file to the HelloWorldWeb directory (the folder above the bin directory).

6. Start Internet Services Manager (from the Start menu, select Programs, then Administrative Tools, then Internet Services Manager).

7. Create a virtual directory in IIS. Make the virtual directory alias SimpleApp and set the source directory to the HelloWorldWeb directory.

The following examples show the remoted object creation code and configuration file for completing these steps, as well as the client XML file for IIS Remoting.

Code Example: IIS Hosting, Remoted Object Creation

```csharp
using System;
using System.Runtime.Remoting;
using System.Security.Principal;
using System.Diagnostics;
using System.Threading;

namespace Server
{
        public class MyObject : MarshalByRefObject
        {
                public MyObject()
                {
                }
                public void TestingCOMPlus()
                {

                        EventLogTraceListener EventListener =
                        new EventLogTraceListener("Application");
                        Trace.Listeners.Add(EventListener);

                        //Per Q306158 INFO: Implementing Impersonation in an
                        //ASP.NET Application

                        //Cast the principal identity
                        WindowsIdentity MyID =
                          (WindowsIdentity)Thread.CurrentPrincipal.Identity;
                        WindowsImpersonationContext impersonationContext =
                          MyID.Impersonate();

                        impersonationContext.Undo();
                }
        }
}
```

Code Example: IIS Hosting, Configuration File

```
<configuration>
        <system.runtime.remoting>
                <application>
                        <system.web>
                                <identity impersonate="true"
                        </system.web>
                        <channels>
                                <channel ref="tcp" port="9999">
                                <serverProviders>
                                        <formatter ref="binary"
                                            typeFilterLevel="Full"/>
                                </serverProviders>
                                </channel>
                        </channels>
                        <service>
                                <wellknown mode="Singleton"
                                    type="Server.MyObject,
                                    Server" objectUri="MyObject.soap" />
                        </service>
                </application>
        </system.runtime.remoting>
</configuration>
```

Code Example: Client XML File

```
<configuration>
        <system.runtime.remoting>
                <application>
                        <channels>
                                <channel ref="http"
                                    useDefaultCredentials="true"/>
                        </channels>
                        <client>
                                <wellknown type="Server.MyObject, server"
                                    url="http://localhost/AuthTest/MyObject.soap" />
                        </client>
                </application>
        </system.runtime.remoting>
</configuration>
```

Hosting Process for a Service

The following example shows how to set up a service to host a remoted object. Use installutil.exe to install this executable as a service. Place the configuration file in the *<Windir>*System32 directory, or use the following code to place the configuration file in the application install directory:

```
RemotingConfiguration.Configure
    (AppDomain.CurrentDomain.SetupInformation.Configuration.File);
```

Code Example: Simple Hosting Process Code, Service

```
using System;
using System.Diagnostics;
using System.ServiceProcess;
using System.Runtime.Remoting;
namespace RemotingWindowsService
{
        //You must inherit ServiceBase to be a service application
        class RemotingService :System.ServiceProcess.ServiceBase
        {
            private static EventLog MyEvent = new EventLog("Application");
            public static string SVC_NAME = "My Remoting Service";
            public RemotingService()
            {
                    this.ServiceName = SVC_NAME;
            }
            static void Main(string[] args)
            {
                    MyEvent.Source = SVC_NAME;
                    MyEvent.WriteEntry("Remoting Service Initializing");
                    ServiceBase.Run(new RemotingService());
            }
            protected override void OnStart(string[] args)
            {
                    MyEvent.WriteEntry("Starting Remoting Service");
                    string ConfigFile = "RemotingWindowsService.exe.config";
                    RemotingConfiguration.Configure(ConfigFile);
            }
            protected override void OnStop()
            {
                    MyEvent.WriteEntry("Stooping Service");
            }
        }
}
```

Creating Remoted Objects

As noted earlier, MarshalByValue objects, which are created on the client, have the [Serializable] attribute or inherit from the ISerializable interface. MarshalByRefObject objects can be service activated (SAO) or client activated (CAO). SAOs are either SingleCall or Singleton. The following examples demonstrate how to create these types of remoted objects.

Code Example: Creating a MarshalByValue [Serializable] Object

```
using System;
using System.Runtime.Remoting.Lifetime;

namespace RemoteObject
{
        //Allows an object to be passed by value
        [Serializable]
        public class MyObject : System.MarshalByRefObject
        {
                public MyObject()
                {
                        Console.WriteLine("Constructor Called ...");
                }
                public void HelloWorld()
                {
                        Console.WriteLine("Hello World!!!");
                }
        }
}
```

Code Example: Creating a MarshalByRefObject, Server Activated Object (SAO)

```
using System;
using System.Runtime.Remoting.Lifetime;


namespace RemoteObject
{
        //MarshalByRefObject allows you to pass an object by ref
        public class MyObject : System.MarshalByRefObject
        {
                public MyObject()
                {
                        Console.WriteLine("Constructor Called ...");
                }
                public void HelloWorld()
                {
                        Console.WriteLine("Hello World!!!");
                }
        }
}
```

Code Example: Creating a MarshalByRefObject, Client Activated Object (CAO)

```
using System;
using System.Runtime.Remoting.Lifetime;
namespace RemoteObject
{
        public class MyObject : System.MarshalByRefObject
        {
                public int MyRefCount;
                public MyObject()
                {
                        Console.WriteLine("Constructor Called ...");
                        MyRefCount++;
                }
                public void HelloWorld()
                {
                        Console.WriteLine("Hello World!!!");

                }
        }
}
```

Server Programmatic Design for Remoting

When creating a Remoting server, you can choose to programmatically configure Remoting. The most common reason for using a programmatic design is that it's easier to deploy, because you do not need to provide a separate configuration file. (The next section describes how to use a configuration file design to configure Remoting.)

The following examples show server code for using the various types of remoted objects.

Code Example: Server Code, Programmatic Design for a SingleCall SAO

```csharp
using System;
using System.Collections;
using System.Runtime.Remoting;
using System.Runtime.Remoting.Channels;
using System.Runtime.Remoting.Channels.Tcp;
using RemoteObject;

namespace Server
{

        class RemoteClient
        {
                static void Main(string[] args)
                {
                        IDictionary props = new Hashtable();
                        props["typeFilterLevel"] = "Full";
                        BinaryServerFormatterSinkProvider BinFormatter =
                          new BinaryServerFormatterSinkProvider(props, null);
                        TcpServerChannel channel =
                          new TcpServerChannel("TCP Channel", 9999, BinFormatter);

                        ChannelServices.RegisterChannel(channel);
                        WellKnownServiceTypeEntry MyObj =
                            new WellKnownServiceTypeEntry(typeof(MyObject),
                            "Server/MyObject",
                            SingleCall);
                    //Listens for calls
                        RemotingConfiguration.RegisterWellKnownServiceType(MyObj);
```

```
                        Console.ReadLine();
            }
        }
}
```

Code Example: Server Code, Programmatic Design for a Singleton SAO

```
using System;
using System.Collections;
using System.Runtime.Remoting;
using System.Runtime.Remoting.Channels;
using System.Runtime.Remoting.Channels.Tcp;
using RemoteObject;

namespace Server
{
        class RemoteClient
        {

                static void Main(string[] args)
                {
                        IDictionary props = new Hashtable();
                        props["typeFilterLevel"] = "Full";
                        BinaryServerFormatterSinkProvider BinFormatter =
                          newBinaryServerFormatterSinkProvider(props, null);
                        TcpServerChannel channel = new TcpServerChannel(
                          "TCP Channel", 9999, BinFormatter);

                        ChannelServices.RegisterChannel(channel);
                        WellKnownServiceTypeEntry MyObj =
                          new WellKnownServiceTypeEntry(typeof(MyObject),
                          "Server/MyObject",Sngleton);
                        //Listens for calls
                        RemotingConfiguration.RegisterWellKnownServiceType(MyObj);

                        Console.ReadLine();
                }
        }
}
```

Code Example: Server Code, Programmatic Design for a CAO

```csharp
using System;
using System.Collections;
using System.Runtime.Remoting;
using System.Runtime.Remoting.Channels;
using System.Runtime.Remoting.Channels.Tcp;
using RemoteObject;

namespace Server
{

        class RemotingServer
        {
            static void Main(string[] args)
            {
                    Console.WriteLine("Configuring Host . . .");
                    IDictionary props = new Hashtable();
                    props["typeFilterLevel"] = "Full";
                    BinaryServerFormatterSinkProvider BinFormatter =
                        new BinaryServerFormatterSinkProvider(props, null);
                    TcpServerChannel channel = new TcpServerChannel(
                        "TCP Channel", 9999, BinFormatter);

                    ChannelServices.RegisterChannel(channel);
                    //Listens for calls
                    RemotingConfiguration.RegisterActivatedServiceType(
                    typeof(MyObject));
                    Console.WriteLine("Press Return To Exit");
                    Console.ReadLine();

            }
        }
}
```

Server Configuration File Design for Remoting

Using a configuration file to set up Remoting is the most popular approach, because it allows you to modify the Remoting settings without recompiling the application.

The following examples show server code for reading configuration files, as well as the XML configuration files, for using the various types of remoted objects.

Code Example: Server Code, Configuration File Design for a SingleCall SAO

```
using System.Runtime.Remoting;
using RemoteObject;
namespace Server
{

        class RemotingServer
        {

                static void Main(string[] args)
                {
                        Console.WriteLine("Configuring Host . . .");
                        //Reads config file for Remoting information
                        RemotingConfiguration.Configure("Server.exe.config");
                        Console.WriteLine("Press Return To Exit");
                        Console.ReadLine();
                }
        }
}
```

XML Server Configuration File

```
<configuration>
        <system.runtime.remoting>
                <application>
                        <channels>
                                <channel ref="tcp" port="9999">
                                        <serverProviders>
                                                <formatter ref="binary"
                                                        typeFilterLevel="Full"/>
                                        </serverProviders>
                                        </channel>
                                </channel>
                        </channels>
                        <service>
                                <wellknown mode="SingleCall"
                                        type="RemoteObject.MyObject,RemoteObject"
                                        objectUri="RemoteObject.soap"/>
                        </service>
                </application>
        </system.runtime.remoting>
</configuration>
```

Code Example: Server Code, Configuration File Design for a Singleton SAO

```
using System;
using System.Runtime.Remoting;
using RemoteObject;
namespace Server
{

        class RemotingServer
        {
                static void Main(string[] args)
                {
                        Console.WriteLine("Configuring Host . . .");
                        RemotingConfiguration.Configure("Server.exe.config");
                        Console.WriteLine("Press Return To Exit");
                        Console.ReadLine();

                }
        }
}
```

XML Server Configuration File

```xml
<configuration>
        <system.runtime.remoting>
                <application>
                        <channels>
                                <channel ref="tcp" port="9999">
                                        <serverProviders>
                                                <formatter ref="binary"
                                                    typeFilterLevel="Full"/>
                                        </serverProviders>
                                </channel>
                        </channels>
                        <service>
                                <wellknown mode="Singleton"
                                        type="RemoteObject.MyObject,RemoteObject"
                                        objectUri="RemoteObject.soap"/>
                        </service>
                </application>
        </system.runtime.remoting>
</configuration>
```

Code Example: Server Code, Configuration File Design for a CAO

```csharp
using System;
using System.Runtime.Remoting;
using RemoteObject;

namespace Server
{

        class RemotingServer
        {

                static void Main(string[] args)
                {
                        Console.WriteLine("Configuring Host . . .");
                        RemotingConfiguration.Configure("Server.exe.config");
                        Console.WriteLine("Press Return To Exit");
                        Console.ReadLine();


                }
        }
}
```

XML Server, Client-Activated Server Configuration File

```
<configuration>
        <system.runtime.remoting>
                <application>
                        <channels>
                                <channel ref="tcp" port="9999">
                                        <serverProviders>
                                                <formatter ref="binary"
                                                    typeFilterLevel="Full"/>

                                        </serverProviders>
                                </channel>
                        </channels>
                        <service>
                                <activated type="RemObj.MyObject,RemObj"/>
                        </service>
                </application>
        </system.runtime.remoting>
</configuration>
```

Client Programmatic Design for Remoting

Just as with writing your server application, you can use a programmatic design or a configuration file for setting up Remoting in your client application.

The following examples show client code for using the various types of remoted objects. Using configuration files is demonstrated in the next section.

Code Example: Client Code, Programmatic Design for a SingleCall SAO

```
using System;
using System.Runtime.Remoting;
using System.Runtime.Remoting.Channels;
using System.Runtime.Remoting.Channels.Tcp;
using RemoteObject;

namespace Client
{

    class RemoteClient
    {
        static void Main(string[] args)
        {
            TcpClientChannel channel = new TcpClientChannel();
            ChannelServices.RegisterChannel(channel);
            WellKnownClientTypeEntry MyObj =
                new WellKnownClientTypeEntry(typeof(MyObject),
                "tcp://localhost:10000/Server/MyObject");
            RemotingConfiguration.RegisterWellKnownClientType(MyObj);
            //Creates a new instance of a single call object
            MyObject Obj = new MyObject();
            Obj.HelloWorld();
        }
    }
}
```

NOTE You could use RemotingConfiguration.
RegisterWellKnownClientType(GetType(MyObj),
"tcp://localhost:10000/server/MyObject").

Code Example: Client Code, Programmatic Design for a Singleton SAO

```
using System;
using System.Runtime.Remoting;
using System.Runtime.Remoting.Channels;
using System.Runtime.Remoting.Channels.Tcp;
using RemoteObject;

namespace Client
{

    class RemoteClient
    {
        static void Main(string[] args)
        {
            TcpClientChannel channel = new TcpClientChannel();
            ChannelServices.RegisterChannel(channel);
            WellKnownClientTypeEntry MyObj =
              new WellKnownClientTypeEntry(typeof(MyObject),
              "tcp://localhost:10000/Server/MyObject");
            RemotingConfiguration.RegisterWellKnownClientType(MyObj);
            //Creates a new instance of a singleton
            MyObject Obj = new MyObject();
            Obj.HelloWorld();
        }
    }
}
```

Code Example: Client Code, Programmatic Design for a CAO

```csharp
using System;
using System.Runtime.Remoting;
using System.Runtime.Remoting.Channels;
using System.Runtime.Remoting.Channels.Tcp;
using RemoteObject;

namespace Client
{

    class RemoteClient
    {

        static void Main(string[] args)
        {
            TcpClientChannel channel = new TcpClientChannel();
            ChannelServices.RegisterChannel(channel);
            RemotingConfiguration.RegisterActivatedClientType(
              typeof(MyObject),
             "tcp://localhost:10000 ");
            //Creates a new instance of a CAO
            MyObject Obj = new MyObject();
            Obj.HelloWorld();
        }
    }
}
```

Client Configuration File Design for Remoting

When you use a configuration file to set up Remoting in the client, you can modify the Remoting settings without recompiling the application.

The following examples show client code for reading configuration files, as well as the XML configuration files, for using the various types of remoted objects.

Code Example: Client Code, Configuration File Design for a SingleCall SAO

```
using System;
using System.Runtime.Remoting;
using RemoteObject;

namespace Client
{
        class RemoteClient
        {
                static void Main(string[] args)
                {
                        //Reads config file for Remoting information
                        RemotingConfiguration.Configure("Client.exe.config");
                        MyObject Obj = new MyObject();
                        Obj.HelloWorld();
                }
        }
}
```

XML Client Configuration File

```
<configuration>
        <system.runtime.remoting>
                <application>
                        <channels>
                                <channel ref="http"/>
                        </channels>
                        <client>
                                <wellknown
                                        type="RemoteObject.MyObject,RemoteObject"
                                        url="http://localhost:9000/RemoteObject.soap"/>
                        </client>
                </application>
        </system.runtime.remoting>
</configuration>
```

Code Example: Client Code, Configuration File Design for a Singleton SAO

```csharp
using System;
using System.Runtime.Remoting;
using RemoteObject;
namespace Client
{
        class RemoteClient
        {
            static void Main(string[] args)
            {
                    RemotingConfiguration.Configure("Client.exe.config");
                    MyObject Obj = new MyObject();
                    Obj.HelloWorld();
            }
        }
}
```

XML Client Configuration File

```xml
<configuration>
        <system.runtime.remoting>
                <application>
                        <channels>
                                <channel ref="http"/>
                        </channels>
                        <client>
                                <wellknown
                                    type="RemoteObject.MyObject,RemoteObject"
                                    url="http://localhost:9000/RemoteObject.soap"/>
                        </client>
                </application>
        </system.runtime.remoting>
</configuration>
```

Code Example: Client Code, Configuration File Design for a CAO

```
using System;
using System.Runtime.Remoting;
using RemoteObject;

namespace Client
{

    class RemoteClient
    {
        static void Main(string[] args)
        {
            RemotingConfiguration.Configure("Client.exe.config");
            MyObject Obj = new MyObject();
            Obj.HelloWorld();
        }
    }
}
```

Configuration File

```
<configuration>
    <system.runtime.remoting>
        <application>
            <channels>
                <channel ref="http"/>
            </channels>
            <client url="http://localhost:9000">
                <activated type="RemObj.MyObject, RemObj"/>
            </client>
        </application>
    </system.runtime.remoting>
</configuration>
```

Managing Object Lifetimes

Lifetime management is one of the most important aspects of Remoting configuration. By default, a remoted object will be freed if it is not used for five minutes. You should always control the lifetime of your remoted objects.

The following examples show how to control object lifetimes with code and with a configuration file.

Code Example: Setting the Lifetime of an Object Programmatically

```
using System;
using System.Runtime.Remoting.Lifetime;
namespace RemoteObject
{
        public class MyObject : System.MarshalByRefObject
        {
                public MyObject()
                {
                        Console.WriteLine("Constructor Called ...");
                        this.NumberOfCalls = NumberOfCalls;
                }
                public void HelloWorld()
                {
                        Console.WriteLine("Hello World!!!");
                }
                //Allows you to set the lifetime of an object programmatically
                public override object InitializeLifetimeService()
                {
                        ILease lease = (ILease) base.InitializeLifetimeService();
                        if(lease.CurrentState == LeaseState.Initial)
                        {
                                lease.InitialLeaseTime = TimeSpan.FromMinutes(1);
                                lease.RenewOnCallTime = TimeSpan.FromSeconds(20);
                        }
                        return lease;
                }
                private int NumberOfCalls;
                public int NumberofCalls
                {
                        get {return NumberOfCalls;}
                        set {NumberOfCalls = value;}
                }
        }
}
```

Code Example: Setting the Lifetime of an Object in an XML Server
Configuration File

```
<configuration>
        <system.runtime.remoting>
                <application name = "server.exe">
                        //Sets lifetime of object via config file
                        <lifetime
                                leaseTime = "15M"
                                sponsorshipTimeOut = "4M"
                                renewOnCallTime = "3M"
                                pollTime = "30S"
                        />
                </application>
        </system.runtime.remoting>
</configuration>
```

Using Client-Side Sponsors

Sponsors allow you to control the lifetime of a remoted object. You can create sponsors on the client, the server, or third-party process. At its most basic level, a sponsor is a remoted object itself (which requires lifetime management), whose purpose is to renew the lifetime of another remoted object.

```
using System;
using System.Collections;
using RemObj;
using System.Runtime.Remoting;
using System.Runtime.Remoting.Lifetime;
using System.Runtime.Remoting.Channels;
using System.Runtime.Remoting.Channels.Tcp;
using System.Windows.Forms;

namespace Client
{
        class RemoteClient
        {
                static void Main(string[] args)
                {
                        IDictionary FormatterProps = new Hashtable();
                        FormatterProps["typeFilterLevel"] = "Full";
                        BinaryServerFormatterSinkProvider ServerBinFormatter =
                          new BinaryServerFormatterSinkProvider
                              (FormatterProps, null);
                        BinaryClientFormatterSinkProvider ClientBinFormatter =
                           new BinaryClientFormatterSinkProvider();

                        IDictionary ChannelProps = new Hashtable();
                        ChannelProps["port"] = "9998";
                        TcpChannel channel =
                         new TcpChannel(ChannelProps,
                         ClientBinFormatter, ServerBinFormatter);
                        ChannelServices.RegisterChannel(channel);
                        RemotingConfiguration.RegisterActivatedClientType(
                         typeof(MyObject), "tcp://localhost:10000");

                        MyObject Obj = new MyObject();
                        Console.WriteLine("{0} - Create CAO", DateTime.Now);
                        ILease MyLease = (ILease) Obj.GetLifetimeService();
                        MyLease.Register(new MySponsor());
```

```
                    Obj.DoSomething();
                    Application.Run();
        }
}
public class MySponsor : MarshalByRefObject, ISponsor
{
        public MySponsor() {}
        public bool CheckConditions()
        {
            return true;

        }
        public TimeSpan Renewal(ILease lease)
        {
            if(CheckConditions())
            {
                Console.WriteLine("{0} - Sponsor Renewed",
                    DateTime.Now);
                return TimeSpan.FromSeconds(20);
            }
            else
            {
                Console.WriteLine("{0} - Sponsor Stopped",
                    DateTime.Now);
                return TimeSpan.Zero;
            }
        }
    }
}
```

Calling Remoted Methods Asynchronously

Calling remoted methods asynchronously allows you to make the call and continue to do work on the thread. Then, at your leisure, you can recover the response.

The following examples demonstrate how to call a remoted method asynchronously and how to make an asynchronous call to a remoted method and allow it to make a callback when the method has completed its work.

Code Example: Client Code, Calling a Remoted Method Asynchronously

```
using System;
using System.Runtime.Remoting;
using RemoteObject;

namespace Client
{

    class RemoteClient
    {
        private delegate int MyDelegate();
        static void Main(string[] args)
        {
            RemotingConfiguration.Configure("Client.exe.config");
            MyObject Obj = new MyObject();
            MyDelegate d = new MyDelegate(Obj.HelloWorld);
            //Start the method Async
            IAsyncResult ar = d.BeginInvoke(null, null);
            //To get the result
            ar.AsyncWaitHandle.WaitOne()
            if(ar.IsCompleted)
            {
                Console.WriteLine("HelloWorld Finished");
                int result = d.EndInvoke(ar);
                Console.WriteLine("result: " + result);
            }
        }
    }
}
```

Code Example: Client Code, Using Callbacks with Delegates

```
using System;
using System.Runtime.Remoting;
using RemoteObject;

namespace Client
{

    class RemoteClient
    {
        private delegate int MyDelegate();
        private static  MyDelegate d;
        public static int MyDelegateCallback(IAsyncResult ar)
        {
            if(ar.IsCompleted)
            {
                Console.WriteLine("HelloWorld Finished");
                int result = d.EndInvoke(ar);
                Console.WriteLine("result: " + result);
            }
        }


        static void Main(string[] args)
        {
            RemotingConfiguration.Configure("Client.exe.config");
            MyObject Obj = new MyObject();
            MyDelegate d = new MyDelegate(Obj.HelloWorld);

            AsyncCallback Mycb =
              new AsyncCallback(Client.MyDelegateCallback);
            IAsyncResult ar = d.BeginInvoke(cb, null);
            Console.WriteLine("Start call!");
        }
    }
}
```

Using Call Context

Call context works a lot like Thread Local Storage (TLS) did in Win32 programming. It allows you to associate specific data with a thread. Call context goes the next step and allows the data to transfer across threads and processes.

The following examples demonstrate using call context.

Code Example: Using Call Context, Client Side

```
using System;
using System.Runtime.Remoting;
using System.Runtime.Remoting.Messaging;
using RemoteObject;

namespace Client
{
        class RemoteClient
        {
                static void Main(string[] args)
                {
                        RemotingConfiguration.Configure("Client.exe.config");
                        MyObject Obj = new MyObject();
                        String MyName = "Gregory MacBeth";
                        //Adds data to the call context
                        CallContext.SetData("Name", MyName);
                        Obj.HelloWorld();
                }
        }
}
```

Code Example: Using Call Context, Remoted Object

```
using System;
using System.Runtime.Remoting;
using System.Runtime.Remoting.Messaging;
namespace RemoteObject
{
        public class MyObject : System.MarshalByRefObject
        {
                public MyObject()
                {

                }
                public void HelloWorld()
                {
                        //Reads data from the call context
                        string MyName = (string)CallContext.GetData("Name");
                }
        }
}
```

Using Sinks

Remoting is one of the most controllable technologies in .NET. It allows you to write your own transport, dynamic, or formatting sinks. This means that you can add encryption, do custom formatting, and so on.

The following examples demonstrate how to use dynamic sinks and add sinks programmatically.

Code Example: Using Dynamic Sinks

```
using System;
using System.Runtime.Remoting.Messaging;
using System.Runtime.Remoting.Contexts;
//The following code adds this sink at runtime
//Context ctx = Context.DefaultContext;
//IDynamicProperty prp = new MyDynamicSinkProvider;
//Context.RegisterDynamicProperty(prp,null,ctx);

namespace Utilities.Remoting.Sinks
{

        public class MyDynamicSinkProvider: IDynamicProperty,
                                            IContributeDynamicSink
        {
                public string Name
                {
                        get {return "MyDynmaicSinkProvider";}
                }
                public IDynamicMessageSink GetDynamicSink()
                {
                        return new MyDynamicSink();
                }
        }
```

```
public class MyDynamicSink : IDynamicMessageSink
{
        public void ProcessMessageStart(IMessage reqMsg,
            bool bCliSide, bool bAsync)
        {
            //TODO-Add your custom code here
        }
        public void ProcessMessageFinish(IMessage replyMsg,
            bool bCliSide, bool bAsync)
        {
            //TODO-Add your custom code here
        }
    }
}
```

Code Example: Programmatically Adding Sinks, Client Side

```
BinaryClientFormatterSinkProvider MyBinFormatter =
   new BinaryClientFormatterSinkProvider();
RemObj.SampleClientProvider MySink = new SampleClientProvider(null, null);
MySink. _nextProvider = MyBinFormatter;
TcpClientChannel channel = new TcpClientChannel("My TCP Channel", MySink);
ChannelServices.RegisterChannel(channel);
```

Code Example: Programmatically Adding Sinks, Server Side

```
BinaryServerFormatterSinkProvider MyBinFormatter =
   new BinaryServerFormatterSinkProvider();
RemObj.SampleServerProvider MySink = new SampleServerProvider(null, null);
MySink. _nextProvider = MyBinFormatter;
TcpServerChannel channel = new TcpServerChannel("My TCP Channel", 9000, MySink);

ChannelServices.RegisterChannel(channel);
```

Remoting and Threading Issues

It is natural that as the server load increases, there will also be an increase in the response time; after all, resources are finite. In fact, if the server has more client demand than its capacity, at some point, it will start rejecting requests. There are no issues related to TCP channel scalability, but its behavior in concurrent scenarios might not be totally obvious. Most likely, the response time problems that you may be experiencing are related to suboptimal impedance between user code and the Remoting stack. Take into account that TcpServerChannel and HttpServerChannel both rely on I/O completion port socket handlers bound to System.Threading.Threadpool, which uses 0 as the concurrency number for the port.

The NumberOfConcurrentThreads value sets the maximum number of threads that the operating system allows to concurrently process I/O completion packets for the I/O completion port. If this parameter is 0, the system allows as many concurrently running threads as there are processors in the system.

Although any number of threads can call the GetQueuedCompletionStatus function to wait for an I/O completion port, each thread is associated with only one completion port at a time. That port is the port that was last checked by the thread.

When a packet is queued to a port, the system first checks how many threads associated with the port are running. If the number of threads running is less than the value of NumberOfConcurrentThreads, then one of the waiting threads is allowed to process the packet. When a running thread completes its processing, it calls GetQueuedCompletionStatus again, at which point the system can allow another waiting thread to process a packet.

 NOTE See http://msdn.microsoft.com/library/en-us/fileio/base/ getqueuedcompletionstatus.asp for a reference to the GetQueuedCompletionStatus function.

The system also allows a waiting IO thread to process a packet if a running thread enters any wait state. When the thread in the wait state begins running again, there may be a brief period when the number of active threads exceeds the NumberOfConcurrentThreads value. However, the system quickly reduces the number by not allowing any new active threads until the number of active threads falls below the specified value.

This is a feature, since it is intended to keep the number of thread switches low. However, it might be seen as a bug in some situations where worker threads take a long time to execute without entering a wait state. Increasing the concurrency, when in fact there are no machine resources to deal with the load, might not be desirable.

Sample code that can be used to control the thread pool thread settings can be found at `http://staff.develop.com/woodring/dotnet/#tpcontrol`. This will allow you to set `ThreadPool` specifics such as the concurrency limit.

Using Custom Serialization

To use the default serialization, you must mark a class with the [Serializable] attribute. You can use the [NonSerialized] attribute to prevent an object from being serialized.

Under the hood, we use the ObjectIDGenerator class to generate unique ID for objects that we serialize and ObjectManager to track objects as they are being deserialized.

The following example demonstrates custom serialization.

Code Example: Custom Serialization

```
using System;
using System.IO;
using System.Collections;
using System.Runtime.Serialization;
using System.Runtime.Serialization.Formatters;
using System.Runtime.Serialization.Formatters.Binary;
using System.Security.Permissions;

namespace Test.Ch17
{
        public class MyMain
        {
                public static int Main()
                {
                        MyMain M = new MyMain();
                        M.ToFile();
                        M.FromFile();
                        return 0;
                }
```

```
public void ToFile()
{
        Console.WriteLine("ToFile");
        Foo F = new Foo();
        F.a = 5;
        F.b = 10;
        F.c = "HelloWorld!";
        Foo F1 = new Foo();
        F1.a = 20;
        F1.b = 30;
        F1.c = "Greg";
        Console.WriteLine("The value of Foo.a is: {0}", F.a);
        Console.WriteLine("The value of Foo.b is: {0}", F.b);
        Console.WriteLine("The value of Foo.c is: {0}", F.c);
        IFormatter MyFormatter = new BinaryFormatter();
        Stream MyStream = new FileStream("Foo.xml",
          FileMode.Create, FileAccess.Write, FileShare.None);
        MyFormatter.Serialize(MyStream, F);
        MyFormatter.Serialize(MyStream, F1);
        MyStream.Close();
}
public void FromFile()
{
        Console.WriteLine("FromFile");
        IFormatter MyFormatter = new BinaryFormatter();
        Stream MyStream = new FileStream("Foo.xml",
                FileMode.Open, FileAccess.Read,
                FileShare.Read);
        Foo F1 = (Foo)MyFormatter.Deserialize(MyStream);
        Foo F = (Foo)MyFormatter.Deserialize(MyStream);

        MyStream.Close();
        Console.WriteLine("The value of Foo1.a is: {0}", F1.a);
        Console.WriteLine("The value of Foo1.b is: {0}", F1.b);
        Console.WriteLine("The value of Foo1.c is: {0}", F1.c);
        Console.WriteLine("The value of Foo.a is: {0}", F.a);
        Console.WriteLine("The value of Foo.b is: {0}", F.b);
        Console.WriteLine("The value of Foo.c is: {0}", F.c);

}
}
```

```
[Serializable]
public class Foo : ISerializable
{
      public int a,b;
      public string c = "HelloWorld!";
      public Foo(){}
    //Allows for custom deserialization
      public Foo(SerializationInfo si, StreamingContext context)
      {
            c = si.GetString("c");
            a = si.GetInt32("a");
            b = si.GetInt32("b");
      }
    //Allows for custom serialization
      public void GetObjectData(SerializationInfo si,
                                StreamingContext context)
      {
            si.AddValue("a", a);
            si.AddValue("b", b);
            si.AddValue("c", c);
          //Type T = Foo.GetType();
          //si.AddValue("Type", T);
      }
}
}
```

CHAPTER 18

Web Services

- Web Services Basics

- Creating a Simple Web Service

- Creating a Web Service Client

- Golden Rules for Web Services

Web Services Basics

Web Services is the sister distributed application component to Remoting, designed specifically for Internet solutions that require platform generic implementations. This technology is based on stateless HTTP, XML, and SOAP.

The general idea is that clients of any type can make requests to a Web Service and receive that data back via XML. Web Services are published to the world via directories at places like UDDI.org, Xmethods.com, and UDDI.microsoft.com. Clients can query this directory and receive what is called a DISCO file, which contains information about the service in XML format. After receiving this information, the client can then query the service via the Web Services Description Language (WSDL). The client can then produce a proxy, which allows it to call methods on the service and retrieve data. This proxy is what does the magic of converting the method calls into SOAP and finally sending this data to the server via HTML.

Creating a Simple Web Service

The following example is a simple Hello World Web Service that you can create. When you're finished entering the code, simply save the file as an .asmx file. To access this page, just go to the following URL:

```
http://www.macbeth.com/HelloWorld.asmx
```

Code Example: A Simple Hello World Web Service

```
<@ WebService Language="C#" Class="HelloThere" @>
using System.Web.Services

public class HelloThere
{
        [WebMethod]
        public string HelloWorld()
        {
                return "Hello World";
        }
}
```

Creating a Web Service Client

To create a Web Service client, first you must build a proxy for the service. There are several tools that you can use to do this:

- Visual Studio's Add Web Reference functionality

- SoapSuds

- The WSDL command-line tool

To generate a proxy via the WSDL tool, you should do the following:

```
WSDL/l:CS /n:HelloThereNS
/out:HelloThere.cs http://www.macbeth.com/HelloThere.asmx?WSDL
```

Then just add the HelloThere.cs file and reference the namespace in your client. The client code itself is simple, as shown in the following example.

Code Example: A Web Service Client

```
using System;
using HelloThereNS;

namespace MyNamespace
{
        class MyMainClass
        {
                static void Main(string[] args)
                {
                        HelloThere H = new HelloThere()
                        string Hello = H.HelloWorld();
                }

        }
}
```

Golden Rules for Web Services

To design successful Web Services applications, you need to follow the "golden rules" presented here. To explain these rules, we'll use a scenario of a Web Service making calls to another Web Service. We have the client connecting to Web Service (Pink), connecting to Web Service (Blue).

The golden rules are as follows:

- The `minFreeThreads`, `maxConnections`, `maxIOThreads`, and `maxWorkerThreads` settings must be optimized, based on the application.

- The connection timeout of the Web Service call must be less than the `executionTimeout` of the Pink tier.

- If the Pink tier times out, the call to the Blue tier must be aborted.

- Do not write Web methods that do work in a tight loop (applies to version 1.0 of the framework).

- Do not call STA objects from Web Services.

We'll take a closer look at each of these rules in the following sections.

Golden Rule 1: Understanding Settings

The following is the threading model for a Web Service making calls to another Web Service:

Thread 1[IO/Worker]: Request is made to the Pink tier .asmx, which in turn calls the Web Service on the Blue tier.

Thread 1[IO/Worker]: Sends a POST request and blocks on `ws2_32!Send`.

 NOTE   With IIS 5, Thread 1 would most likely be an IO thread. With IIS 6, Thread 1 would be a worker thread.

Thread 2[IO]: Receives HTTP 100 Continue via `WSARecv`.

Thread 3[Worker]: Sends SOAP envelope via `WSASend`.

Thread 2[IO]: Receives the result of Web Services via `WSARecv`.

Thread 1[IO/Worker]: Returns from `ws2_32!Send`.

 **NOTE** If security was used to call the Web Service on the Blue tier, there is the potential to use a fourth thread.

Table 18-1 describes the Web Services settings and shows some simple formulas for determining the proper settings.

Table 18-1. Web Services Settings

Setting	Description	Proper Setting
maxConnections	Sets the maximum concurrent outbound Web Service calls per IP address.	Set to the number of simultaneous outbound connections to a specific IP address that you expect. Should be incremented in steps of 4 to determine optimum settings for application and hardware.
minFreeThreads	Preserves a set number of threads for outbound Web Service calls. In the example presented here, we use three threads for each Web Service call, and possibly one more if security is involved.	maxConnections times 3 (use 4 if security is being used).
minLocalFreeThreads	Same as minFreeThreads, but focuses on requests that are outbound to the same server.	
maxIOThreads	Determines the total number of IO threads available in the thread pool that can service requests.	Needs to be greater than maxConnections + minFreeThreads.
maxWorkerThreads	Determines the total number of worker threads available in the thread pool that can service requests.	Needs to be greater than maxConnections + minFreeThreads.

NOTE   When the number of threads running in the thread pool exceed the value of `minFreeThreads`, you will begin to queue inbound requests.

To tune the thread pool performance, if your CPU utilization is low and you are queuing requests, you should increase the value of `maxIOThreads` and `maxWorkerThreads`. On the other hand, if you CPU utilization is high, you should lower these settings.

NOTE   When CPU utilization exceeds 95 percent, you do not create additional threads. When CPU utilization is below 80 percent, you free unused threads.

Golden Rule 2: Understanding Timeout Settings

The connection timeout setting for a Web Service proxy should always be less than the settings defined by `HttpRuntime.executionTimeout`. If you do not follow this pattern, you will leak socket connections.

You must also be aware of how time is spent in your methods. For example, if you have configured your `executionTimeout` on the Pink tier to 90 seconds and have also configured the Web Service proxy to 70 seconds, you can run into problems. Let's say the incoming request to the Pink tier consumes 50 seconds before it makes the call to the Blue tier. This would allow you approximately 20 seconds to run the Web Service call to the Blue tier.

The recommendation is to make sure that the `executionTimeout` setting is no less than the time it takes to get to your Web method call plus the proxy timeout. So in our example, if testing proved these numbers to be consistent, our `executionTimeout` should be no less than the value defined in testing to be the amount of time it takes to get to the Web Service call, plus the maximum amount of time it takes to execute the call.

To recap, given a call to a Web method on the Pink tier, determine the appropriate timeout setting as follows:

1. Define the time it takes from the beginning of the Web method in the Pink tier to the call to the Web method on the Blue tier. Let's call this A.

2. Define the maximum amount of time we are going to set for the Web Service proxy (Blue). Let's call this B.

3. Set the value of executionTimeout as greater than the value of A + B.

Golden Rule 3: If a Timeout Occurs in One Tier, Abort Outbound Web Service Calls to the Other Tier

Use GetWebRequest to get the current request, as follows:

```
Private WebRequest -request;
Protected override WebRequest GetWebRequest(Uri uri)
{
        _request = base.GetWebRequest(uri);
        return _request;
}
```

Then do the following in the method that invokes the Web Service:

```
Public string SleepItOff(int sleepTime)
{
        Bool timeout = true;
        Try
        {
                Object[] results =
                  this.invoke("SleepItOff", new object[]{sleepTime});
                Timeout = false;
                Return ((string)(result[0]));
        }
        Finally
        {
                If(timeout && _request!=null)
                _request.Abort();
        }
}
```

NOTE You must place the abort code in the `finally` block, because when `executionTimeout` is reached, you call `ThreadAbortException`, which can be caught in a `catch` block.

Golden Rule 4: Do Not Write a Web Service Method That Works in a Tight Loop

The design in version 1.0 of the framework was that inbound requests were handled by I/O threads. By design, the IO completion port will allow only the number of threads executing to be equal to the concurrency value. If you have a Web method that enters a tight loop or takes a sufficiently long period of time to execute without entering a wait state, the scalability of your Web Service will be impacted.

If you need to use a Web method that works in a tight loop, you should queue the work to a worker thread, via the following call:

```
ThreadPool.QueueUserWorkItem(new WaitCallback(DoBackgroundWorkLong));
```

This will place the IO thread in a proper sleep, allowing for other IO threads to get execution time.

Golden Rule 5: Do Not Call STA Objects from Web Services

Accessing STA objects from a Web Service is not supported for the simple reason that STA objects provide automatic synchronization to all clients. There are some workarounds that can be found in the Microsoft Knowledge Base article "XML Web Services and Apartment Objects," which you can find at http://support.microsoft.com/?id=303375.

Office Integration

- Automating Office Basics

- Creating a New Instance of an Office Application

- Using the ROT, File Monikers, and the Shell

- Modifying Office Document Properties

- Creating Command Bars

- Using Events in Office

- Sending E-Mail

Automating Office Basics

The current approach to Office automation is to use existing COM objects provided by Microsoft Office. This means that to use C# in conjunction with Microsoft Office, you must add references to the existing COM libraries:

- Microsoft Word Object Library

- Microsoft Outlook Object Library

- Microsoft Excel Object Library

- Microsoft PowerPoint Object Library

There are multiple ways to start or access Microsoft Office products, as demonstrated in this chapter.

Creating a New Instance of an Office Application

One way to start an Office application is to create an instance of an Office application programmatically. The following example demonstrates how to create an instance of Microsoft Word. Notice that it sets the value of Visible to true. If you do not do this, a copy of Word will start, but you will have no GUI.

Code Example: Creating an Office Application Instance

```
using System;
using System.Windows.Forms;
using System.Runtime.InteropServices;
using Word;

namespace Client.Chapter_19___Office_Integration
{
        class CreatingOfficeApplications
        {
                [STAThread]
                static void Main(string[] args)
                {
                        Word.ApplicationClass MyWord = new Word.ApplicationClass();
                        MyWord.Visible = true;
                        System.Windows.Forms.Application.Run();
                }
        }
}
```

Using the ROT and File Monikers

The Running Object Table (ROT) is used to store instances of running COM servers. File monikers are used to identify objects that are saved into a file.

The following examples show how to use the ROT and file monikers.

Code Example: Using the ROT

```csharp
using System;
using System.Runtime.InteropServices;
using Microsoft.Office.Core;

namespace Client.Chapter_19___Office_Integration
{
        class Class1
        {
                [STAThread]
                static void Main(string[] args)
                {
                        Word.Application MyWord;
                        MyWord = (Word.Application)Marshal.GetActiveObject(
                            "Word.Application");
                        MyWord.Visible = true;
                        MyWord.ShowStartupDialog = true;
                        MyWord.ActiveDocument.PrintPreview();
                }
        }
}
```

Code Example: Using File Monikers

```
using System;
using System.Runtime.InteropServices;
using System.Windows.Forms;
using Excel;

namespace Client.Chapter_19___Office_Integration
{
        class Class1
        {
                [STAThread]
                static void Main(string[] args)
                {
                        Excel.Workbook MyWorkBook;
                        Excel.Worksheet MyWorkSheet;
                        string FileName = @"C:\Cases\Test\bin\Debug\Mybook.xls";
                        MyWorkBook = (Excel.Workbook)Marshal.BindToMoniker(
                          FileName);
                        MyWorkSheet = (Excel.Worksheet)MyWorkBook.ActiveSheet;
                        System.Windows.Forms.Application.Run();
                }
        }
}
```

Modifying Office Document Properties

You can programmatically modify the properties of an Office document. The following shows an example of setting the Author property in a Word document.

Code Example: Modifying Document Properties

```csharp
using System;
using System.Windows.Forms;
using System.Runtime.InteropServices;
using System.Reflection;
using Word;

namespace Client.Chapter_19___Office_Integration
{
        class Class1
        {
                [STAThread]
                static void Main(string[] args)
                {
                        object Missing = Missing.Value;
                        object BuiltInProps;
                        object CustomProps;
                        Word._Document Doc;
                        Word.ApplicationClass MyWord = new Word.ApplicationClass();
                        MyWord.Visible = true;
                        Doc = MyWord.Documents.Add(ref Missing,
                           ref Missing, ref Missing, ref Missing);
                        BuiltInProps = Doc.BuiltInDocumentProperties;
                        Type TypeBuiltingProp = BuiltInProps.GetType();
                        //Setting a built-in property
                        string Prop = "Author";
                        string PropValue;
                        object AuthorProp = TypeBuiltingProp.InvokeMember("item",
                           BindingFlags.Default | BindingFlags.GetProperty,
                           null, BuiltInProps, new Object[] { Prop });
                        Type TypeAuthorProp = AuthorProp.GetType();
                        PropValue = TypeAuthorProp.InvokeMember("Value",
                           BindingFlags.Default | BindingFlags.GetProperty, null,
                           AuthorProp, new Object[]{}).ToString();
                        System.Windows.Forms.Application.Run();
                }
        }
}
```

Creating Command Bars

You can also work with Office application command bars. The following example demonstrates how to create a button on a command bar.

Code Example: Creating Command Bars

```
using System;
using System.Windows.Forms;
using System.Runtime.InteropServices;
using System.Reflection;
using Word;
using Office = Microsoft.Office.Core;

namespace Client.Chapter_19___Office_Integration
{
        class Class1
        {
                [STAThread]
                static void Main(string[] args)
                {
                        Office.CommandBarButton Button;
                        Office.CommandBar CommandBar;
                        object Missing = System.Reflection.Missing.Value;
                        Office._CommandBarButtonEvents_ClickEventHandler
                          ButtonHandler;
                        Word.ApplicationClass MyWord = new Word.ApplicationClass();
                        MyWord.Visible = true;
                        CommandBar = MyWord.CommandBars.Add("MyCommandBar",
                          Missing, Missing, Missing);
                        Button =
                        (Office.CommandBarButton)CommandBar.Controls.
                         Add(Office.MsoControlType.msoControlButton, Missing,
                        Missing,  Missing, Missing);
                        Button.Caption = "MyButton";
                        Button.FaceId = 1845;
                        ButtonHandler =
                          new     Office._CommandBarButtonEvents_ClickEventHandler(
                          OnClick_Button);
                        Button.Click += ButtonHandler;
                        System.Windows.Forms.Application.Run();
                }
```

```
private void OnClick_Button(Office.CommandBarButton ctrl,
                                ref bool cancel)
{
    MessageBox.Show("This Worked!!!");
}
    }
}
```

Using Events in Office

The following example shows how to signal Office-level events. This allows your code to be notified when a specific operation has taken place in an Office application.

Code Example: Using Events

```csharp
using System;
using Excel;
using System.Reflection;
namespace Client.Chapter_19___Office_Integration
{
        class TestClass
        {
                public static
                AppEvents_WorkbookBeforeCloseEventHandler Event_BeforeBookClose;
                public static DocEvents_ChangeEventHandler Event_ChangeEvent;
                static void Main(string[] args)
                {
                    Application MyExcel = new ApplicationClass();
                  Workbook MyWorkbook = MyExcel.Workbooks.Add(Missing.Value);
                  MyWorkbook.Windows.get_Item(1).Caption = "Using Delegates";
                   Worksheet MyWorksheet1 =
                      (Worksheet)MyWorkbook.Worksheets.get_Item(1);
                   Worksheet MyWorksheet2 =
                      (Worksheet)MyWorkbook.Worksheets.get_Item(2);
                   Worksheet MyWorksheet3 =
                      (Worksheet)MyWorkbook.Worksheets.get_Item(3);
                   MyWorksheet1.Activate();
                  //Add event handler for the BeforeClose event
                   Event_BeforeBookClose =
                      new AppEvents_WorkbookBeforeCloseEventHandler(
                      BeforeBookClose);
                   MyExcel.WorkbookBeforeClose += Event_BeforeBookClose;
                  //Add event handler for the ChangeEvent event
                   Event_ChangeEvent =
                      new DocEvents_ChangeEventHandler(CellChange);
                   MyWorksheet1.Change += Event_ChangeEvent;
                   MyWorksheet2.Change += Event_ChangeEvent;
                   MyWorksheet3.Change += Event_ChangeEvent;
                   MyExcel.Visible = true;
                   MyExcel.UserControl = true;
                }
```

```
private static void CellChange(Range Target)
{
        //Gets called when you change a cell
}
private static void BeforeBookClose(Workbook MyWorkbook,
                                ref bool Cancel)
{
        //Gets called before closing a workbook
}
    }
}
```

Sending E-Mail

This section shows how to create e-mail using some Office and Exchange COM objects:

- CDOEx is provided by Exchange 2000 Server.

- CDO is provided by Office.

- The System.Web.Mail interface is provided with the .NET Framework.

Each of these components is unique, but they have overlapping functionality. For instance, CDO is a COM wrapper to MAPI. You can review the following MSDN link for more information:

ms-help://MS.VSCC.2003/MS.MSDNQTR.2003FEB.1033/dncdsys/html/cdo_roadmap.htm

Code Example: Sending E-mail Using CDOEx

```csharp
using System;
using CDO;
using ADODB;

namespace Client.Chapter_19___Office_Integration
{
    class TestClass
    {
        static void Main(string[] args)
        {
            Message MyMessage = new MessageClass();
            Configuration MyConfig = MyMessage.Configuration;
            Fields MyFields = MyConfig.Fields;
            MyFields[@http://schemas.microsoft.com/cdo/"
              + "configuration/sendusing"].Value = 2;
            MyFields[@http://schemas.microsoft.com/cdo/
              + "configuration/smtpserverport"].Value = 25;
            MyFields[@http://schemas.microsoft.com/cdo/
              + "configuration/smtpserver"].Value = "smarthost";
            MyFields.Update();
            MyMessage.Configuration = MyConfig;
            MyMessage.TextBody = "This is a test message";
            MyMessage.Subject = "Testing";
            MyMessage.From = "gregmcb@microsoft.com";
            MyMessage.To = "pmacbeth@comporium.com";
            MyMessage.Send();
        }
    }
}
```

Code Example: Sending E-mail Using CDO 1.21

```csharp
using System;
using System.Reflection;

namespace Test
{
        class TestClass
        {
                [STAThread]
                static void Main(string[] args)
                {
                        Object vEmpty = Missing.Value;
                        string sReplyUserAlias = "ReplyTMyRecipient";
                        try
                        {
                            //Create MAPI session and logon
                             MAPI.Session MySession = new MAPI.Session();
                             MySession.Logon(vEmpty, vEmpty, true,
                                true, 0, true, vEmpty);

                            //Get the Outbox
                             MAPI.Folder MyFolder = (MAPI.Folder)MySession.Outbox;
                             Console.WriteLine("Folder: {0}", MyFolder.Name);
                            //Create a new message
                            MAPI.Messages MyMsgs = (MAPI.Messages)MyFolder.Messages;
                             MAPI.Message MyMsg = (MAPI.Message)MyMsgs.Add(
                                vEmpty, vEmpty, vEmpty, vEmpty);
                             MyMsg.Subject = "Send Using C#";
                             MyMsg.Text = "Hello World";
                            //Add a recipient
                            MAPI.Recipients MyRecips =
                                (MAPI.Recipients)MyMsg.Recipients;
                            MAPI.Recipient MyRecip = (MAPI.Recipient)MyRecips.Add(
                                vEmpty, vEmpty, vEmpty, vEmpty);
                            MyRecip.Name = "TestRecipient";  //TODO: Set recipient
                             MyRecip.Resolve(false);
                            //Set the user to whom mail will be replied
                            //We can't create a new recipient object,
                            //so we add this recipient to the
                            //message just long enough to resolve it.
                             MAPI.Recipient MyTempRecip =
                                (MAPI.Recipient)MyRecips.Add(
                                    vEmpty, vEmpty, vEmpty, vEmpty);
                             MyTempRecip.Name = sReplyUserAlias;
                             MyTempRecip.Resolve(false);
```

```csharp
//Hash the ID into a string that looks like a
//FLATENTRYLIST structure.
//Calculate the length of a string converted
//hex representation of the

//Alt Recip's EntryID.
//Divide this value by 2 to calculate
//how long this will appear to
//MAPI when it views it as binary
//rather than as a string.
 int nID = MyTempRecip.ID.ToString().Length/2;
//Concatenate members of the FLATENTRY structure:
//A) Length of entire FLATENTRY structure
//B) Padding
//C) ENTRYID of Alt Recip
 String mID = Convert.ToString(nID, 16) +
    "000000" + MyTempRecip.ID;

//Now calculate the length of the
//entire FLATENTRY structure as a
//string and again divide by 2 to
//determine length when viewed as binary.
 String StructureLength =
    Convert.ToString(mID.Length/2, 16);
//Assemble the components of the
//FLATENTRYLIST structure:
//A) "01000000" ' defines how many
//FLATENTRY structures there are in
//the FLATENTRYLIST (plus padding) —
//There is only 1 in this sample.
//B) Length of the first (and only)
//FLATENTRY array member
//C) More padding
//D) EntryID of Alt Recip (as a string)
 String sBlock = "01000000" +
    StructureLength + "000000" + mID;
 MAPI.Fields MyFlds;
 MyFlds = (MAPI.Fields)MyMsg.Fields;
```

```
        //Write the values to the fields
          MyFlds.Add(
           MAPI.CdoPropTags.CdoPR_REPLY_RECIPIENT_NAMES,
           MyTempRecip.Name, vEmpty, vEmpty);
          MyFlds.Add(
             MAPI.CdoPropTags.CdoPR_REPLY_RECIPIENT_ENTRIES,
             sBlock, vEmpty, vEmpty);
        //Remove the temporary recipient
          MyTempRecip.Delete();
        //Send mail
          MyMsg.Send(vEmpty, vEmpty, vEmpty);
        //Logoff
          MySession.Logoff();

        //Clean up
          MyRecip = null;
          MyRecips = null;
          MyMsgs = null;
          MyMsg = null;
          MyFolder = null;
          MySession = null;
      }
      catch (Exception e)
      {
          Console.WriteLine("{0} Exception caught.", e);
      }
    }
  }
}
```

Code Example: Sending E-mail Using System.Web

```csharp
using System;
using System.Web.Mail;

namespace Test
{
        class TestClass
        {
                [STAThread]
                static void Main(string[] args)
                {
                        MailMessage Message = new MailMessage();
                        Message.From = "sender@somewhere.com";
                        Message.To = "recipient@somewhere.com";
                        Message.Subject = "Send Using Web Mail";
                        Message.BodyFormat = MailFormat.Html;
                        Message.Body =
                          "<HTML><BODY><B>Hello World!</B></BODY></HTML>";
                        String sFile = @"C:\temp\Hello.txt";
                        MailAttachment Attach =
                            new MailAttachment(sFile, MailEncoding.Base64);
                        Message.Attachments.Add(Attach);
                        SmtpMail.SmtpServer = "MySMTPServer";
                        SmtpMail.Send(Message);
                }

        }
}
```

CHAPTER 20

Windows Forms

- Basic Windows Forms

- Common Controls, Properties, and Events

- Alternatives for Creating Windows Forms

- Message Windows

- Windows Form Changes from 1.0 to 1.1 of the Framework

Basic Windows Forms

It's easy to create a Windows form in C#. All you need to do is use the Windows
Application Wizard, and you have a form. Then you just add controls by dragging
them onto the form and manipulating their properties and events. After you place
the controls on the form, you can modify the controls using their properties and
events at runtime.

The following example shows a form created with the wizard. It contains a
simple label, text box, and command button.

Code Example: Creating a Form with the Wizard

```
using System;
using System.Drawing;
using System.Collections;
using System.ComponentModel;
using System.Windows.Forms;
using System.Data;

namespace SimpleWinForm
{
        public class Form1 : System.Windows.Forms.Form
        {
            private System.Windows.Forms.Label label1;
            private System.Windows.Forms.TextBox textBox1;
            private System.Windows.Forms.Button button1;
            private System.ComponentModel.Container components = null;
            public Form1()
            {
                //
                //Required for Windows Form Designer support
                //
                 InitializeComponent();
                //
                //TODO: Add any constructor code after
                //InitializeComponent call
                //
            }
```

```
 protected override void Dispose( bool disposing )
{
      if( disposing )
      {
            if (components != null)
            {
                  components.Dispose();
             }
      }
      base.Dispose( disposing );
 }
 #region Windows Form Designer generated code
 private void InitializeComponent()
 {
         this.label1 = new System.Windows.Forms.Label();
         this.textBox1 = new System.Windows.Forms.TextBox();
         this.button1 = new System.Windows.Forms.Button();
         this.SuspendLayout();
        //
        //label1
        //
      this.label1.Location = new System.Drawing.Point(120, 40);
         this.label1.Name = "label1";
         this.label1.TabIndex = 0;
         this.label1.Text = "label1";
        //
        //textBox1
        //
         this.textBox1.Location =
           new System.Drawing.Point(96, 88);
         this.textBox1.Name = "textBox1";
         this.textBox1.TabIndex = 1;
         this.textBox1.Text = "textBox1";
        //
        //button1
        //
         this.button1.Location =
           new System.Drawing.Point(136, 160);
         this.button1.Name = "button1";
         this.button1.TabIndex = 2;
         this.button1.Text = "button1";
```

```
                        //
                        //Form1
                        //
                          this.AutoScaleBaseSize =
                             new System.Drawing.Size(5, 13);
                          this.ClientSize = new System.Drawing.Size(292, 266);
                          this.Controls.AddRange(
                             new System.Windows.Forms.Control[] {
                          this.button1,
                          this.textBox1,
                          this.label1});
                          this.Name = "Form1";
                          this.Text = "Form1";
                          this.ResumeLayout(false);
                  }
                  #endregion

                  [STAThread]
                  static void Main()
                  {
                        Application.Run(new Form1());
                  }
            }
      }
```

Common Controls, Properties, and Events

As you can see, Windows forms are made up of Windows controls. The controls have properties, which describe the state of the object, and events, which describe the actions that happen to the control. Table 20-1 describes the common controls. Tables 20-2 and 20-3 show the properties and events of controls.

Table 20-1. Common Form Controls

Control Name	Description
Button	Used to execute a path of code that realizes the intent of the button
Calendar	Provides a picture of a calendar in which you can select a date and month
Check Box	Provides an on/off, yes/no, include/exclude capability
Combo Box	Combines the features of a Text Box and a List Box; the three styles are drop-down (simple), always display list, and drop-down complex
Date/Time Picker	A Text Box that allows a user to choose a date and time from a calendar view
Group Box	Allows you to group other controls that have a common purpose
Label	Displays text
List Box	Displays an array of strings that a user can choose from
Main Menu	Creates a main menu
Picture	Allows you to place a picture on a form
Pointer	The icon used for the mouse pointer
Progress	Allows you to display the progress of a specific action
Radio Button	Allows the user to make a single selection from a group
Horizontal Scroll Bar	Allows the user to scroll left and right
Vertical Scroll Bar	Allows the user to scroll up and down
Text Box	Allows the user to enter text
Timer	This control is not visible and is used to start specific events

Table 20-2. Common Control Properties

Property	Description
Name	The programmatic name of the control
AutoCheck	When true, a radio button changes state automatically when clicked
AutoScale	When true, the form scales with the screen font
AutoScroll	Determines if scroll bars appear when a form exceeds the window size
AutoScrollMargin	Enables/disables the margin around a control when scrolling
AutoScrollMinSize	Minimum size for the autoscroll region
AutoSize	Determines if labels or picture controls are resized to fit the contents
BackColor	Sets the background color of a form
BackgroundImages	Sets the background image of a form
BorderStyle	Controls the border of a form
CancelButton	Sets the control as the Cancel button for the form, which makes it the same as pressing the Esc key
CheckAlign	Sets the location of a Check Box control within another control
Checked	Indicates if a control is checked
ContextMenu	Determines the shortcut menu displayed when a user right-clicks a control
ControlBox	Sets the Control/System Menu for a form
Cursor	Sets the cursor when the mouse pointer is over a control
DrawGrid	Determines if the drawing grid is displayed on a form
Enabled	Determines if a control is enabled on a form
FlatStyle	Determines how a control is displayed when a user moves the mouse over a control; the three settings are flat, pop-up, and standard
Font	Sets the font used in the control
ForeColor	Determines the foreground color when displaying text and graphics on a control

Table 20-2. Common Control Properties (Continued)

Property	Description
HelpButton	Displays a Help button on a form's caption bar
Icon	Sets the icon on a form when a form is minimized
Image	Sets the image displayed on the face of a control for radio buttons, buttons, check boxes, or picture boxes
ImageAlign	Sets the alignment of an image on the face of a control
ImageIndex	Index value of an image when it is displayed on the face of a control
ImageList	List used to select an image to display on a control's face
Interval	Sets the number of milliseconds in a timer's countdown; zero disables the timer
Items	Sets or returns the list of items in a combo, list, directory, drive, or file list
Large/Small Change	Used by scroll bars to determine the change when a user clicks a control
Location	Sets the X and Y values of a control
Locked	Prevents a control from being moved or resized
Maximize/Minimize Box	Determines if a Maximize or Minimize box is displayed
Maximum/Minimum	Used by horizontal/vertical scroll bars to determine a bar's maximum or minimum value
MultiLine	Read-only property that determines if a text box can hold more than one line
Opacity	Sets a form to be opaque (100) or transparent (0)
RightToLeft	Sets the direction of writing text in a text box
Scrollbars	Determines if a text box has horizontal/vertical scroll bars
Size	Sets the size of a control in pixels
Sorted	Used by combo and list boxes to set if the data is sorted
StartPosition	Sets the control's position on a form when it first appears
TabIndex	Sets the control's position in the tab order of the parent form
TabStop	Determines if the control is included in tabbing stops

Table 20-2. Common Control Properties (Continued)

Property	Description
Text	Sets the value/text of a control
TextAlign	Sets the alignment of text within a control
Visible	Sets the visibility of a control (true or false)
WindowState	Returns the state of a form: Minimized or Maximized

Table 20-3. Common Control Events

Event	Description
Activate	Triggered when a form is controlled
ButtonClick	Triggered by clicking a toolbar button
ButtonDropDown	Triggered by clicking a drop-down button style
CheckStateChanged	Triggered when a control's checked state has changed
CheckedChanged	Triggered by changing a control's Checked property
Click	Triggered by a mouse click
Closed	Triggered when a form control is closed
CloseUp	Triggered by the Date/Time Picker control when a date is selected
Closing	Triggered during the process of closing a form
DateChanged	Triggered by the Calendar control when the range of dates changes
DateSelected	Triggered by the Calendar control when a date or range of dates is selected
Deactivated	Triggered when a form is deactivated
DoubleClick	Triggered by a double-click of the mouse on a control
DragDrop	Triggered by dragging and dropping a control on a form
DragEnter	Triggered by dragging a control into a control's client area
DragLeave	Triggered when the mouse drags an item outside a client control area
DragOver	Triggered when a drag-and-drop operation is in progress and an item is over a client area of a control
DrawItem	Triggered when a panel on a status bar needs to be repainted
Enter	Triggered when a control becomes the active control
Format	Triggered when a control wants text to be displayed in a callback field
FormatQuery	Triggered by a control querying how to draw or paint a custom string
GiveFeedback	Triggered when a mouse drags an item

Table 20-3. Common Control Events (Continued)

Event	Description
Help	Triggered by a user requesting help for a control
InputLangChange	Triggered when the input language of a form is changed
InputLangChangedRequest	Triggered when the system changes the input language
KeyDown	Triggered when a key is first pressed
KeyPress	Triggered when a key is first released
KeyUp	Triggered when a key is released
Layout	Triggered when a control first lays out its contents
Leave	Triggered when a control is no longer active
MDIChildActivate	Triggered when an MDI child window is activated
MenuComplete	Triggered when menu selection is finished
MenuStart	Triggered when a menu is started
MouseDown	Triggered when a mouse button is clicked
MouseEnter	Triggered when the mouse first moves into a control's client area
MouseHover	Triggered when a mouse remains in a control's client area
MouseLeave	Triggered when the mouse leaves a client control
MouseMove	Triggered by mouse movement
MouseUp	Triggered by releasing a mouse button
Move	Triggered when a control is moved
PanelClick	Triggered by clicking a panel in a status bar
QueryContinueDrag	Triggered by dragging a control with the mouse
Resize	Triggered when a control is resized
Scroll	Triggered by moving a scroll bar's thumb
TextChanged	Triggered when the Text property is changed
UserString	Triggered when a control wants to parse a string
Validated	Triggered when a control is validated
Validating	Triggered when a control is being validated
ValueChange	Triggered when the value of a control is changed

Alternatives for Creating Windows Forms

There are two main alternatives to using the Windows Application Wizard for creating a form:

- Build a form from scratch

- Use form inheritance

To starting from scratch, follow this procedure:

1. Create an empty solution.

2. Add a new class and call it `main`. It will include all the code you need to start the application.

3. Add another new item, but this time, add a new Windows `Form`.

4. Add a reference to the project for `System.Windows.Forms.dll`.

5. Add a `using` statement for `System.Windows.Forms`.

6. In the `main` class, call this static method:

   ```
   Application.Run(new Form1());
   ```

Another method is to use form inheritance. The cool thing about this approach is that you only need to add an existing form as an inherited class, just as when you use class inheritance.

Message Windows

This following example demonstrates how to send messages to the Windows XP Desktop, resulting in a balloon-type window appearing in the lower-right corner. These windows are commonly used by applications such as Instant Messenger.

Code Example: XP Bubbles

```
using System;
using System.Runtime.InteropServices;
using System.Windows.Forms;
//Add this functionality by using these methods
/*
private void Info_Click(object sender, System.EventArgs e)
{
        XPSystrayBubble.XPBubble.INotification("Info Greg!");
}
private void OnLoad(object sender, System.EventArgs e)
{
        XPSystrayBubble.XPBubble.AddIcon(this);
}
private void OnClose(object sender, System.EventArgs e)
{
        XPSystrayBubble.XPBubble.RemoveIcon(this);
}
private void Warning_Click(object sender, System.EventArgs e)
{
        XPSystrayBubble.XPBubble.INotification("Warning Greg!");
}
private void Error_Click(object sender, System.EventArgs e)
{
        XPSystrayBubble.XPBubble.INotification("Error Greg!");
}
```

```
*/
namespace XPSystrayBubble
{
      [StructLayout(LayoutKind.Sequential)] public struct NOTIFYICONDATA
      {
            public int cbSize;
            public IntPtr hwnd;
            public int uID;
            public int uFlags;
            public IntPtr uCallbackMessage;
            public IntPtr hIcon;
            [MarshalAs(UnmanagedType.ByValTStr, SizeConst=128)]
            public string szTip;
            public int dwState;
            public int dwStateMask;
            [MarshalAs(UnmanagedType.ByValTStr, SizeConst=256)]
            public string szInfo;
            public int uVersion;
            [MarshalAs(UnmanagedType.ByValTStr, SizeConst=64)]
            public string szInfoTitle;
            public int dwInfoFlags;
      }

      public class XPBubble
      {
            static public bool Result;
            public const int NIF_MESSAGE = 0x1;
            public const int NIF_ICON = 0x2;
            public const int NIF_TIP = 0x4;
            public const int NIF_STATE = 0x8;
            public const int NIF_INFO = 0x10;
            public const int NIF_GUID = 0x20;

            public const int NIM_ADD = 0x0;
            public const int NIM_MODIFY =  0x1;
            public const int NIM_DELETE = 0x2;
            public const int NIM_SETFOCUS =  0x3;
            public const int NIM_SETVERSION = 0x4;
            public const int NOTIFYICON_VERSION = 0x3;
            public const int NIS_HIDDEN = 0x1;
            public const int NIS_SHAREDICON = 0x2;
            public const int NIIF_NONE = 0x0;
            public const int NIIF_INFO = 0x1;
            public const int NIIF_WARNING = 0x2;
            public const int NIIF_ERROR = 0x3;
```

```
[DllImport("shell32.dll")]
public static extern bool Shell_NotifyIcon(int dwMessage,
                              ref NOTIFYICONDATA lpData);
public static NOTIFYICONDATA NIF = new NOTIFYICONDATA();
public static void WNotification(string sMessage)
{
      NIF.uFlags = NIF_INFO;
      NIF.uVersion = 2000;
      NIF.szInfoTitle = "Warning";
      NIF.szInfo = sMessage;
      NIF.dwInfoFlags = NIIF_WARNING;
      Result = Shell_NotifyIcon(NIM_MODIFY, ref NIF);
}
public static void ENotification(string sMessage)
{
      NIF.uFlags = NIF_INFO;
      NIF.uVersion = 2000;
      NIF.szInfoTitle = "Error";
      NIF.szInfo = sMessage;
      NIF.dwInfoFlags = NIIF_ERROR;
      Result = Shell_NotifyIcon(NIM_MODIFY, ref NIF);
}
public static void INotification(string sMessage)
{
      NIF.uFlags = NIF_INFO;
      NIF.uVersion = 2000;
      NIF.szInfoTitle = "Info";
      NIF.szInfo = sMessage;
      NIF.dwInfoFlags = NIIF_INFO;
      Result = Shell_NotifyIcon(NIM_MODIFY, ref NIF);
}
```

```
public static void RemoveIcon(System.Windows.Forms.Form X)
{
    NIF.cbSize = Marshal.SizeOf(NIF);
    NIF.hwnd = X.Handle;
    NIF.uID = 1;
    Result = Shell_NotifyIcon(NIM_DELETE, ref NIF);
}
public static void AddIcon(System.Windows.Forms.Form X)
{
    NIF.cbSize = Marshal.SizeOf(NIF);
    NIF.hwnd = X.Handle;
    NIF.uID = 1;
    NIF.uCallbackMessage = new IntPtr(0x500);
    NIF.uVersion = NOTIFYICON_VERSION;
    NIF.hIcon = X.Icon.Handle;

    Result = Shell_NotifyIcon(NIM_ADD, ref NIF);
}
}
}
```

Windows Form Changes from 1.0 to 1.1 of the Framework

The following are some of the differences between versions 1.0 and 1.1 of the framework that relate to Windows forms:

- Calling Form.Close in the Load event of a modal form now closes the form.

- The Validating event no longer fires twice when closing a form.

- Adding a nonserializable object to the Clipboard now generates an exception.

- The ListView object no longer fires the MouseUp event when the ListItem is dragged.

- The TreeView object raises the MouseUp event correctly when the mouse button is released.

- The TrackBar control now raises ValueChangedEvents when the value is changed via the mouse scroll wheel.

- Setting the DataSource property of a ListBox or ComboBox to Null will now clear the contents of the control.

- A data-bound ComboBox with its DropDownStyle property set to DropDownList now finds items by programmatically setting the Text property.

- When a form is closed, the Validating event does not fire for the control that has focus if that control is in a UserControl.

Part Three
ASP.NET

HTML Basics

- Why HTML in a Book on C#?

- Creating a Basic HTML Page

- Making Text Look Better

- Working with Lists

- Using Tables to Build Pages

- Using Controls

- Using Scripts

- Using Style Sheets (CSS)

- HTML Quick Reference

Why HTML in a Book on C#?

You might wonder why I have included a chapter on HTML in a book that describes how to use a real programming language like C#. The answer is simple: You must know basic HTML so you can write good ASP.NET pages using C#.

Creating a Basic HTML Page

The following is a basic HTML page (see Figure 21-1):

```
<html>
     <head>
          <title> This is a basic Web Page! </title>
     </head>
     <body>
          <p>Hello World! </p>
     </body>
</html>
```

Figure 21-1. A basic HTML page

 CAUTION   The <body> tag supports a background attribute that can be used to supply a watermark-type display to the whole page. When you use this attribute, make sure that your text contrasts with the background appropriately.

The following shows how to use the prebuilt heading tags (see Figure 21-2):

```
<html>
    <head>
        <title> This is a basic Web Page! </title>
    </head>
     <body>
            <h1>Hello World! h1</h1>
            <h2>Hello World! h2 </h2>
            <h3>Hello World! h3 </h3>
            <h4>Hello World! h4 </h4>
            <h5>Hello World! h5 </h5>
            <h6>Hello World! h6 </h6>
    </body>
</html>
```

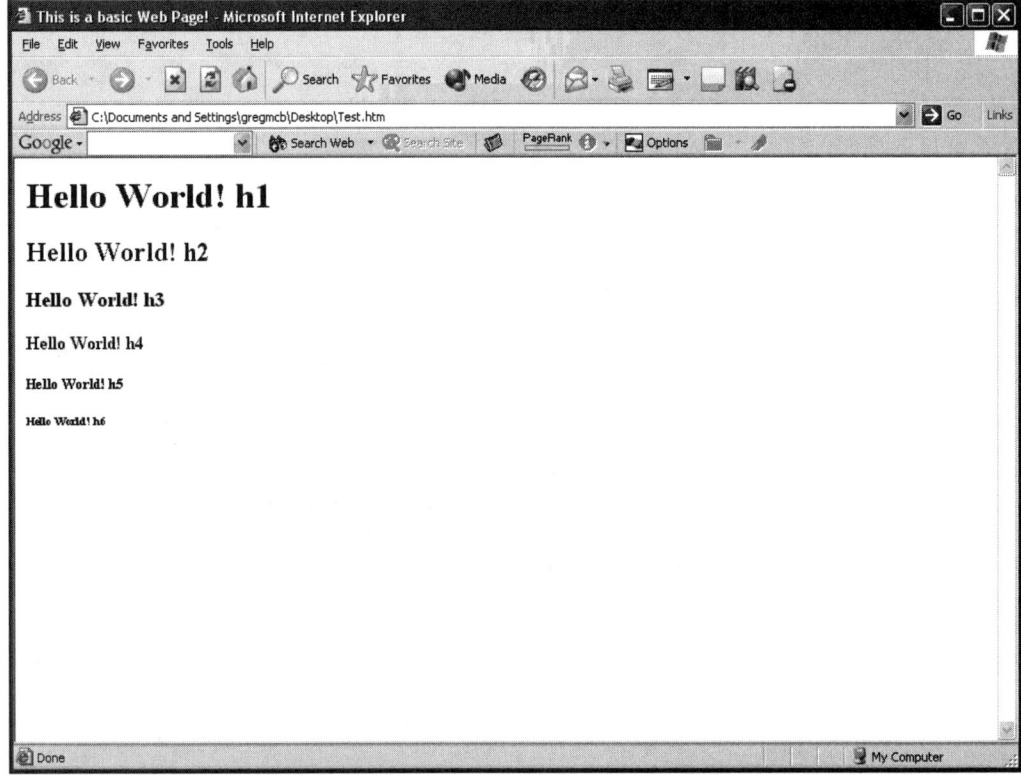

Figure 21-2. A basic HTML page with headings

Another basic element of an HTML page is an image. The following demonstrates adding a aimple image (see Figure 21-3):

```
<html>
    <head>
        <title> This is a basic Web Page! </title>
    </head>
    <body>
        <img src="dotnet.gif" align="top">
    </body>
</html>
```

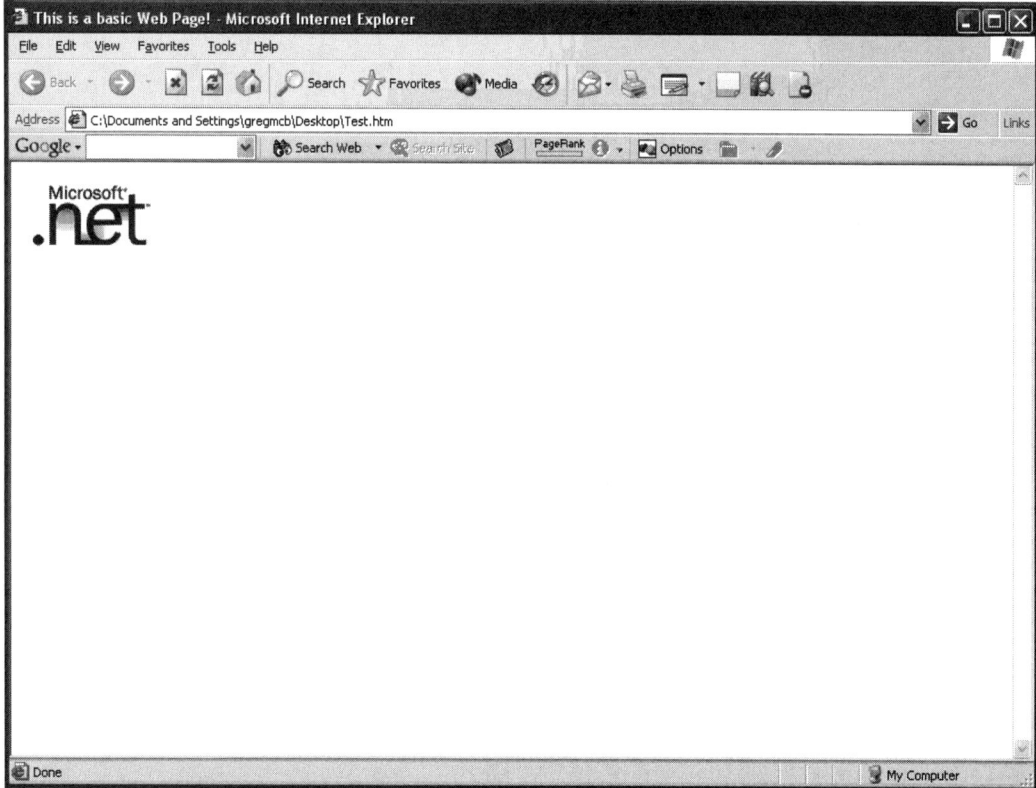

Figure 21-3. A basic HTML page with a simple image

This example uses the `align` attribute to place the image at the top of the page. Other `align` values include `left`, `right`, `middle`, `center`, and `bottom`. Two useful attributes you can use with images are `width` and `height`. You can also use the `border` attribute to give the image a border.

CAUTION Be very cautious in using the `width` and `height` attributes, because you can distort the image when you change its size.

HTML pages also typically have hyperlinks. The following demonstrates creating a simple hyperlink (see Figure 21-4):

```
<html>
     <head>
          <title> This is a basic Web Page! </title>
     </head>
     <body>
          <a href="http://www.drudgereport.com"> Drudge Report </a> <br>
          <a href="mailto:gmacbeath@comproium.net" > E-mail me </a>
     </body>
</html>
```

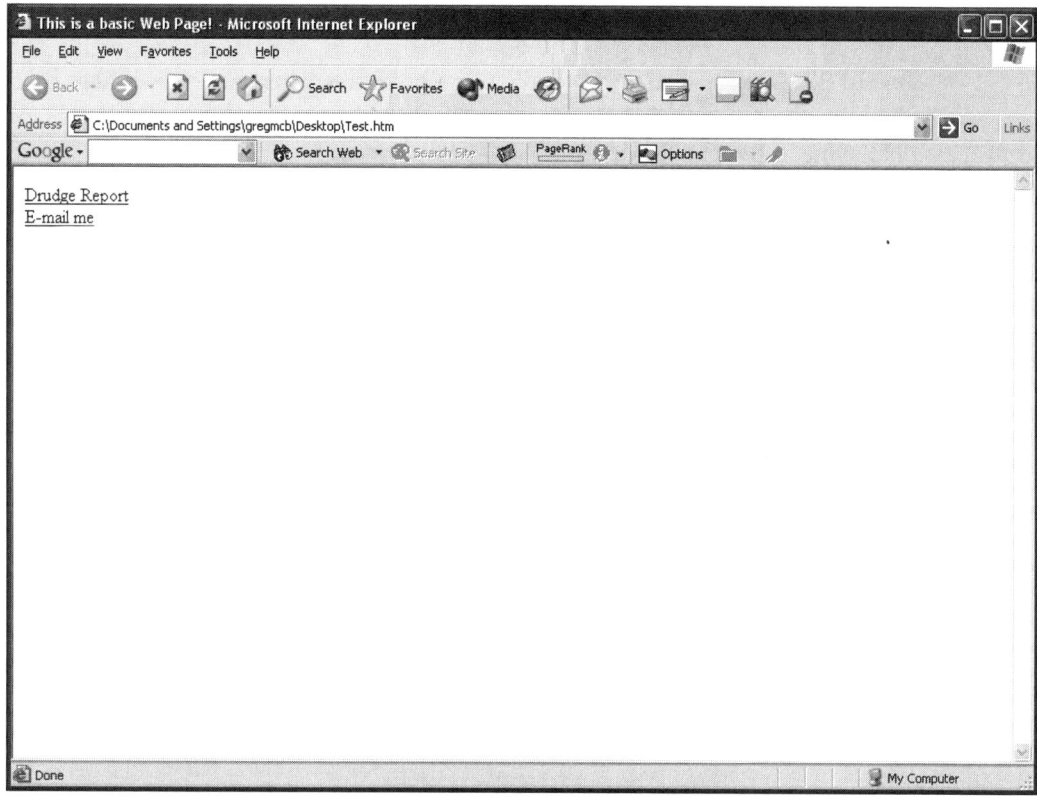

Figure 21-4. Hyperlinks added to an HTML page

Making Text Look Better

Text in HTML pages can be dressed up in many ways. There are built-in tags that allow you to show text as a specific type. Table 21-1 shows some common tags for displaying different types of text.

Table 21-1. Built-in Tags for Text Types

Tag	Description
<cite>	Bibliographic citation
<code>	Source code
<dfn>	Definition
<em>	Emphasis
<kbd>	Text typed on a keyboard
<samp>	Sequence of literal characters
<strong>	Strong emphasis
<var>	Variable in code

You can also use other tags to enhance the appearance of text. Table 21-2 lists common text formatting tags.

Table 21-2. Built-in Tags for Text Formats

Tag	Description
<b>	Bold
<big>	Increase the default font size
<i>	Italicize the text
<small>	Decrease the default font size
<sub>	Subscript
<sup>	Superscript
<tt>	Monospaced font
<u>	Underline text

Working with Lists

To add a list to an HTML page, use the `<ul>` tag for unordered (bulleted) lists or the `<ol>` tag for ordered (numbered) lists, with the `<li>` tags for list items. Here is an example (see Figure 21-5):

```
<html>
    <head>
        <title> This is a basic Web Page! </title>
    </head>
    <body>
        <ul>
            <li>Queen</li>
            <li>Genisis</li>
            <li>Van Halen</li>
        </ul>
        <ol>
            <li>Queen</li>
            <li>Genisis</li>
            <li>Van Halen</li>
        </ol>
        <dl>
            <dt> Rock </dt>
            <dd>Great Music!</dd>
        </dl>
    </body>
</html>
```

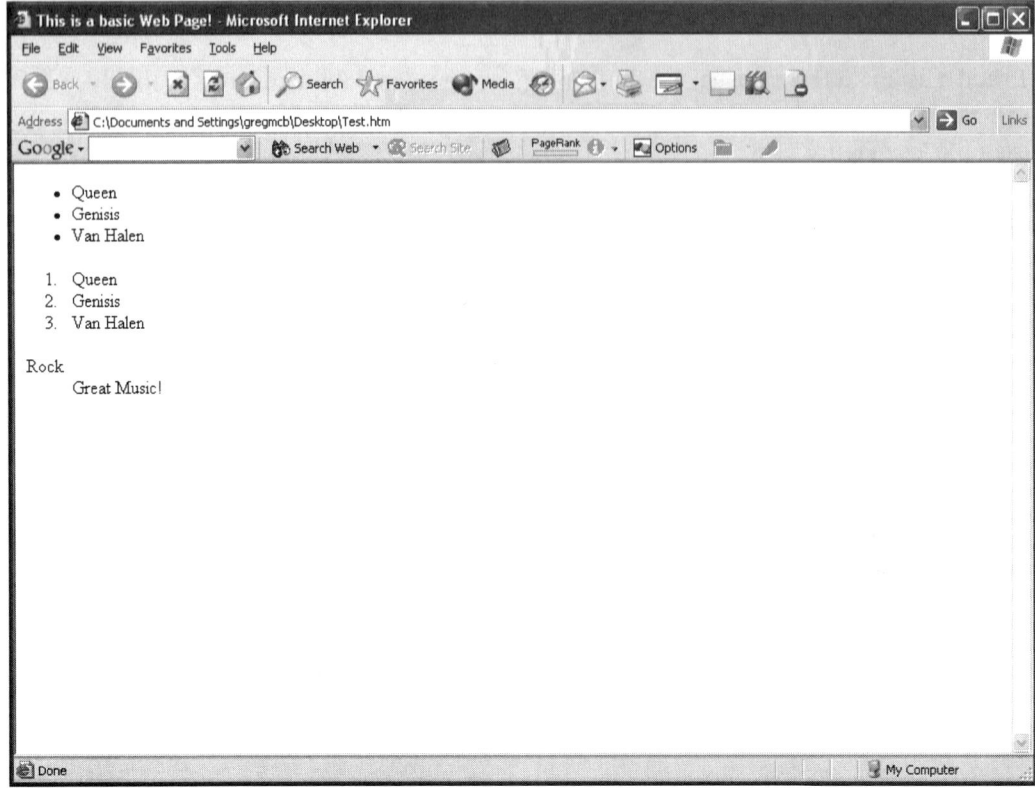

Figure 21-5. Lists added to an HTML page

With unordered lists, you can use the `type` attribute to describe what your bullets look like. The valid values are `disc`, `circle`, and `square`.

With numbered lists, the `type` attribute controls the numbering. The valid possibilities are as follows:

`1`, which displays 1, 2, 3, 4, 5, and so on

`A`, which displays A, B, C, D, E, and so on

`a`, which displays a, b, c, d, e, and so on

`I`, which displays I, II, III, IV, V, and so on

`i`, which displays i, ii, iii, iv, v, and so on

You can also use the `start` attribute to control the number with which to start the numbered list. For example, the following starts the list with the letter *F*:

```
<ol type="A" start="5"/>
```

Using Tables to Build Pages

If you want your page to appear in a tabular format, you can use the table tags to build the page. Here is an example (see Figure 21-6):

```
<html>
      <head>
            <title> This is a basic Web Page! </title>
      </head>
      <body>
            <table width="100%" border="1">
            <tr>
                <td width="25%" rowspan="3">My Navigation Bar</td>
                <td width="75%">PageTitle</td>
            </tr>
            <tr>
                <td>
                    <table width="100%" border="1">
                    <tr>
                        <td width="50%"> Column One </td>
                        <td width="50%"> Column Two </td>
                    </tr>
                    </table>
                </td>
            </tr>
            <tr>
                <td>Footer</td>
            </tr>
            </table>
      </body>
</html>
```

The rowspan attribute can be applied to a <td> tag (also known as a cell tag) to combine several rows into a single cell. Similarly, the colspan attribute combines several columns.

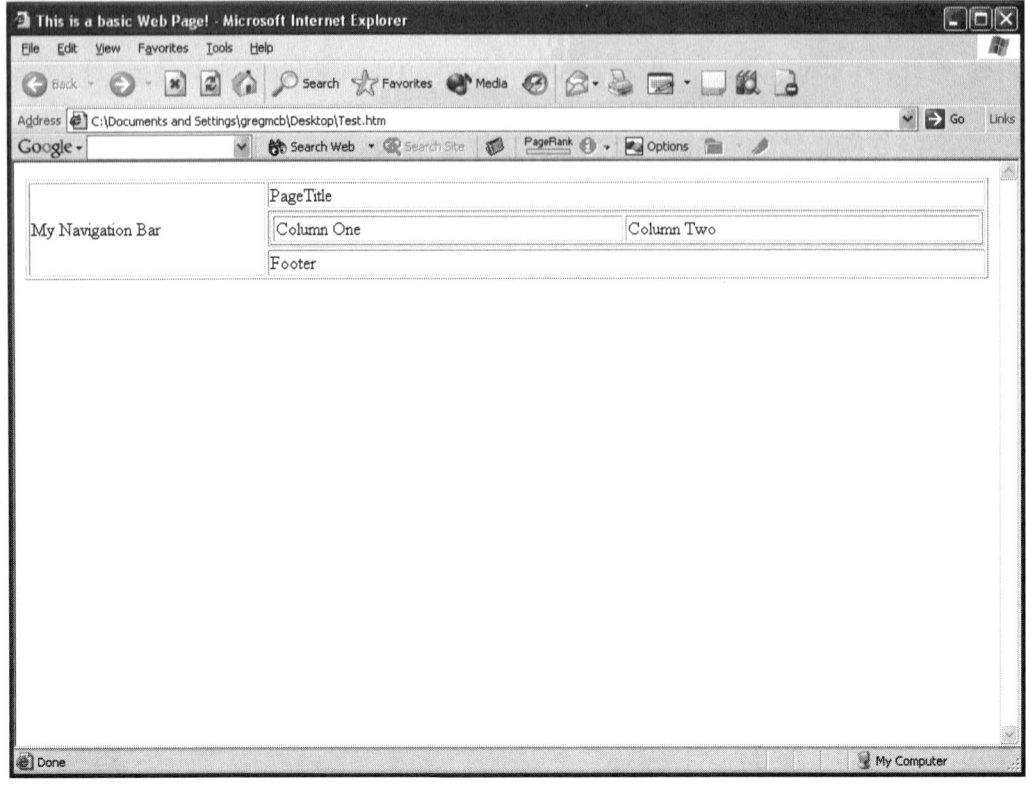

Figure 21-6. A table added to an HTML page

Using Controls

Of course, you can add many types of controls to an HTML page. Here, we will look at examples of using text box, password box, text area, check box, radio button, menu, and command button controls.

Text Boxes and Password Boxes

The following demonstrates using text and password box controls (see Figure 21-7).

```
<html>
      <head>
            <title> This is a basic Web Page! </title>
      </head>
      <body>
            UserName: <input type="text" name="username" value=""/> <br>
            Password: <input type="password" name="password" value=""/>
      </body>
</html>
```

Figure 21-7. A text box and password box added to an HTML page

With text box and password box controls, you set attributes to specify the number of characters allowed and the number of characters displayed. The size attribute determines the maximum numbers of characters that can be entered into the control. The maxlength attribute determines how many characters can be seen.

Text Areas

The text area control provides for a larger area of text than a text box. The following is an example of using a text area control (see Figure 21-8):

```
<html>
      <head>
            <title> This is a basic Web Page! </title>
      </head>
      <body>
            Comments: <br>
            <textarea name="Comments" rows="4" cols="55" wrap="">
            Enter Your Comments Here!
            </textarea>
      </body>
</html>
```

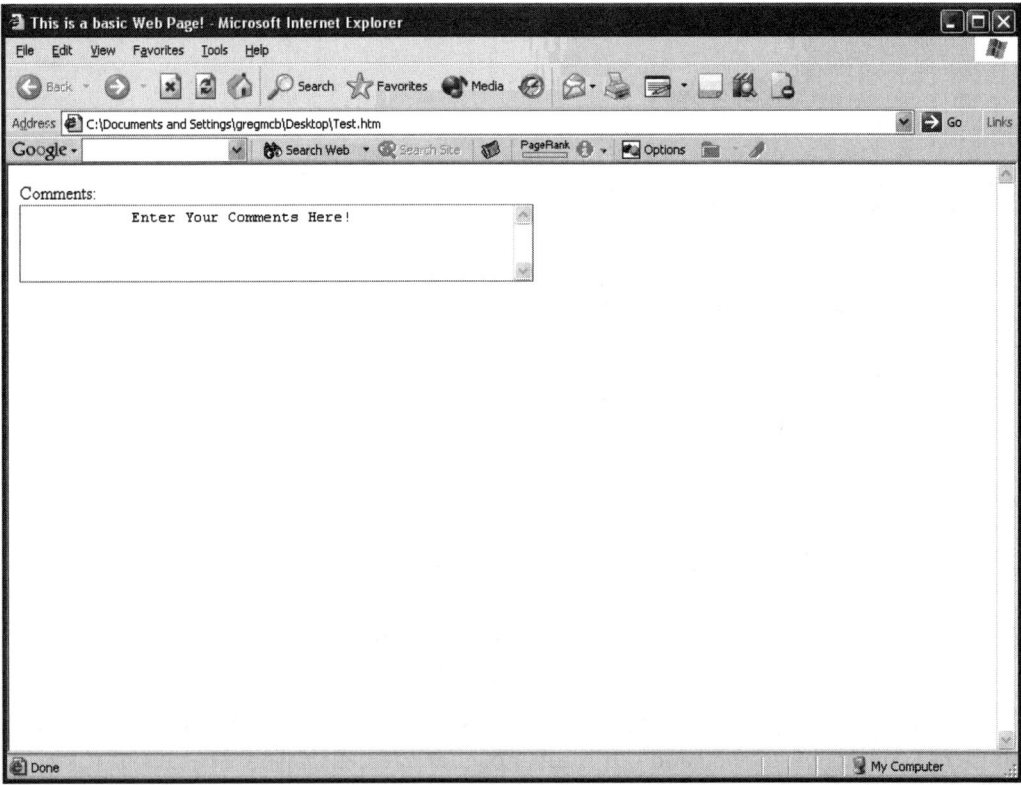

Figure 21-8. A text area added to an HTML page

Check Boxes

To add check boxes to an HTML page, use checkbox as the input type. The following is an example of using check boxes:

```
<html>
     <head>
          <title> This is a basic Web Page! </title>
     </head>
     <body>
          Who is the best Football Team: <br>
          <input type="checkbox" name="FootballTeams"
            value="Dolphins" check=""> Dolphins <br>
          <input type="checkbox" name="FootballTeams"
            value="Patriots" > Patriots  <br>
          <input type="checkbox" name="FootballTeams" value="Jets" > Jets <br>
          <input type="checkbox" name="FootballTeams" value="Bills" > Bills <br>
     </body>
</html>
```

Radio Buttons

To add radio buttons, use radio as the input type. The following is an example of using radio buttons:

```
<html>
     <head>
          <title> This is a basic Web Page! </title>
     </head>
     <body>
          Who is the best Quarterback: <br>
          <input type="radio" name="Quarterbacks"
            value="Marino" check=""> Marino <br>
          <input type="radio" name="Quarterbacks" value="Manning" > Manning <br>
          <input type="radio" name="Quarterbacks" value="Montana" > Montana <br>
          <input type="radio" name="Quarterbacks" value="Griese" > Griese <br>
     </body>
</html>
```

Menu Controls

Use the <select> tag to display a menu and <option> tags to populate the menu.
The following is an example of including a menu on an HTML page:

```
<html>
     <head>
          <title> This is a basic Web Page! </title>
     </head>
     <body>
          What is the best Color:<br>
          <select name="Colors">
                              <option value="red"> Red</option>
                              <option value="blue"> Blue</option>
                              <option value="green"> Green</option>
                              <option value="yellow"> Yellow</option>
          </select>
     </body>
</html>
```

Command Buttons

To add command buttons, specify the type of button, such as submit or reset,
as the input type. The following is an example of using command buttons:

```
<html>
     <head>
          <title> This is a basic Web Page! </title>
     </head>
     <body>
          <form enctype="text/plain" action="mailto:gmacbeth@comporium.net"
             method="post">
          <input type="submit" value="submit">
          <input type="reset" value="reset">
          </form>
     </body>
</html>
```

Using Scripts

Scripts are extremely useful for making your Web pages dynamic. In fact, in the old days of ASP, this is how you accessed COM objects and provided custom results to users.

The following shows an example of the HTML for using a script:

```
<html>
    <head>
        <script language="javascript" src="Test.js">
        </script>
        <title> This is a basic Web Page! </title>
    </head>
    <body>
        <input type="button" value="Click Me"
          onclick="ThrowDialogBox('Hello World')"/>
    </body>
</html>
```

In this example, the Test.js file includes the following Java script code:

```
function ThrowDialogBox(str)
{
    alert(str);
}
```

There are numerous events that you can handle with scripts. Table 21-3 shows some of these events.

Table 21-3. Form Events

Event	Description
onload	Browser loads an object
onkeydown	User presses a key
onkeyup	User releases a key
onmousedown	User presses a mouse button on an object
onmouseover	User moves a pointer over an object
onclick	User left-clicks an object

Using Style Sheets (CSS)

Using Cascading Style Sheets (CSS), you can apply styles in many ways. The following example shows how to set the style of a paragraph to a specific format (see Figure 21-9). This would apply to all <p> tags in this document. However, you can override these settings by placing comments directly in a <p> tag.

```
<html>
      <head>
            <link rel="stylesheet" type="text/css" href="styles.css" >
            <title> This is a basic Web Page! </title>
      </head>
      <body>
            <p class="Test">
                              This should be bold and green
            </p>
            <p style="color:blue; font-size:36pt;">
                                          This should be big blue text
            </p>
      </body>
</html>
```

And the style sheet styles.css file contains this:

```
p.Test{ color:green; font-weight:bold}
```

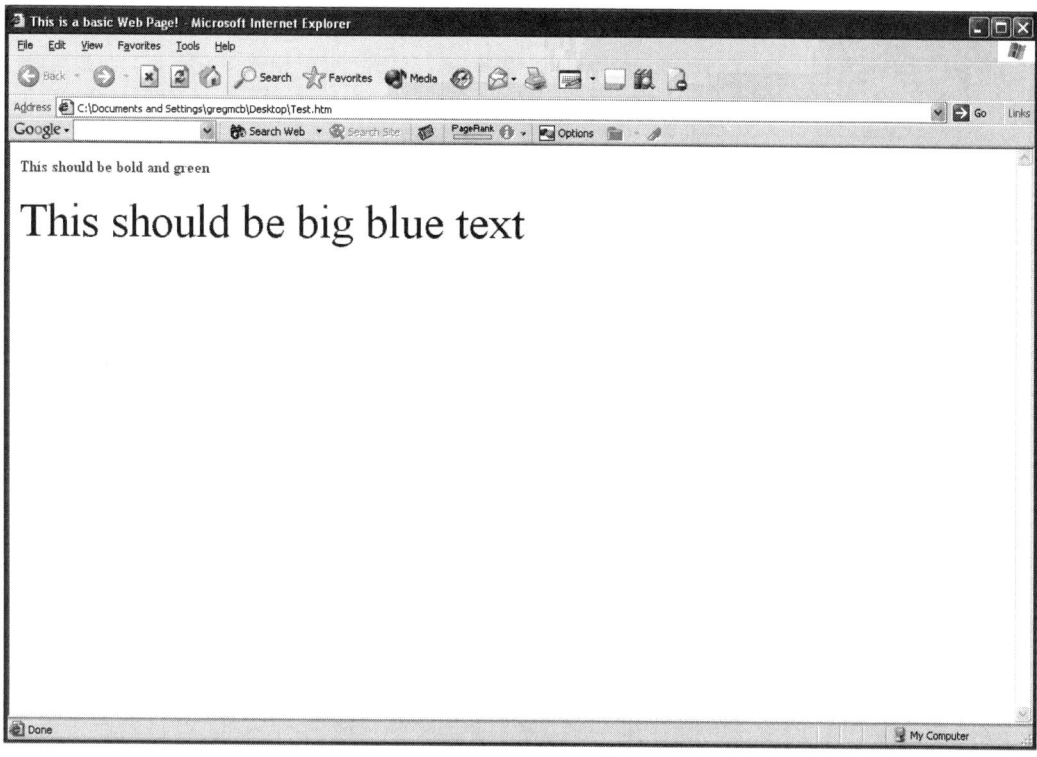

Figure 21-9. Using CSS to apply styles

Table 21-4 shows the common style properties that can be used for text.

Table 21-4. Common Style Properties for Text

Property	Description
font	Describes font settings
font-style	Sets the font style
font-weight	Sets the font thickness
font-size	Sets the font size
font-family	Specifies the font family
color	Sets the color of text
background-color	Sets the background color of text
background-image	Sets the background image of text
background-repeat	Determines how the background image for text is placed
letter-spacing	Adjusts spacing between text
text-indent	Sets the indentation of the first line in text
text-align	Positions text horizontally
margin-top	Sets the top margin of text
margin-right	Sets the right margin of text
margin-bottom	Sets the bottom margin of text
margin-left	Sets the left margin of text
text-decoration	Sets the highlight of text
text-transform	Sets the case of text
cursor	Sets the mouse pointer icon when the mouse hovers

Table 21-5 shows the properties that can be used for image positioning.

Table 21-5. Common Style Properties for Images

Property	Description
position	Declares the type of positioning, relative or absolute
top	Specifies the top offset
right	Specifies the right offset
left	Specifies the left offset
bottom	Specifies the bottom offset
width	Determines the width of an element
height	Sets the height of an element
display	Hides or shows an element
border-width	Sets the border width
border-style	Sets the border style
border-color	Sets the border color

HTML Quick Reference

Table 21-6 provides a quick reference to common tags used to build HTML pages.

Table 21-6. Common HTML Tags

Tag	Description
STRUCTURAL	
<html> </html>	Encloses HTML script
<head> </head>	Head of the page
<title> </title>	Title of the page in the browser
<body> </body>	Body of the page
<!--	Comments
TEXT	
<p> </p>	Paragraph text
<div> </div>	Block of content
<span> </span>	Inline content
 	Line break
<hr/>	Horizontal line (rule)
<font> </font>	Font for text
<b> </b>	Bold
<i> </i>	Italics
<h1>..</h6>	Headers
<tt> </tt>	Typewriter text
LIST	
<ul> </ul>	Unordered bulleted list
<ol> </ol>	Ordered numbered list
<li> </li> Item in a list	
<dl> </dl>	Definition list
<dt> </dt>	Term in a definition list
<dd> </dd>	Definition in a definition list

Table 21-6. Common HTML Tags (Continued)

Tag	Description
TABLE	
`<table> </table>`	Table
`<tr> </tr>`	Table row
`<td> </td>`	Cell
`<th> </th>`	Table heading
`<caption> </caption>`	Table caption
FORM	
`<form> </form>`	Form
`<input> </input>`	Input field
`<select> </select>`	Selection list
`<option> </option>`	Option form
`<textarea> </textarea>`	Scrolling, multiline text field
MISCELLANEOUS	
`<img> </img>`	Image
`<a> </a>`	Anchor hyperlink
`<map> </map>`	Image map
`<area> </area>`	Area within an image map
`<meta> </meta>`	Page information
`<style> </style>`	Style sheet
`<link/>`	Link to an external file

XML

- XML Basics

- Reading XML: From Files, Streams, and URLs

- Writing XML to a File

- Loading an XML Document

XML Basics

XML is a language that provides a way to standardize the way in which we structure data via a *metalanguage*.

The `System.Xml` namespace defines the built-in classes that allow you to control and manipulate XML. Table 22-1 describes these classes.

Table 22-1. System.Xml Namespace Classes

Class	Description
XmlTextReader	Provides, fast, noncached, forward-only access to XML
XmlNodeReader	Reads a given DOM node
XmlValidatingReader	Provides DTD, XDR, and XSD schema validation
XmlTextWriter	Provides fast-forward-only way to create XML
XmlDocument	Implements an XML document
XmlDataDocument	Provides an XML document that can be associated with a `DataSet`
XmlPathDocument	Provides a fast cache for processing an XML document for XSLT

Reading XML

To read XML, you use XmlTextReader. You can read XML from a file, a stream, or a URL, as demonstrated in the following examples.

Code Example: Reading XML from a File

```csharp
using System;
using System.IO;
using System.Xml;

namespace Client.Chapter_22___XML
{
        class Test
        {
                private const string doc = "Test.xml";
                static void Main(string[] args)
                {
                    XmlTextReader reader = null;
                    //Load the file with an XmlTextReader
                    reader = new XmlTextReader(doc);
                    //Read the file
                    while (reader.Read())
                    {
                        //TODO -
                    }
                    if (reader != null)
                       reader.Close();
                }
        }
}
```

Code Example: Reading XML from a Stream

```csharp
using System;
using System.IO;
using System.Xml;

namespace Client.Chapter_22___XML
{
    class Test
    {
        static void Main(string[] args)
        {
            StringReader stream;
            XmlTextReader reader = null;
            stream = new StringReader("  XML File Text");
            //Load the XmlTextReader from the stream
            reader = new XmlTextReader(stream);
            while (reader.Read())
            {
                //TODO -
            }
            if (reader != null)
                reader.Close();
        }
    }
}
```

Code Example: Reading XML from a URL

```csharp
using System;
using System.IO;
using System.Xml;

namespace Client.Chapter_22___XML
{
        class Test
        {
            static void Main(string[] args)
            {
                    string localURL = "http:\\Test\\Test.xml";
                    XmlTextReader myXmlURLreader = null;
                    myXmlURLreader = new XmlTextReader (localURL);
                    while (myXmlURLreader.Read())
                    {
                            //TODO -
                    }
                    if (myXmlURLreader != null)
                            myXmlURLreader.Close();
            }
        }
}
```

Writing XML to a File

You can write XML to a file by using XmlTextWriter. For example, you might use this method to add information to a database, as demonstrated in the following example.

Code Example: Writing XML to a File

```
using System;
using System.IO;
using System.Xml;
using System.Xml.Schema;

namespace Client.Chapter_22___XML
{
        class Test
        {
                static void Main(string[] args)
                {
                        string document = "newbooks.xml";
                        XmlTextWriter myXmlTextWriter = null;
                        XmlTextReader myXmlTextReader = null;
                        myXmlTextWriter = new XmlTextWriter(args[1], null);
                        myXmlTextWriter.Formatting = Formatting.Indented;
                        myXmlTextWriter.WriteStartDocument(false);
                        myXmlTextWriter.WriteDocType("bookstore", null,
                           "books.dtd", null);
                        myXmlTextWriter.WriteComment("This file represents" +
                           " another fragment of a book store inventory database");
                        myXmlTextWriter.WriteStartElement("bookstore");
                        myXmlTextWriter.WriteStartElement("book", null);
                        myXmlTextWriter.WriteAttributeString("genre", "software");
                        myXmlTextWriter.WriteAttributeString("publicationdate",
                           "2003");
                        myXmlTextWriter.WriteAttributeString("ISBN",
                           "1-3333-3333-0");
                        myXmlTextWriter.WriteElementString("title", null,
                           "The C# Programmer's Handbook");
                        myXmlTextWriter.WriteStartElement("Author", null);
                        myXmlTextWriter.WriteElementString("first-name", "Greg");
                        myXmlTextWriter.WriteElementString("last-name", "MacBeth");
                        myXmlTextWriter.WriteEndElement();
                        myXmlTextWriter.WriteElementString("price", "29.99");
                        myXmlTextWriter.WriteEndElement();
                        myXmlTextWriter.WriteEndElement();
```

```
        //Write the XML to file and close the writer
        myXmlTextWriter.Flush();
        myXmlTextWriter.Close();
        if (myXmlTextWriter != null)
            myXmlTextWriter.Close();
    }
}
}
```

Loading an XML Document

Finally, you can load an XML document by declaring a new XmlDataDocument and specifying the data. The following example demonstrates loading and displaying an XML document.

Code Example: Loading an XML Document

```
using System;
using System.IO;
using System.Xml;

namespace Client.Chapter_22___XML
{
        public class LoadXmlDocumentSample
        {
                private const String document = "books.xml";
                public static void Main()
                {
                        LoadXmlDocumentSample myLoadXmlDocumentSample =
                            new LoadXmlDocumentSample();
                        myLoadXmlDocumentSample.Run(document);
                }
                public void Run(String args)
                {
                    try
                    {
                        //Load the XML from file
                         Console.WriteLine();
                         Console.WriteLine("Loading file {0} ...", args);
                        XmlDataDocument myXmlDocument = new XmlDataDocument();
                         myXmlDocument.Load(args);
                         Console.WriteLine("XmlDataDocument loaded" +
                         "with XML data successfully ...");
                        //Display the XML document
                         myXmlDocument.Save(Console.Out);
                    }
                    catch (Exception e)
                    {
                            Console.WriteLine("Exception: {0}", e.ToString());
                    }
                }
        }
}
```

ASP.NET

- ASP.NET Basics

- ASP.NET Directives

- Application State

- ASP.NET Common Events

- ASP.NET Configuration

- User Sessions: Browser Cookies

- User Sessions: Session State

- Cookieless Sessions

- ASP.NET Caching

- Forms-Based Authentication

- Windows-Based Authentication

- ASP.NET Controls

ASP.NET Basics

The big benefit of ASP is that it allows you to add dynamic content to a Web site. As you saw in Chapter 21, HTML is great for adding static data, but if you want to add data on the fly, you have a problem.

The solution to this problem is ASP, or ASP.NET in terms of this book. With this technology, you can produce dynamic Web sites that display data from databases or other sources, allowing your users to see the latest and greatest details of your business.

ASP.NET Directives

There are many directives that you can use in your Web applications. The directive types include `application`, `assembly`, `control`, `implements`, `import`, `OutputCache`, `Page`, `Reference`, and `Register`. Table 23-1 lists some of the most common ones and on which objects they can be used.

Table 23-1. ASP.NET Directives

Directive	Description
Application	Used to define application-level attributes
Assembly	Links an assembly to the application
Control	Used by controls
Implements	Allows a page to implement a COM interface
Import	Imports a namespace into a page
OutputCache	Used to cache pages, controls, or data
Page	Defines page-specific attributes
Reference	Links another page or control to this page
Register	Associates an alias with a user control

The Page directive is probably the most important, and it has some specific attributes, which are listed in Table 23-2.

Table 23-2. Page Directive Attributes

Attribute	Description
AutoEventWireup	Sets event postbacks
Buffer	Sets up response buffering
ClassName	Sets the page class name
ClientTarget	Targets user agents where controls should be rendered
CodeBehind	Sets the .cs file that runs the code for the page
Debug	Sets compiling with symbols
Description	Provides a description
EnableSessionState	Enables or disables SessionState
EnableViewState	Enables or disables ViewState

NOTE ViewState allows controls on a Web page to maintain their values and state between postbacks. When a button is clicked and it results in a round-trip from the client to server, the value of the controls with ViewState enabled will be maintained.

Application State

Application state allows you to add information that will be available to all users that access your Web site. In short, these are *global* variables.

You can add data to the application state by doing the following:

```
Application("MyGlobal") = "Greg's web site";
```

You can retrieve specific data from this cache with code similar to the following:

```
Response.Write(Application("MyGlobal"));
```

To remove items, use the RemoveAll or Remove method, as follows:

```
Application.RemoveAll();
Application.Remove("MyGlobal");
```

The big problem with application data is that you must protect it from synchronization problems. This is done by using Application.Lock and Application.Unlock.

```
Application.Lock();
   Application("UserCount") += 1;
Application.Unlock();
```

CAUTION   When locking the application state, it is important to realize that when you lock the state, it locks all members of the application state. There is no way to lock specific members of the state.

Common ASP.NET Events

All of the ASP.NET events are stored in the global.aspx file. When you modify this file, the application will automatically restart. Table 23-3 lists the common ASP.NET events.

Table 23-3. Common ASP.NET Events

Event	Description
Application_AuthenticationRequest	Raised before authenticating a user
Application_AuthorizeRequest	Raised before authorizing a user
Application_BeginRequest	Raised by every request to the server
Application_End	Raised before the end of all application instances
Application_EndRequest	Raised at the end of every request to the server
Application_Error	Raised when an unhandled error occurs
Application_PreSendRequestContent	Raised before sending data/content to the browser
Application_PreSendRequestHeaders	Raised before sending headers to the browser
Application_Start	Raised when the first application is started (occurs only once)
Dispose	Raised before the end of an application
Init	Raised after an application instance is created

ASP.NET Configuration

There are two files that you can use to control ASP.NET pages:

- The Machine.config file influences all ASP.NET applications.

- The Web.config file affects only the site that contains the Web.config file.

To make matters even muddier, you can place Web.config files in each folder or virtual directory of your site, and those settings will override settings in higher Web.config files.

Configuration File Elements

There are many elements that can be added to the System.Web section of your configuration files, as shown in Table 23-4.

Table 23-4. Configuration File System, Web Section Elements

Element	Description
trace	Controls page and application tracing
globalizations	Specifies character encodings to use with requests and responses
httpRunTime	Specifies the maximum time a page can execute, the maximum size of a request, and if fully qualified names should be used for client redirects
compilation	Specifies the default programming language for pages, whether a page is compiled in debug mode or release mode, and the assemblies available to the application
pages	Specifies configuration information for a page
customErrors	Determines how errors are displayed
authentication	Specifies authentication settings
identity	Configures user account settings for impersonation
authorization	Determines the users and roles that can access pages
machineKey	Used to share encryption key information across a Web farm
trust	Sets security policy settings

Table 23-4. Configuration File System, Web Section Elements (Continued)

Element	Description
securityPolicy	Contains a list of security policies
sessionState	Sets session state information such as in-process, out-of-process, or cookieless
httpHandlers	Associates a particular HTTP handler with a specific page path and request verb
httpModules	Lists the modules involved in page requests
processModel	Contains process-wide settings that control the aspnet_wp processes
webControls	Sets the location of client-side scripts used with Web controls
clientTarget	Lists values that are used by the ClientTarget property
browserCaps	Lists information about the capabilities of individual browser types
webServices	Configures settings for Web Services

The Web.config file provides for a Location property, which lets you set specific pages or specific paths.

```
<configuration>
            <location path="MyVirtualDirectory">
                    <system.web>
                    </system.web>
            </location>
            <location path="MyPage.aspx" allowOverrides="false">
                    <system.web>
                    </system.web>
            </location>
</configuration>
```

Configuration Attributes

You can set various attributes for the configuration file elements. Tables 23-5 through 23-8 show the attributes for the node, httpRuntime, processModel, and trace elements.

Table 23-5. Authentication Attributes for the Node Element

Value	Description
Windows	Uses credentials provided by IIS. The authorization element can be used to control access further.
Forms	Provides for custom authorization.
Passport	Allows for the use of passport authentication.
None	Disables authentication at the ASP.NET level.

Table 23-6. httpRuntime Attributes

Attributes	Description
appRequestQueueLimit	Specifies the limit for request queuing. Once this limit is reached, the server returns 503 errors. The default value is 100.
executionTimeout	Sets the amount of time that a request can execute before timing out. The default is 90 seconds.
MaxRequestLength	Sets the maximum file size that can be uploaded. The default value is 4KB. This is primarily used to prevent denial-of-service attacks.
MinFreeLocalRequestFreeThreads	Sets the minimum number of threads reserved for local requests. The default is 4.
minFreeThreads	Sets the minimum number of threads reserved for requests that require additional threads. The default is 8.
useFullyQualifiedRedirectUrl	Determines if URLs sent to the client are fully qualified or relative.

Table 23-7. processModel Attributes

Attribute	Description
Enable	Determines if process model settings are used.
Timeout	Sets the lifespan of the process. The default level is infinite.
idleTimeout	Sets the lifespan of an aspnet_wp process when idle. The default is infinite.
shutdownTimeout	Sets the amount of time the process can be shut down gracefully. The default is 5 seconds.
requestLimit	Sets the number of requests that can be processed by ASP.NET before it is shut down. The default is infinite.
requestQueueLimit	Sets the number of requests that can be queued before the process is shut down. The default is 50000.
memoryLimit	Sets the amount of memory that can be used by the aspnet_wp process before it will be recycled. The default is 60 percent.
cpuMask	Used in a Web garden where aspnet_wp affinity is set on processors.
webGarden	Enables Web gardening.
Username	Sets the username that an aspnet_wp process runs under.
comAuthenticationLevel	Sets the DCOM authentication level.
comImpersonationLevel	Sets the DCOM impersonation level.
responseRestartDeadlockInterval	Sets the amount of time that will be allowed between process restarts due to deadlocking. The default is 9 minutes.
responseDeadlockInterval	Sets the amount of time allowed without a response when requests are queued. The default is 3 minutes.
maxWorkerThreads	Sets the maximum limit of worker threads per CPU in the thread pool.
maxIoThreads	Set the maximum limit on the number of IO threads per processor.

Table 23-8. Trace Attributes

Attribute	Description
Enabled	Enables tracing. The default is false.
localOnly	Determines if tracing can be viewed remotely. The default is true.
pageOutput	Sets whether trace output is rendered at the bottom of the page or available via trace.axd. The default is false.
requestLimit	Sets the number of traces that can be stored in the trace buffer and be viewed by trace.axd. The default is 10.
traceMode	Sets the sort order of trace items. The default is SortByTime.

AppSettings Configurations

You can add your own custom settings by using the appSettings elements. To do this, configure your Web.config file as follows:

```
<configuration>
          <appSettings>
                    <add key="MyName" value="Greg MacBeth" />
          </appSettings>
</configuration>
```

You can read these settings with the following code:

```
string Name = ConfigurationSettings.AppSettings("MyName");
```

Important HTTP Classes

There are two important HTTP classes. One handles responses, and the other handles requests.

- HttpRequest allows the gathering of data from the Web client. For example, you can get the authentication method, hostname, and address.

- HttpResponse exposes data that will be sent to the client browser.

User Sessions: Browser Cookies

Cookies are used to store small amounts of data on the user's browser. This data is limited to 4KB and must be a string.

Adding and Retrieving Cookies

There are two types of cookies:

- *Temporary cookies* are stored in the browser's memory. You can add a temporary cookie by doing the following:

```
HttpCookie myCookie = new HttpCookie("MyName", "Gregory MacBeth");
Response.Cookies.AddImyCookie);
```

- *Persistent cookies* are stored on the hard drive. You can add a permanent cookie by doing the following:

```
HttpCookie myCookie = new HttpCookie("MyName", "Gregory MacBeth");
myCookie.Expires = DateTime.MaxValue; //Or a specific date
Response.Cookies.AddImyCookie);
```

The only difference between these two cookie types is that a persistent cookie has an expiration date. Once a cookie is created, it is automatically sent to and from the browser via the HTTP headers. HttpCookie contains some common properties that you can set. These properties are listed in Table 23-9.

Table 23-9. Common HttpCookie Properties

Key	Description
Domain	Indicates the domain associated with the cookie
Expires	Indicates the expiration date of the cookie
HasKeys(bool)	Indicates if a cookie contains a dictionary
Name	Defines the name of a cookie
Path	Indicates the path associated with a cookie (the default value is /)
Secure	Indicates if the cookie should be sent over an encrypted connection only
Value	Stores the value of the cookie
Values	Named value pair that stores key and value pairs in a dictionary

You can retrieve a cookie value by using the following code:

```
Response.Write(Request.Cookies("MyName").Value);
```

Using a Dictionary in a Cookie

A dictionary allows you to populate a cookie with multiple types of information, ranging from strings to numbers and more.

Here is an example of using a dictionary in a cookie:

```
HttpCookie myCookie = new HttpCookie("myContactInfo");
myCookie.Values("Name") = "Greg MacBeth";
myCookie.Values("Address") = "111 139th Street.";
myCookie.Values("City") = "Fort Mill";
Response.Cookies.Add(myCookie);
```

You can read a dictionary cookie via the following code:

```
if(myCookie.HasKeys = "true")
{
    foreach(string Info in myCookie.Values);
    {
        Response.Write(myCookie.Values("Info"));
     }
}
```

User Sessions: Session State

If you do not want to store session information on the client, you have the option of storing the information using the session state. There are some major differences between using session state and using cookies:

- The session state information is stored on the server.

- You are not limited to storing string objects. You can store any object type in session state.

NOTE   Under the covers, even when you use session state, you still send one cookie to the client. This cookie identifies the session.

Modifying the Session State Timeout Value

The data added to the session state stays for the duration of the client browser's connection to the server or until the timeout period expires, which defaults to 20 minutes.

You can modify the session timeout value using the following code:

```
Session.Timeout = 30; //Sets the timeout to 30 minutes
```

Alternatively, you can change the session state timeout value in the Web.config file:

```
<system.web>
        <sessionState timeout="30 />
</system.web>
```

Adding, Retrieving, and Removing Session State Items

You can work with session state items as follows:

- You can add items to the session state with the following code:

```
Session("MyName") = "Greg MacBeth";
```

- You can retrieve items via this code:

```
Response.Write(Session("MyName"));
```

- You can remove or delete items using Remove or RemoveAll:

```
Session.Remove("MyName");
Session.RemoveAll();
```

Session State Storage

Session state can be stored in one of three locations: in-process (default), out-of-process in the ASP.NET State Service, or in a SQL database. The benefit to using in-process storage is performance. The benefit to storing session state in a SQL database or in the ASP.NET State Service is redundancy.

If you want to store session state in-process, you do not need to do anything, because this is the default setting. However, if you wish to use out-of-process storage or a SQL database, you must make configuration settings.

- **ASP.NET State Service:** To store session state, start the ASP.NET State Service and modify the Web.config file to the following:

```
<sessionState>
        mode="StateServer"
        stateConnectionString="tcp=127.0.0.1:42424"
</sessionState>
```

- **SQL database:** To store session state in SQL, run SQL Query Analyzer and open and run the script InstallSqlState.sql batch. This batch file creates a database that will be used to store the session state. Also, modify the Web.config to the following:

```
<sessionState>
        mode="SqlServer"
        stateConnectionString="tcp=127.0.0.1;UID=sa;PWD=password"
</sessionState>
```

Disabling Session State

You can disable session state by modifying the Web.config, as follows:

```
<sessionState>
        mode="Off"
</sessionState>
```

User Sessions: Cookieless

Since some users have disabled cookies completely, we still have a problem, even when using session state. This is because session state relies on the session ID cookie being placed on the client.

We can work around this problem on computers that have disabled cookies by modifying the Web.config file, as follows:

```
<sessionState cookieless="true" />
```

The net result of this is that the session ID will be stored in the URL, rather than in a cookie. For example, if you visit http://www.macbeth.com/default.aspx, you will actually see the URL as http://www.macbeth.com/(xxxxxxxxxxxxxx)/ default.aspx.

CAUTION   There is one significant limitation to using this method of storing session IDs in URLs: You cannot use absolute URLs when linking between pages.

ASP.NET Caching

You can dramatically improve performance in your Web application by using caching. The idea is simple: Cache Web pages so you do not need to do the work to retrieve the page again. For example, this might be useful for a Web site that presents a list of courses offered by a school. Since this data is unlikely to change often, you can enhance performance by caching this static data, thus preventing several round-trips to the database.

You can cache entire pages, page fragments, or page data, as described in the following sections.

Page Output Caching

To enable page output caching, you must add the following page directive to the top of your page:

```
<%@ OutputCache Duration="60" VaryByParam="none" @>
```

You can be even more specific and cache pages based on parameters, as in this example:

```
<%@ OutputCache Duration="60" VaryByParam="ProductID" @>
```

This allows you to cache a version of the page for each product ID. For example, the following requests will result in separate pages being cached:

```
http://www.macbeth.com/products.aspz?ProductID=1
http://www.macbeth.com/products.aspz?ProductID=2
```

If you wish to cache by any parameter, set the value of VaryByParam to "*". There are two other attributes that you can use to control caching:

- VaryByHeader allows you to cache different versions of the page by browser.

- VaryByCustom allows you to cache by page based on a specific string.

By default, the pages are cached on both the client and server. You can control the location of the cache by using the `Location` attribute in the `OutputCache` directive, which can have the following values:

`Any`	Default
`Client`	Page is cached on the client
`Downstream`	Page is cached on a downstream server
`None`	Disables caching
`Server`	Page is cached only on the server

Finally, you can control caching behavior with even more granularity by using the `HttpCachePolicy` object.

Page Fragment Caching

Page fragment caching allows you to cache specific parts of a page. This feature is implemented via a user control's own `OutputCache` directive.

The syntax is the same as using the page output cache, except the directive is applied to the control.

```
<%@ OutputCache Duration="60" VaryByParam="none" @>
```

CAUTION   A big limitation of enabling page fragment caching is that you lose the ability to programmatically access the control via the containing page.

Page Data Caching

In situations where caching the data of the page makes more sense than caching the actual page, you have the option of using page data caching. To do this, you use the `Cache` object to store data.

You can add items to the data cache by doing the following:

```
Cache("MyName") = "Greg MacBeth";
```

For more complex types, use the following:

```
HashTable MyTable = new HashTable();
MyTable.Add("MyData", ds); //Where ds is a DataSet
MyTable.Add("MyName", "Greg MacBeth");
Cache("MyInfo") = MyTable;
```

You can retrieve data from the cache via the following code:

```
string Name = Cache("MyName");
```

Forms-Based Authentication

Forms-based authentication allows your users to be prompted for credentials, and those credentials will be used to access the site. When you are using forms-based authentication, you are not using Active Directory to authenticate your users. Instead, you are using a third-party database, such as the Web.config file, an XML file, or a database with credentials and password.

To enable forms-based authentication, you should modify the Web.config file as follows:

```
<system.web>
<authentication      mode="Form"
                     loginUrl=http://www.macbeth.com/login.aspx
                     timeout="45"
                     />
</system.web>
Deny Access to the anonymous account
<system.web>
     <authorization>
         <deny users="?" />
     </authorization>
</system.web>
```

Create a login page that allows a user to enter a username and password. You can authenticate against the Web.config file, as follows:

```
<credentials passwordFormat="Clear">
     <user name="gregmcb" password="Password"/>
</credentials>
```

You can authenticate against a database by matching the credentials supplied.

The identity of a user that logs on this way is represented by the FormsIdentity class. You can use this object to find out the authentication type (which always returns forms), if the user was authenticated, and ticket information.

Windows-Based Authentication

When you use Windows-based authentication, you are using Active Directory and the credentials supplied by the client. To use this form of authentication, you must disable anonymous access via IIS security settings. Then you must configure your Web.config file as follows:

```
<system.web>
        <identity impersonate="true" />
        <authentication mode="Windows" />
            <authorization>
                    <deny users="?"/>
                    <allow roles="MyDomain\MyGroup"/>
                    <deny users="MyDomain\gregmcb" />
                    <allow users="*"/>
            <authorization>
</system.web>
```

Once this is done, you can control access via normal IIS permissions combined with using the `<authorization>` element in the Web.config file.

ASP.NET Controls

HTML server controls are nothing more than regular HTML controls that run on the server. They always have the property `runat="server"` set on them. Web Server controls provide a richer functionality as well as following the XML syntax.

Tables 23-10 through 23-13 show the HTML server controls, Web server controls, common control properties, and the events that are common to every control.

Table 23-10. HTML Server Controls

Control	Description
HtmlForm	Equivalent to the `<form>` tag
HtmlInputText	Equivalent to the `<input type="text">` tag
HtmlInputCheckBox	Equivalent to the `<input type="checkbox">` tag
HtmlInputFile	Equivalent to the `<input type="file">` tag
HtmlInputHidden	Equivalent to the `<input type="hidden">` tag
HtmlInputImage	Equivalent to the `<input type="image">` tag
HtmlInputRadioButton	Equivalent to the `<input type="radio">` tag
HtmlInputButton	Equivalent to the `<input type="button">` tag
HtmlButton	Equivalent to the `<button>` tag
HtmlSelect	Equivalent to the `<select>` tag
HtmlImage	Equivalent to the `<image>` tag
HtmlTextArea	Equivalent to the `<textarea>` tag
HtmlGenericControl	Equivalent to the `<body>`, `<div>`, `<span>`, or `<font>` tag
HtmlAnchor	Equivalent to the `<a>` or `<anchor>` tag
HtmlTable	Equivalent to the `<table>` tag
HtmlTableCell	Equivalent to the `<td>` tag
HtmlTableRow	Equivalent to the `<tr>` tag

Table 23-11. Web Server Controls

Control	Description	Example
TextBox	Input control	`<asp:TextBox … />`
Label	Read-only control that is delivered as a `<span>` tag	`<asp:Label … />`
Button	Control that causes an action	`<asp:Button … />`
CheckBox	Input control that provides multiple selections	`<asp:CheckBox … />`
RadioButton	Input control that provides a single selection given multiple options	`<asp:RadioButton … />`
ImageButton	Button control that provides an image and is rendered as the `<img>` tag	`<asp:ImageButton … />`
LinkButton	Action control that behaves like a hyperlink	`<asp:LinkButton … />`
HyperLink	Control that behaves like a hyperlink that is rendered as an `<a>` or `<anchor>` tag	`<asp:HyperLink … />`
Image	Control that displays an image and is rendered as an `<img>` tag	`<asp:Image … />`
ListBox	Input control that is rendered as a `<select>` command	`<asp:ListBox … />`
DropDownList	Control that creates a simple selection list and is rendered as the `<select>` command	`<asp:DropDownList … />`
RadioButtonList	Creates a control that displays a series of radio button options	`<asp:RadioButtonList … />`
DataList	List control that provides for good customization	`<asp:DataList … />`
DataGrid	Control rendered as a table that allows for detailed customization	`<asp:DataGrid … />`
Repeater	Allows for the display of multiple images	`<asp:Repeater … />`
Table	Draws a table	`<asp:Table … />`
TableCell	Creates a cell in a table	`<asp:TableCell … />`

Table 23-11. Web Server Controls (Continued)

Control	Description	Example
TableRow	Creates a row in a table	`<asp:TableRow … />`
PlaceHolder	Container control that can be used to host other controls	`<asp:PlaceHolder … />`
Literal	Displays static text	`<asp:Literal … />`
Panel	Control used to contain other objects and is rendered as a `<span>` tag	`<asp:Panel … />`
AdRotator	Displays advertisements	`<asp:AdRotator … />`
Calendar	Displays a calendar	`<asp:Calendar … />`
XML	XML transformation control	Presents XML data

Table 23-12. Common Control Properties

Property	Description
AccessKey	Assigns a shortcut key to a control
Attributes	Provides access to the attributes of a control
BackColor	Provides the background color of a control
BorderColor	Provides the border color of a control
BorderWidth	Changes the border width of a control
BorderStyle	Changes the border style of a control
CssClass	Sets the CSS class name
Style	Sets the CSS style
Enabled	Enables or disables the control
Font	Sets the font of the control
ForeColor	Sets the foreground color of the control
Height	Sets the height of the control
TabIndex	Sets the tab index of the control
Tool	Sets the tooltip help text
Width	Sets the width of the control

Table 23-13. Common Control Events

Event	Description
DataBinding	Raised when the DataBind method is called
Disposed	Occurs when the control is released from memory
Init	Occurs when the control is first initialized
Load	Occurs when the control is loaded into the page object
PreRender	Occurs just prior to when the control's Render method is called
Unload	Occurs when the control is unloaded from memory

Part Four

Appendixes

C# Tools and Resources

THE FOLLOWING ARE USEFUL TOOLS for the C# programmer. They are all built into the .NET Framework SDK.

- **Csc.exe:** Command-line compiler.

- **Ildasm.exe:** Allows you to read IL code for a given assembly.

- **Ilasm.exe:** Allows you to create an assembly given IL code.

- **Instalutil.exe:** Allows you to install an assembly as a service.

- **Regasm.exe:** Creates a .tlb file and registers it for COM Interop.

- **Regsvcs.exe:** Allows you to register a managed assembly into COM+.

- **Soapsuds.exe:** Allows you to read type information from a Web Service or remoted object.

- **Tlbexp.exe:** Creates a .tlb file for a given assembly.

- **Tlbimp.exe:** Generates a RCW for a given COM library

The following sites offer resources for C# developers. They contain sample code and discussions of specific topics. These resources may help you get answers to questions that arise while you are planning and developing your projects.

- http://www.gotdotnet.com

- http://blogs.gotdotnet.com

- http://www.dotnetremoting.com

- http://www.csharphelp.com

- http://support.microsoft.com

- http://msdn.microsoft.com

Exam 70-315

Developing and Implementing Web Applications with Microsoft Visual C# .NET and Microsoft Visual Studio .NET

THIS APPENDIX CONTAINS information that will help you prepare for Exam 70-315, Developing and Implementing Web Applications with Microsoft Visual C# .NET and Microsoft Visual Studio .NET. This is a Microsoft Certified Professional (MCP) exam, and it also provides credit for the certifications Microsoft Certified Solution Developer (MCSD), Microsoft Certified Application Developer (MCAD) for Microsoft .NET, and Microsoft Certified Database Administrator (MCDBA) on Microsoft SQL Server 2000.

Creating User Services

This section describes directives, controls, validation, and events, as well as other information related to creating user services.

Common Directives

Table B-1 shows the common directives used for developing Web applications.

Table B-1. Common Web Application Directives

Directive	Description
@Page	Defines page-specific attributes (only in .aspx)
@Control	Defines control-specific attributes (only in .ascx)
@Import	Imports a namespace
@Implements	Declares a specific interface implemented
@Register	Creates aliases
@Assembly	Links an assembly
@OutputCache	Controls the output caching
@Reference	Links a page or user control

Setting the AutoEventWireup attribute to true in the @Page directive of the page automatically associates Web page events with server-side methods.

The following code needs to be placed in the .aspx file to link a class in a codebehind page:

```
<%@Page Inherits="ClassName"%>
```

The following directive allows an ASP.NET page to access COM objects:

```
<@Page ASPCompat="true" >
```

After you have converted all COM objects to .NET, you can remove the ASPCompat attribute of the <%@Page %> directive, which will increase performance substantially.

To include a disclaimer page on every page in your Web site, you should add the following code:

```
<%@Register TagPrefix="MyCo" TagName=Disclaimer" Src="Disclaim.ascx" %>
```

Common Control Types

Table B-2 shows the common types of controls used for developing Web applications.

Table B-2. Common Web Application Controls

Control	Description
HTML control	Regular HTML control
HTML server control	HTML control with `runat="server"` set
Web control	A true ASP.NET control

Table B-3 compares Web user controls with Web custom controls.

Table B-3. Differences Between Web User Controls and Web Custom Controls

Web User Control	Web Custom Control
Easier to create	Harder to create
Limited support for consumers who use Visual Studio .NET and cannot be added to the toolbox	Full Visual Studio .NET support and can be inserted in the toolbox
Must be inserted in each application that uses it	There can be only one copy in the GAC
Typically used with static layout	Typically used with dynamic layout

You can load a control dynamically at runtime with the following code:

```
Label MyLabel = new Label();
MyLabel.Text = "Hello World";
Container1.Controls.Add(MyLabel);
```

If you define the following for a Web page:

```
<%@Register TagPrefix="MyControls" Namespace="MyNamespace" Assembly="MyAssembly"%>
```

you can render a control on a page with the following code:

```
<MyControls:CSC1 id="Control1" runat="server"/>
```

To properly render a control defined with the following:

```
<%@Register TagPrefix="UControl" Namespace="MyUserControls"
Assembly="MyControls"%>
```

you need the following code:

```
<MyControl:GridX1 id="Control1" BackColor="Color.White"

   OnMyEvent="Gx-MyEvent" runat="server" />
```

To create an instance of a Web control that has been defined in this way:

```
<%@Register TagPrefix="ABC" Namespace="ReportNS" Assembly="rptctrl" %>
```

do the following:

```
<ABC:myReport PageNumber="42" src="rptctrl" runat="server" />
```

This sets a property of the control to a specific value at creation of the instance of the control.

If you create a user control in an assembly defined as MyCtrl.dll, you must do the following to use it:

```
Using System.
Using System.Web.UI;
Namespace MyCCNamespace{
    Public class MyControl {}
}
```

The following code is used to reference the control described above:

```
<%@Register TagPrefix="CC" Namespace="MyCCNamespace" Assembly"MyCtrl.dll"%>
```

The `IsPostBack` property of a control can be used to determine if the page is being loaded for the first time. If the property is `true`, the page was posted back from the browser. If it is `false`, this is the initial creation of the page, and its default values need to be loaded.

To bind a `DataGrid` to a `DataSource` only when it is first loaded, check the `Page.IsPostBack` property. If the value is `false`, bind the data.

To add an attribute to a cell of a `DataGrid`, use the following:

```
MyCell.Attributes.Add("Class", "HighlightedCell")
```

By default, the `DropDownList` control does not post back to the server when an item is selected. You can change this by setting the `AutoPostBack` property to `true`.

You should use the `AutoPostBack` property of a `DataList` to ensure that the `DataList` is automatically updated when an item is selected.

The following code binds code to a `DataGrid`:

```
MyDataSet ds = new MyDataSet();
MyDataAdapter.Fill(ds);
MyDataGrid.DataSource = ds;
MyDataGrid.DataBind();
```

The `ItemDataBound` event of a `DataGrid` is the best place to implement custom formatting, such as color for a `DataGrid`.

The `DayRender` event of the `Calendar` control can be used to populate the calendar with data.

If you create a custom control that has `TextBox` controls in it, and you want an ASP.NET application to be able to access properties of the `TextBox` control, you should create a `public` property for each `TextBox` property you wish to expose.

The `Literal` control is the best control to use to display formatted text, because it renders the data in its `Text` property directly to an HTML stream.

The following code allows you to execute a client-side method called `GetRegistryString` prior to executing a server method called `GetRate`:

```
<input type="button" runat="server" value="eurobtn"
   onclick="getregistrystring();" onserverclick="GetRate"/>
```

Common Validation Controls

Table B-3 shows the common types of validation controls used in Web applications.

Table B-3. Common Validation Controls

Control	Description
RequiredFieldValidator	The field is required.
CompareValidator	The value of the field is compared against a const value or another property's value. Supported operators are less-than, equal, greater-than, and so on.
RangeValidator	The value must be between a specified lower and upper range.
RegularExpressionValidator	The value of the field must match the given regular expression.
CustomValidator	The value must comply with user-defined rules.

The CustomValidator is the only control that allows you to write custom logic.

To quickly disable server-side validation when a value in a drop-down list is changed, you should set the AutoPostBack property of the DropDownList to false.

You should use the Validate method of a validation control on a TextBox control to validate the data placed in it.

If you want to validate user data and provide descriptions beside controls and detailed descriptions at the bottom of the page, you should do the following:

1. Set the Text property of the validation controls to a brief error.

2. Add a ValidationSummary control to the bottom of the form.

3. Set the ErrorMessage property of the validation control to a detailed error message.

Common Events

Table B-4 shows the common types of events used in Web applications.

Table B-4. Common Web Application Events

Event	Description
APPLICATION	
`Application__Start`	Called when the first user visits the Web application
`Application__End`	Called before the Web application is disposed
`Application__BeginRequest`	Called at the beginning of each request
`Application_EndRequest`	Called at the end of each request
SESSION	
`Session_Start`	Called every time a new user visits a Web application's first page
`Session__End`	Called when the user session times out
PAGE	
`Page__Init`	Called at the beginning of processing of a page to populate server controls with their value from `ViewState`
`Page__Load`	Called when `Page_Init` ends
`Page_PreRender`	Called before rendering a page
`Page_UnLoad`	Called before unloading a page
`Page_Error`	Called if there is an untrapped error
`Page_AbortTransaction`	Called if a transaction is aborted
`Page_CommitTransaction`	Called if a transaction is committed
`Page_DataBinding`	Called when one or more controls is bound to a `DataSource`
`Page_Disposed`	Called when the page is next to be disposed
SERVER	
Postback events	Client-side events that cause a page to be posted back to the server and result in server-side events being raised

Table B-4. Common Web Application Events (Continued)

Event	Description
Cache events	Client-side events that are cached in the ViewState and are processed on postback events
Validation events	Occur at both the client and server

Event handlers should be written in the Web form.

If scripting is disabled on a user's computer, this may result in server-side events not working because they rely on Java scripts.

If an AutoPostBack property is set to true for a control, a form post will take place when the controls Changed event is fired. Otherwise, Changed events do not cause a form post.

The following code snippet will activate when the index changes for a list box:

```
<asp: ListBox id="MyList" AutoPostBack="true"
   OnSelectedIndexChange="MyList_IndexChanged runat="server">
<asp:ListItem Value="A">Apples</asp:ListItem>
<asp:ListItem Value="B">Bannas</asp:ListItem>
<asp:ListItem Value="C">Cherries</asp:ListItem>
</asp:ListBox>
```

The ImageButton.OnMouseOver event can be used to change the image of the control when the mouse hovers over the image.

The following code fires an event anytime a check box is checked:

```
<asp:CheckBox id="MyCheck" AutoPostBack="true"
   onCheckedChanged="MyCheck_Clicked" runat="server" />
```

Events must be declared as public for them to be fired in a custom control class.

The ItemCommand event is raised when any custom button in a DataGrid is clicked. When clicking the Edit button in a DataGrid, you use the EditCommand event.

The SelectionChanged event of a Calendar control can be used to determine the date picked in the control.

More User Services Notes

By saving the global.asax file, you can make changes take effect immediately for all users with the least impact on them.

The `Application_OnEnd` event handler of the global.asax file can be used to handle events that need to occur when the last user of a Web application closes the session.

Code that should be run before or on application startup should be written in the global.asax file in the `Application_OnStart` method. This method can be used to load an application with data.

The fastest way to store state information is to store it in-process.

The following are valid ways to add a value to state information:

```
Session["MyVal"] = 99
Session.Add["MyVal"] = 99
```

Setting the `EnableViewState` property of a control to `false` will improve performance, but it also disables storing state information.

ASP.NET applications should store session state information in SQL Server when state data should be secure and capable of being restored after a Web server restart.

Each processor in a Web garden maintains state information separately; therefore, you must use an out-of-process solution such as a state server or SQL to store state information.

To store session state in an out-of-process component, you should modify the Web.config file in this way:

```
<sessionState mode="StateServer" />
```

By placing the `DataSet` in the cache and placing the name of the selected employee in the session object, you can store data specific to the user between round-trips.

By setting the `Duration` attribute of the `@OutputCache` directive in the Web user control to a smaller number, you will reduce the amount of time the control caches data.

To cache the output of a user control so that subsequent requests are pulled from the cache, use the following code:

```
<%@OutputCache Duration="30"VaryByParam"*" %>
```

The following are three ways to cache a string of data:

```
Cache["MyKey"] = stringValue
Cache.Add("MyKey", stringValue)
Cache.Insert("MyKey", stringValue)
```

The most efficient way to query a database and cache that data is to create a control that caches the data for the Web form. Be sure to use the @OutputCache directive.

To prove the identity of your site to customer, you should use the Signcode.exe tool to sign all assemblies with an Authenticode digital signature.

The following command will sign an assembly:

```
sn -R MyAssembly.dll MyKeys.snk
```

The following will allow developers to continue to work on assemblies when they do not have the private key:

```
<assembly:AssemblyKeyFileAttribute("PublicKey.snk")>
<assembly:AssemblyDelaySignAttribute(true)>
```

By using Wsdl.exe and generating a Web Service proxy, you can allow developers to begin writing code for your service before you release it.

You can use sn.exe to bypass verification of an assembly's strong name. The Vr- switch allows you to temporarily disable the strong-name functionality during testing.

If users complain that an intranet .NET Web application fails to work after Internet Explorer security settings are tightened, you should make sure that you enable JavaScript in the Local Internet Zone setting.

By reading the preferred culture from the properties of a request object, you can allow the proper language Web site to be displayed.

In developing a multilanguage and culture site, you should create a separate satellite assembly for each culture as it is created. Then place the assembly in the bin directory of its own subdirectory.

To display a pop-up window confirming a custom choice, first create a client-side function named VerifyOrder that generates a pop-up window. Then add the following code in the Web page:

```
<input type="Submit" runat="server" Value="
Check Out" onclick="VerifyOrder()" onserverclick="submitbutton_click"/>
```

For an application to communicate with a Web Service, you must do take the following steps:

1. Use Wsdl.exe to create a proxy for the Web Service.

2. Use the Csc.exe compiler to create an assembly from the proxy.

3. Place the resulting assembly in the \bin directory of the Web application.

You can define a namespace using the following methods:

- Change the root namespace in the project's Property dialog box.

- Use the namespace {} keyword.

Creating and Managing Components in .NET Assemblies

To create an XML document in a Web page, you add a using System.Xml statement. Then create the XML document with the following:

```
XmlDocument doc = new XmlDocument()
System.Xml.XmlDocument X = new System.Xml.XmlDocument
```

All assemblies that are used in your Web application must be installed in the bin directory.

You can use Windows Installer and Gacutil to install an assembly into the GAC.

You can link your Web application to shared assemblies in the GAC by adding <add> statements to the <assemblies> section of the Web.config file. You can add an assembly to a specific Web page by adding <@Assembly> to the top of the Web form.

If you create a custom control named MyControl and compile it into an assembly called MyCtrl.dll, you can set the default properties in the control with the following code:

```
[ToolboxData("<{0}: MyControl BackColor='Yellow'
WarningLevel="3"  runat="server"></{0}:MyControl>"]
public class MyControl
```

Properties of a public class that are contained in a control are referred to as *subproperties*. ASP.NET uses hyphenated syntax to access subproperties: object-property.

Suppose that you create a control named wucControl and add it to a form. You want to dynamically set the DataSource at runtime, so you add code such as the following to the Form_Load event:

```
wucControl1.DataSource=MyDataSrc;
```

Then you get compile errors. To fix this, you need to add the following line to the declaration of the Web form:

```
protected wucControl wucControl1
```

A Web custom control is a good choice for a preference editor that will be used by multiple Web applications.

The following code will cache `RegionValue` information:

```
<%@OutputCache Duration="30" VaryByControl="RegionValue" %>
```

If you are trying to create a menu that will be the same for all of your applications, a Web user control is a good choice.

Consuming and Manipulating Data

The best way to create a set of scripts to rebuild data structures on another database is to use Server Explorer. In that utility, click the server that you want to generate the scripts, and then click Generate Create Script.

The best way to store information from an XML Web Service is to store the information in a `DataSet` and then place it in the cache.

If you want to translate a legacy ADO recordset to a .NET `DataSet`, you need to do the following:

1. Use the Type Library Importer to create a .NET compatible assembly (interop).

2. Use an `OleDbDataAdapter` to fill the `DataSet` with rows from the recordset.

By setting the `SmartNavigation` attribute of the `@Page` directive to `true`, you allow the following behavior to take place:

- Retain control focus after a postback.

- Retain scroll position after a postback.

If you merge two data sets with the following command:

```
dsFormer.Merge(dsCurrent)
```

You will find all the data from `dsCurrent` placed in `dsFormer`.

It you have two data sets defined as:

DS1	SystemID	SystemName	
DS2	SystemID	SystemName	SystemType

and you merge them with this command:

```
DS1.Merge(DS2, false, MissingSchemaAction.Ignore);
```

This results in the following two behaviors:

- The value of SystemName in the match row will be the value stored in DS2.

- DS1 will not contain the SystemType column.

If you have two DataSets defined as this:

DS1	SystemID	SystemName	--	Contains 2 rows of data
DS2	SystemID	SystemName	SystemType	Contains 1 row of data

where a row in DS1 and DS2 have the same value for SystemID, and you merge the two with this code:

```
DS1.Merge(DS2, true, MissingSchemaAction.Add);
```

You get the following results:

- DS1 will contain two rows.

- DS1 will add the SystemType column.

The following code will populate a new DataSet with rows from another DataSet that have been modified:

```
dsUpdates = dsMyData.GetChanges()
```

If you wish to change the column name in a DataSet to a name different from the one is stored in the database, you need to do the following:

```
DataTableMappings MapName = MyDataAdapter.TableMappings.Add(
    "MyMap", "ProductsTable");
MapName.ColumnMappings.Add(("pr_ID", "ID");
MapName.ColumnMappings.Add(("pr_Name", "Name");
```

The SCOPE_IDENTITY function of a T-SQL statement can be used to retrieve the value of an identity column.

The following code will retrieve the key of the last row in a table:

```
lastID= MyOleCmd.ExecuteScaler()
```

The following code will read a column of data in a DataSet where you have mapped column names:

```
foreach(DataRow dr in ds.Tables["ProductTable"].Rows)
{
        string MyString = dr.["Name"].ToString();
}
```

The valid methods of the SqlTransaction class are Save, Commit, and Terminate. The following code is the proper way to execute transactions:

```
SqlTransaction TransMain = SqlCommand.BeginTransaction();
SqlCommand cmdMain = new SqlCommand()
cmdMain.Transaction = TransMain;
cmdMain.CommandText = stringFirstCommand;
cmdMain.ExecuteNonQuery();
cmdMain.CommandText = stringSecondCommand;
cmdMain.ExecuteNonQuery();
TransMain.Commit();
ConnMain.Close();
```

If you want to use a transaction to update a database, and if errors occur, you want to free all the resources as well as roll back any changes, you should do the following:

```
try
{
        TransMain.Commit();
}
catch(Exception e)
{
        TransMain.Rollback();
}
finally
{
        ConnMain.Close();
}
```

If you want to see the errors that may exist in any of the rows of a DataSet, you should use the following code:

```
DataRow DataErrors;
If(MyDataSet.Tables["Table1"].HasErrors)
{
    DataErrors = MyDataSet.Tables["Table1"].GetErrors();
    For (int Index = 0 ; Index < DataErrors.Length; Index++)
    {
        Console.WriteLine(DataErrors.RowError);
    }
}
```

If you need to write a query to collect data from the following two tables that results in one table that contains OrderID, CustomerID, and Quantity, you should do this:

```
Orders OrderID CustomerID Date
OrdersDetails OrderID DetailID ProductID Quantity Amount
SELECT CustomerID ProductID Quantity
FROM Orders
INNER JOIN OrderDetails
On Orders.OrderID = OrderDetails.OrderID
```

A DataView object can be used to sort and filter data. Use the DataView.RowFilter property to filter data.

If you want to sort the contents of a DataGrid, you should do the following:

1. Set the Sort property of the DataView to the column you wish to sort by.

2. Bind the DataGrid to the DataView.

The initial catalog parameter of a connection string specifies the database name.

The following statement is used to call stored procedures:

```
SqlCommand.ExecuteScaler
```

The following code can be used to call a stored procedure that returns a value and store that value in a local variable:

```
SqlCommand MyCommand = new SqlCommand("MyStoredProcedureName", myConn);
SqlDataReader MyReader = MyCommand.ExecuteReader();
MyReader.Close();
Long MyVal = MyReader.Parameters["@ReturnVal"].Value;
.Value;
.Parameters["@ReturnVal"]d.ExecuteScaler();
```

The following connection string can be used to specify that a server has no more than 30 seconds to respond and cannot exceed 20 connections in its connection pool:

```
"user id=sa;password=12345;initial catalog =
    MyDB;source = MyServer;Connection Timeout=30;Max PoolSize=20"
```

The following code snippet shows how to delete data from a row in a table and any rows that match in a table that is joined by foreign keys:

```
DataColumn column1, column2;
DataRelation MyRelation;
Column1 = MyDataSet.Tables["Widgets"].Columns["WidgetID"];
Column2 = MyDataSet.Tables["WidgetsData"].Columns["WidgetID"];
MyRelation = new DataRelation("Widgets with components", Column1, Column2);
MyDataSet.Relations.Add(MyRelation);
```

The following shows another way to make sure that rows related via a foreign key are deleted when a row in the main table is deleted:

```
DataColumn Column1, Column2;
ForeignKeyConstraint MyConstraint;
Column1 = MyDataSet.Tables["Widgets"].Columns["WidgetID"];
Column2 = MyDataSet.Tables["WidgetsData"].Columns["WidgetID"];
MyConstraint = new ForeignKeyConstraint((("Widgets with components",
    Column1, Column2);
MyConstraint.UpdateRule = Rule.Cascade;
MyConstraint.DeleteRule = Rule.Cascade;
MyDataSet.Tables["Widgets"].Constraints.Add(MyConstraint);
MyDataSet.EnforceConstraints = true;
```

You can improve performance without affecting security by allowing all users to access a SQL database using one account, and then using .NET security to control access to features of the Web site.

Testing and Debugging

The Locals window in Visual Studio .NET allows you to see the value of a stored procedure parameter while in break mode.

If you enable SQL debugging in the project configurations, you can step into stored procedures.

If you want to see detailed errors while debugging a Web application, you should set the value of the mode attribute `<customErrors>` tag in the Web.config file to off.

The following code writes data to an event log:

```
String MyMessage;
MyEventLog.WriteEntry(MyMessage);
```

If you enable tracing via the following configuration line:

```
<trace enabled="true" pageOutput="false" localonly="false/>
```

you can access the trace via the page `http://Servername/trace.axd`.

If you are debugging a script that has a stop statement, and it does not stop, you should ensure that the Internet Explorer browser you are using has the Disable Script Debugging feature turned off. This setting is in the Advanced tab of Internet Options, accessed from the Tools menu in Internet Explorer.

If you create a Web.config file configured like this:

```
<customErrors mode="RemoteOnly">
    <error statusCode="404" redirect="error404.htm"/>
    <error statusCode="405" redirect="error405.htm"/>
    <error statusCode="406" redirect="error406.htm"/>
</customErrors>
```

and you want to forward users to a custom error page, do the following:

1. Comment out all the error tags.

2. Add the defaultRedirect attribute to the customErrors tag and set its value to MyCustomError.aspx.

If you want to trace the first 20 requests for all the Web pages in your site, at the bottom of the page, configure the Web.config file as follows:

- Trace element is enabled and set to true.

- Trace element requestLimit is set to 20.

- Trace element pageOutput is set to true.

The following will place trace information at the bottom of the page and make it viewable to everyone:

```
<trace enabled="true" pageOutput="true" localOnly="false"/>
```

If you want to make trace information viewable only locally and via the trace.axd tool, configure your Web.config file as follows:

```
<trace enabled="true" localOnly="true"/>
```

The following code will write trace data to the event log:

```
EventLogTraceListener MyEvent = new EventLogTraceListener("Test");
Trace.Listeners.Add(MyEvent);
Trace.WriteLine(string);
```

By specifying the Context property in Trace.Write, you can allow controls to write Trace statements to the page on which they are added.

```
Context.Trace.Write("MyContext", strTraceMessage);
```

If you want to trace every page on your site except for two pages, you should do the following:

1. Set the value of the @Page directive Trace attribute to false.

2. In the Web.config file, set the Trace element's Enabled property to true. Also set the Trace element's pageOutput property to true.

You should do the following during unit testing:

1. Build a demo front end. Execute every method of every component and verify its return values.

2. Verify with third-party Web Service providers that the methods return good values.

3. Inspect the values returned from stored procedures.

Use the output windows to view the results of Debug.WriteLine information.

By setting the mode attribute to RemoteOnly and accessing a Web page locally, you can restrict detailed logging to just that computer.

Deploying a Web Application

If you want to deploy a project that uses a common component in your organization and needs three databases, 1GB of RAM, and 20GB of hard disk space, you should do the following:

1. Create a Web installation project.

2. Create a merge module.

3. Use the Launch Conditions Editor.

4. Use the Custom Action Editor.

5. Set the deployment project's Bootstrapper option to WebBootstrapper.

The best way to install a shared assembly is to use a merge module project.

By not including the Windows Installer Bootstrapper, you reduce and optimize the size of an installation package.

When you use a Web installation package, you will have the add/remove functionality in the Control Panel.

You can use custom actions to upgrade the structure in a SQL database when creating an upgrade project.

Maintaining and Supporting a Web Application

The following are ways to optimize server performance:

- Use caching to store and retrieve data.

- Optimize database queries.

- Use tracing to determine the execution time for each piece of relevant code on a page.

- Disable sessions that are not necessary.

- Use `Response.Write` to concatenate strings.

- Use `Page.IsPostBack` to avoid recalculating parts of a page.

- Limit the use of server controls.

- Limit the use of `ViewState`.

Always use `StringBuilder` to build strings, because it is fast and provides the best performance, especially when building a large string from several records in a database.

If you are deploying a Web application and you want a specific virtual directory created, you should set the `VirtualDirectory` property of the Web application folder in the setup project.

If you receive the following error:

```
it is an error to use a section registered as
allows Definition='MachineToApplication' beyond application level
```

do this:

1. On the Web server, create a virtual directory to store the application.

2. Configure the production server with the same settings as the development server.

Configuring and Securing a Web Application

If you specify a forms element in your Web.config file when using forms authentication, and you do not include loginUrl, users will automatically be forwarded to the default.aspx page.

If you create a Web.config file in a subfolder with the following definition:

```
<authorization>
    <allow roles="Doctors"/>
    <deny users="*"/>
</authorization>
```

only members of the Doctors role will be able to access this folder. However, everyone will be able to access other folders that do not specify a specific authorization section. The * means everyone, and ? means anonymous users.

The following statement denies access to anonymous users:

```
<deny users="?"/>
```

The following authorization section allows access to a folder for user1 and user2, and denies access to user3 and user4:

```
<authorization>
   <allow users="user1, user2"/>
   <deny users="user3, user4"/>
</authorization>
```

If all users are authenticated in your organization and you want to ensure authorization, you should set up IIS to use Integrated Security.

If you wish to use FileAuthorizationModule, you must use Windows Integrated Security.

Exam 70-316

Developing and Implementing Windows-Based Applications with Microsoft Visual C# .NET and Microsoft Visual Studio .NET

THIS APPENDIX CONTAINS information that will help you prepare for Exam 70-316, Developing and Implementing Windows-based Applications with Microsoft Visual C# .NET and Microsoft Visual Studio .NET. This is a Microsoft Certified Professional (MCP) exam, and it also provides credit for the certifications Microsoft Certified Solution Developer (MCSD), Microsoft Certified Application Developer (MCAD) for Microsoft .NET, and Microsoft Certified Database Administrator (MCDBA) on Microsoft SQL Server 2000.

Creating User Services

When making modifications to a base form, you must build the form for inherited forms to reflect the changes.

You can use the IncrementalBuild functionality of project to decrease build times when you are working on new code and existing code does not need to be rebuilt.

When creating a multinational application, you should create a single executable file with the default culture embedded. Then create separate satellite assemblies for culture-specific resource files. You can use the Al.exe tool to compile the resource files into satellite assemblies.

The Invalidate method will cause a control to redraw itself, and thus any changes will be seen after calling this method.

You can use the IDisposable.Dispose method to control resource usage in resource-scarce environments.

If you want methods to be called when an object is created, call those methods in the constructor of a class.

An event may be invoked only by the class that defines it. The following is an example of calling a base class event from an inherited class:

```
if(base.Deceased != null)
    Base.Deceased(this, e)
```

The Select event of a menu item is fired when the mouse points to a menu item or the arrow keys are used to navigate to the item.

When data binding is not being used, a forms Load event handler is used to place data into controls on the form.

The Closing event handler of a form can be used to prevent a form from closing if certain conditions have not been met. This requires the Cancel property of the CancelEventsArgs object to be set to true.

A TextBox TextChanged event handler can be used to examine the contents of a text box when it loses focus.

The QueryPageSettings event occurs before the BeginPrint event and provides you with the opportunity to set properties of the PageSettings object. The PageSettings object allows you to modify settings such as margins, paper source, and printer resolutions.

The following code can be placed in an event handler for a TextBox to set its value:

```
((TextBox)sender).Text = HUMAN_TOKEN
```

By setting the Cancel property of CancelEventArgs to true in a Validating event handler for a control, you suppress further events, and the control maintains the focus.

The Validating event of a control can be used to verify the contents of a control and prevent focus from moving to the next control when the Tab key is pressed. This also requires the Cancel property of the CancelEventArgs object to be set to true.

Setting the Dock property of a control to fill causes the control to fill the entire client area.

Setting the DialogResult property to yes allows for a dialog box to return results and close the form.

The ReshowDelay property determines the amount of time that must elapse before a previously viewed tooltip will allow the tooltip help to be reshown.

When you change the RightToLeft property of a form for countries where languages are read from right to left, the following things will occur:

- Text in each form's caption will be right-aligned.

- Text in `Label` controls will be right-aligned.

- The main menu will move to right side of the form and will appear in reverse order.

- Text in buttons on a toolbar will not change.

The following is true when you set the `DefaultItem` property of a `MenuItem` to `true`:

- The menu item's typeface will be bold.

- Double-clicking a submenu containing the default item will select the default item.

The `AccessibleName` property of a control is spoken when it receives focus. You can restrict the size of a form by using the following code:

```
MyForm.MaximumSize = new Size(150,150);
```

The `MaximumSize` property prevents a form from exceeding the specified size.

The `MaxLength` property can be used to limit the number of characters typed into a text box.

Setting the `TabStop` property of each control on a form will prevent a user from tabbing through the controls on a form.

To use a shortcut key to transfer focus to a control, you must do the following:

- In the label control's `Text` property use the & to set the shortcut (for example, &Phone).

- Set the value of the `TabIndex` of the label to be 1 plus the value of the label's `TabIndex` property.

- Set the `UseMnemonic` property to `true`.

The shortcut key of a `CheckBox` is enabled by placing a % in the `Text` property. The & character should be placed before the letter you wish to be the shortcut. You must also set the `AutoCheck` property to `true`. This will allow a user to use the shortcut to check or uncheck a check box on demand.

The following code can be used to add an existing menu item to a new menu object such as a context menu:

```
PopupMenu.MenuItems.Add(MenuEditItem.Clone()) ;
```

To enable Help on any control that has focus by pressing F1, do the following:

- Add a HelpProvider component to the form.

- Set the HelpString property of the control to the text you want to appear when F1 is pressed.

- Set the ShowHelp property of each control to true.

To bind a column in a DataSet to a Text property of TextBox, use this code:

```
TextBox.Add(new Binding("Text", MyDataSet, "YTD.TotalSales"));
```

To bind a ComboBox to columns in a DataSet, do the following:

```
Combo.ValueMember = "ProcCode";
Combo.DisplayMember = "ProcName";
```

The ValueMember property determines the value that is written. The DisplayMember property determines the column in the DataSet that is displayed.

When the LockControls option is enabled, the only way to set the size of a control in the Forms Designer is to use the width and size properties.

Creating and Managing Components and .NET Assemblies

To ensure that a network share is valid, you should call the Exists method of the Directory class and ensure that it returns true.

You can use regasm to make a C# DLL available to other development environments such as Visual Basic 6, as in this example:

```
regasm /tlb:MyDll.tlb /codebase c:\MyDLL.DLL
```

To use a .NET component in Visual Basic 6, you need to register the component with Regasm.exe.

By changing the apply attribute of the publisherPolicy element in the *Application*.config.exe file to No, a publisher policy can be used to allow an application to run an updated version of an assembly. Otherwise, the application will always load the version of the assembly with which it was compiled.

In order to run an application that uses a specific version of an assembly, you must sign the assembly using sn.exe. This will give the assembly a strong name.

You can use Wsdl.exe to generate proxy classes for exposed Web Services and send them to your customers for use.

If you create a class with this code:

```
ClassA Test = new ClassB();
Test.MyMethod();
```

and `ClassB` is a derived class of `ClassA`, the class type that you are creating with the new class methods will be called.

The `typeof` keyword is used to tell if a class is derived from a base class.

The following are valid constructors for the `MyObject` class:

```
public MyCache()
public MyCache(int MyInt)
```

The following code:

```
object Test = new MyObject()
```

can be optimized like this:

```
MyObject Test = new MyObject()
```

The `sealed` keyword can prevent users from overriding or deriving a new class from this class.

`PathTooLongException` is a `System.IO` exception that can be used when dealing with file access.

When two people using Visual Source Safe (VSS) check out the same file and both have made changes, you should have one user check in his or her changes, and then have another user retrieve the latest code and resolve any conflicts.

You can use the `ToolboxItemFilterAttribute` to add a custom control's icon in the .NET IDE toolbox.

To end a print job, you should set the `HasMorePages` property of the `PrintPageEventArgs` class to `false`. This instructs the `PrintDocument` object to complete the print job and call the `EndPrint` event.

The `CausesValidation` property determines if the `Validating` event fires. If this property is set to `true`, it determines if the `Validating` event can fire the `Validated` and `LostFocus` events.

A form's `Load` event can be used to read configuration options from an XML file.

The `ExecuteNonQuery` method of `SqlCommand` is used to process T-SQL statements that delete, insert, and update. The method returns an `int` with the number of rows that were deleted, inserted, or updated.

Consuming and Manipulating Data

The valid methods of the OleDBCommand class are Cancel, ExecuteScaler, and CreateParameter.

The XmlWriteMode.DiffGram enum can be used in the WriteXml method to determine the format of an XML document.

The XmlValidatingReader class can be used to validate XML with both inline and external schema.

The following is the most efficient way to build an XML file from a DataSet that states the data types in the XML file:

```
FileStream MyStream = new FileStream("export.xml", FileMode.Create);
MyDataSet.WriteXML(MyStream, XmlWriteMode.WriteSchema);
```

The XmlElement.DocumentElement property will return the root node of the XML file.

By calling the MoveToFirstAttribute method and by building a separate error-handling procedure for the ValidationEventHandler event, you can write data to an XML file using an external schema.

The following code will allow you to validate an XML file:

```
XmlTextReader MyReader = new XmlTextReader"//server/xmldata.xml");
XmlValidatingReader MyXMLValidator = new XmlValidatingReader(MyReader);
MyXMLValidator.ValidationType = ValidationType.Schema;
NetworkCredentials MyCredentials =
    new NetworkCredentials(StringUsername, StringPassword, StringDomain);
MyXMLValidator.XmlResolver.Credentials = MyCredentials;
```

The following code will allow you to read data from an XML file into a SQL database when the XML file does not contain schema data:

```
DataSet MyDataSet = new DataSet();
MyDataSet.ReadXml("MyXMLFile.txt", XmlReadMode.InferSchema);
```

The following code can be used to execute a SQL command:

```
MyDataAdapter.Update(MyDataSet, MyTableName);
```

The SqlDataReader class is the most efficient class to use to populate a bunch of Label controls.

The SqlDataAdapter.Update method will apply changes made in a DataSet to a database.

The SqlException.Class property issues a number between 1 to 25 that determines the severity of an exception. The higher the number, the more serious the problem.

When using the SqlDataReader.GetBoolean method to read a particular column, and the column does not contain Boolean data, you will get the InvalidCastException exception.

SqlCommand.Prepare creates an optimized version of a stored procedure that executes more quickly than a stored procedure that is not prepared.

The SqlCommand.ExecuteScaler method can be used to return the first row and first column returned by a query. This method is most appropriate for stored procedures.

The SqlCommandBuilder.DeriveParameter method can be used to retrieve the parameters of a stored procedure.

The following is a valid connection string for a SqlConnection object:

```
"user id=sa;password=ABC;Initial Catalog= Resources(DB Name);"
    + "Data Source=ServerName"
```

The SQL managed provider allows for connection pooling, which will reduce the number of connections.

The following code can be used to create a DataSet:

```
DataSet MyDataSet;
SqlCommand MyCommand = new SqlCommand("SELECT * FROM Employees");
MyCommand.Connection = new SqlConnection("database=MyDB,server=MyServer");
MyCommand.Command = CommandType.Text;
SqlDataAdapter MyAdapter = new SqlDataAdapter();
MyAdapter.SelectCommand–MyCommand;
MyAdapter.Fill(MyDataSet);
```

The following code can be used to create a primary key:

```
DataColumn[] MyColumnArray = {TableNew.Columns["Column1"],
TableNew.Columns["Column2")};
TableNew.PrimaryKey = MyColumnArray;
```

You create a DataView object with the following code:

```
DataView MyData = new DataView(MyDataSet.Tables["PhoneList"],
    "Name, Number, State");
```

By creating a `DataView` object with a `DataSet` and setting the `RowStateFilter` property to `DataViewRowState.ModifiedOriginal`, you can allow one `DataGrid` to see changes made in another `DataGrid` when both grids are bound to the same `DataSet`.

The following can be used to bind a `DataGrid` to a `DataSet`:

```
MyGrid.SetDataBinding(MyDataSet, "TableName");
```

The following code will create a `ParameterObject`:

```
SqlParameter MyParam = MyCommand.Parameters.Add("@Param1", SqlDbType.Int);
```

The following code is used to generate a `DataReader` object:

```
SqlCommand MyCommand = new SqlCommand("StoredProcedureMain", MyConnection);
SqlDataReader MyReader = MyCommand.ExecuteReader;
MyCommand.Parameters("@InputValues").Value = MyLong;
```

If you wish to update data in a table and create two parameters, an input parameter and an output parameter, use the following code:

```
MyDataAdapter.UpdateCommand.Parameters.Add("@Category",
    SqlDbType.Nchar, 15, "CategoryName");
SqlParameter MyParam = MyDataAdapter.UpdateCommand.Parameters.Add(
    "@NumRows", SqlDbType.Int, 0, "");
MyParam.Direction = ParameterDirection.Output;
```

The enum member `TransactionIsolationLevel.Serializable` specifies that no user can read or modify rows in a `DataSet` while a transaction is open.

The `UniqueConstraint` class can be used to ensure the values in one or more columns are unique.

The most efficient way to load an unbound control with read-only data is to use a `DataReader` object, as in this example:

```
MyCommand.CommandText = MyCommandString;
MyCommand.CommandType = CommandType.Text;
SqlDataReader MyReader = MyCommand.ExecuteReader;
while(MyReader.Read())
{
    MyListBox.Items.Add(MyReader.GetString(0));
}
```

The following code should be placed in a `ComboBox` `Click` event to update a `DataGrid` control:

```
MyDataView.RowFilter = "DrinkName  = '" + comboDrink.Text + "'";
```

The `RowChanged` event of a `DataTable` object is raised when a `DataRow` object is modified.

`DataTable.Copy` can be used to create an exact copy of a `DataTable`, including the table's object constraints, data, and schema.

Data can be viewed in a combo box based on a `DataView` by using the following code:

```
MyDataView.Sort = MyCombo.Text + "ASC"
```

This sorts the data in ascending order. Use `DESC` to sort the data in descending order.

The following code will retrieve and sort rows in a `DataView`:

```
DataView MyDataView = new DataView(MyDataSet.Tables["MyTable"]);
MyDataView.Sort = "Category, Temp ASC";
MyDataView.RowFilter = "Category = '"
                +MyCombo.Text + "', Tempo = '" + MyCombo.Text + "'";
```

The following code will return a single row based on a name with a state:

```
MyDataView.RowFilter = "Name = '" + StringName + "', State ='" +StringState + "'";
```

When edits are made to a `DataView` object, the `EndEdit` method of the `DataRowView` object must be called to apply the changes to the underlying data table.

The following code snippet will allow a user to enter data in a `TextBox` that will be used to query data in database and populate a `ListBox`:

```
SqlConnection MyConnection = SqlConnection(ConnectionString);
SqlCommand MyCommand = new SqlCommand("SELECT Location FROM Parts WHERE"
    + "PartName = '" + TextBox.Text + "'", MyConnection);
SqlDataReader MyReader;
MyReader = MyCommand.ExecuteReader();
while(MyReader.Read())
{
    MyListBox.Items.Add(MyReader.GetString(0));
    }
```

The following code will set a TextBox.Text property to the @TotalSales output parameter:

```
MyTextBox.Text = (string)MyCommand.Parameters("@TotalSales").Value;
```

Testing and Debugging

ArithmeticException is thrown for errors like divide-by-zero.

The following code will downcast a long to an int and throw an exception if the value is greater than what an int can hold:

```
Int MyInt = checked((int)MyLong);
```

The following is an example of a method that could display exception information for all exceptions:

```
Debug.WriteLine("ERROR:" + e.Message + " at " + e.Source);
    if(e.InnerException != null)
        DisplayError(e.InnerException);
```

By calling the throw command inside a catch block of a base class with no parameters, you essentially cause the exception to be sent to the caller and not the base class.

Visual Studio allows you to set breakpoints based on an interval of times a breakpoint is hit.

By setting a breakpoint with a condition, you can enable the application to break into the debugger when a value of a variable is modified.

.NET breakpoints can do the following:

- Stop execution at a specific line of code based on the number of times that code has been run.

- Stop execution of code based on a specific line number and a multiple of a specific number of times the code has been run.

- Break when a specific variable is set to a specific value in a specific line of code.

You can use the `Assert` method of the `Debug` or `Trace` class to instantly provide a stack trace when a certain condition is met.

`Trace.WriteLine` can be used to log information to the event log after creating an `EventLogTraceListener`.

By not adding a `TraceListener` to the `Listeners` collection, you can prevent the `TraceListener` object from receiving messages.

Server Explorer can be used to debug SQL stored procedures.

If you wish to enable tracing of a server-based application that does not have its own configuration file for a single computer, you should modify the Machine.config file on the single computer and set the trace level of the application in the file.

In the Machine.config file, you can use the following to set application-specific settings:

```
<add key="Application Name", value=MyApp>
```

The following will enable tracing in a C# application:

- Add #define `TRACE` to the top of the source file.

- Add a `<switches>` element to an application's configuration file.

The App.config file can be used to modify tracing outside the application. When using trace switches, you can set the value from 0 (minimum) to 4 (maximum).

By editing an App.config file and setting the trace level to 4, you can get verbose information when using the `<switches>` option.

The following App.config file will disable tracing:

```
<configuration>
    <system.diagnostics>
        <switches>
            <add name="MySwitch" value ="0"/>
        </switches>
    </system.diagnostics>
</configuration>
```

The Output window is the best place to examine syntax errors when building an application.

The easiest way to identify all the syntax errors of an application is to use the Task List and remove or set the filter for build errors.

All comments that start with `TODO` automatically show up in the Task List of Visual Studio.

To share information about what work needs to be done with another user, you can do the following:

- Add TODO comments in the source code where work needs to be done. These will then show up in the Task List.

- Filter the Task List by policy tasks by choosing ShowTask from the Task List pop-up window and choosing Policy.

- Tell the other user to view the Task List to see items that need work.

Visual Studio .NET offers the following windows:

- The This window shows the properties of the currently executing object.

- The Autos window shows all the variables referenced in the current and previous line of code.

- The Locals window shows the values of all local objects and variables.

The following are examples of unit testing:

- Building a demo front end that executes every method of every component and verifies the return values

- Inspecting the values returned from each stored procedure

You can use Dotnetfx.exe to repair a .NET Framework installation when you encounter running .NET applications.

Deploying a Windows-Based Application

Use the <probing> element of an App.config file to set the location of an assembly.
You can modify an App.config file in such a way that it will always use a specific version of an assembly.
The CLR searches for an assembly in the following order:

1. GAC

2. <codebase>

3. <probing>

The most appropriate tool to use to install an assembly into the GAC is the Microsoft Windows Installer 2.0.

You can use the File Types Editor to associate extension types (.greg or .slk) with an application.

By configuring all the settings in the Registry Editor and by using the `Condition` property of the entries to control which settings are entered, you can allow users to make settings to the Registry during installation.

The easiest way to beta test an application in such a way as to ensure all users are running the same version of the software on a network is to install the application on a network share and create an installation procedure that places a shortcut to the network on the user's desktop.

You still must install the .NET Framework on individual computers, even if you deploy the .NET application to a share.

The following steps should be taken when deploying an assembly to every computer:

1. Give the assembly a strong name using the sn.exe tool.

2. Create an installation program for the assembly.

3. Log on to the computer as the Administrator account.

4. Install the assembly into the GAC.

A `MergeModule` project can be used to simplify deployment. This type of project is a setup project that can be called only by other setup projects.

The File System Editor can be used to deploy specific fonts.

The most efficient way to create installation files that can be used on a Zip disk is to use the Build property page and change the `PackageFile` property to `InCabinetFiles`. Then change the `CabFile Size` property to the desired size in kilobytes.

You can use NGen.exe to make an application start faster.

Maintaining and Supporting a Windows-Based Application

The following are benefits of deploying an application using a hub-and-spoke model:

-   Your application will not need to be recompiled when changes are made to satellite assemblies.

-   You do not need to wait for the completion of all satellite assemblies before deploying your application.

-   The CLR will use a fallback process if a satellite assembly cannot be found.

You should use an XCOPY means of deploying an application when installing an application that contains a private assembly to a server on the Internet.

Configuring and Securing a Windows-Based Application

You can use the Caspol.exe utility to add a publisher condition to the ALL_CODE group at the enterprise level, and then import the company's certificate into the condition. This will allow you to prevent users from running unauthorized .NET applications.

By using the Caspol utility and setting the Exclusive attribute on the default setting, you can ensure that no other settings that are greater than your settings can be granted.

Caspol can be used to set the permissions on a specific assembly when you receive messages that a user does not have the permissions to run an assembly.

You can control the availability of controls on a form by using the following code and using Windows NT security groups.

```
MyForm M = new MyForm();
WindowsIdentity Me = WindowsIdentity.GetCurrent();
WindowsPrincipal Principal = new WindowsPrincipal(Me);
if(Principal.IsInRole("DomainName\GroupName"))
{
    M.ShowAdvancedFeatures();
}
M.Show();
```

To require an application to use a specific version of an assembly, you should modify the *Application*.exe.config file. The requiredRuntime node can be used to set a specific version of the assembly required to run.

One route to troubleshoot a TypeLoadException is to make sure the assembly is in the same folder as the EXE, install the assembly into the GAC, and then use the following:

```
<probing privatePath="Path" />
```

You can call methods of a Web Service asynchronously using WSDL by calling `BeginMethodName` and `EndMethodName`.

If you install a new version of an assembly and you discover that the older version of the assembly is always being used, it is most likely because the assembly is being set in the configuration file.

Identity objects represent the user on whose behalf the code is running. If you wish to use a customized identity, you can use a `CustomIdentity` class.

You can assure people that software comes from a specific developer or company by using the Signcode.exe tool to digitally sign an assembly.

Index

Symbols

-- decrement operator 31, 32, 125

- subtraction operator 31

% modulus division operator 31, 32

(!) NOT bitwise operator 38

(!) NOT logical operator 37

(!=) not equal operator 36

(&&) AND logical operator 37

(&) AND bitwise operator 38

(.) dot operator 46

(^) XOR bitwise operator 38

({}) curly braces scope 25

(|) OR bitwise operator 38

(||) OR logical operator 37

(<<) shift left operator 40

(>>) shift right operator 40

* multiplication operator 31

*= multiplication assignment operator 31, 32

/ division operator 31

/= division assignment operator 31, 32

@Page directive

   SmartNavigate attribute 514

\ backslash escape character 16

\' single quote escape character 16

\0 null termination escape character 16

\a alert escape character 16

\b backspace escape character 16

\f form feed escape character 16

\n new line escape character 16

\r carriage return escape character 16

\t horizontal tab escape character 16

\v vertical tab escape character 16

+ addition operator 31

++ increment operator 31, 32, 125

+= addition assignment operator 31, 32

< comparison operator 36

<= comparison operator 36

-= subtraction assignment operator 31, 32

== equivalence operator 36

> comparison operator 36

>= comparison operator 36

A

Abort method, Thread class 273

abstraction 92

access specifiers 81

activated service and client and attributes 359

Active Directory

   accessing 214

   changing password 222

   connecting and binding to 215

   deleting objects 223

   Directory caching 226-227

   reading attributes of an object 217-218

   searching directory 224-225

   traversing objects in 216

   writing and modifying attributes of object 220-221

   writing new objects to 219

Add method, ArrayLists class 54

Add method, Hashtable class 56

addition assignment operator += 31, 32

addition operator + 31

Remove method, ArrayLists class 54

Remove method, DirectoryEntry class

   deleting objects 223

Remove method, Hashtable class 57

Remove method, String class 14

RemoveAt method, ArrayLists class 54

Replace method, String class 14

reserved memory 122

ResetEvent class

   threading 283

Resolve method, Dns class 263

resources 501

Resume method, Thread class 275

Reverse method, ArrayLists class 54

role based security. *See* RBS

ROT (Running Object Table) 410

RowChanged event, DataTable class 533

RowFilter property, DataView class 517

Running Object Table. *See* ROT

Runtime Callable Wrapper. *See* RCW

S

safe arrays 186

SAFEARRAYS

   and COM 161

SAO (Server Activated Objects) 355

sbyte value type 8

SCOPE_IDENTITY function 515

scopes 25

scripts and HTML 457

sealed keyword 529

SELECT statement 245

selection statements 66-69

SelectionChanged event, Calendar
   control 510

Server Activated Objects. *See* SAO

session state

   adding, retrieving and removing items 487

   disabling 488

   modifying timeout value 486

   storage 487

shift left operator (<<) 40

shift operators 40

   example 41

   precedence table 44

shift right operator (>>) 40

short value type 8

   storing whole numbers 11

single quote escape character \' 16

single-dimensional array 50

single-threaded apartment. *See* STA

size attribute 453

SizeOf method, Marshal class 160

sizeof operator 160

Sleep method, Thread class 275

SmartNavigate attribute, @Page directive 514

SoapSuds 355, 400

socket connections

   creating 260

   listening for 262

Sort property, DataView class 517

SortedList class, System.Collections
   namespace

   IDictionary interface used to create 57

SOS tool

   !ClrStack command 320

   !COMSTATE command 319

   !DumpClass command 321-322

   !DumpDomain command 323

   !DumpHeap command 324-325

   !DumpMD command 324

   !DumpMT command 328

   !DumpMule command 329

ToArray method, ArrayLists class 54

ToCharArray method, String class 15

ToLower method, String class 15, 110

tools 501

ToString method, ArrayLists class 54

ToString method, Object class 79

ToUpper method, String class 15, 110

Trace class, System.Diagnostics
namespace 290

TraceSwitch class

controling tracing with configuration
file 290, 295

tracing 290-296

TrackBar control, changes 438

transactions 249

TreeView control, changes 438

Trim method, String class 15, 117

TrimEnd method, String class 15, 117

trimming strings 117

TrimStart method, String class 15, 117

try/catch statements 142-144

T-SQL statements

SCOPE_IDENTITY function 515

type attribute 450

U

uint value type 8

storing whole numbers 11

<ul> tag 449

ulong value type 8

storing whole numbers 11

unary operators 33

example 34

precedence table 43

unboxing

converting reference types 22

unchecked statement 11

Unicode, manipulation of strings to ASCII 13

unions 46

UniqueConstraint class 532

Unlock method, Application class 477

unordered lists 449-450

Update method, SqlDataReader class 530

UPDATE statement 245

UsePropertyCache property,
DirectoryEntry class 226

ushort value type 8

storing whole numbers 11

using keyword 140, 161

V

Validating event, changes 438

validation controls 508

value types

common methods 8

common value types, table 8

values

assigning to variable 6

constant and static 23

variables

assigning a value to 6

declaring 6

example of using 7

varying arrays 186

vertical tab escape character \v 16

virtual keyword 95

virtual memory 122

virtual methods 95-96

Visual Studio

Add Web Reference functionality 400

breakpoints 534

creating strong-typed DataSet 240

Locals window 519

Output window 535

W